Sue Kay & Vaughan Jones
Carmen Cadierno & Mabel Soracco
additional material by Jon Hird

Inside Out

Student's Book
Contains preparation materials for the level III examination of the Escuelas Oficiales de Idiomas

Level III

Units & topics	Speaking & writing	Reading & listening texts	Grammar, lexis & Pronunciation
1 Friends Famous people Family Friendship page 4	Talking about friends, relatives & famous people Using basic question forms in conversation **Game:** *Noughts & Crosses* **Anecdote:** talking about a friend Writing an e-mail and an informal letter about yourself	Interview with Jade Jagger Article: *That Was Then This Is Now* – do university students stay friends forever? Conversation about a close friend Song: *You've Got a Friend* – by the Brand New Heavies	**G** Question forms in the main tenses and with modals Subject v. object questions Questions ending with prepositions **L** Friendship expressions English in pop songs **P** Stress in questions Long & short vowels
2 Relax Stress & relaxation Books, films & music page 14	Talking about stress & ways of relaxing Giving opinions **Anecdote:** books, films & music Writing a film review	People talking about their lives & *The Little Book of Calm* Article: a busy mother's reaction to *The Little Book of Calm* People talking about books, films & music Web-page: *Web Movies* – film information & reviews	**G** Adverbs & adverb phrases of frequency Present simple for habits & routines; present continuous for temporary activities; present perfect for past with present relevance **L** Expressions about stress, mannerisms & self control Adjectives ending in *-ed/-ing* Vocabulary of books, films & music
3 Dating Relationships Personality page 24	Talking about 'firsts' Talking about how couples meet Talking about the qualities of an ideal partner	Article: how two couples began their relationship Interview to find out if the relationships survived one year later Text: couples talking about how they met Article: *Ki Astrology* – personality types in Chinese astrology Conversation about a new boyfriend Article: a boyfriend's worst nightmare	**G** Past simple for finished time contrasted with present perfect for time-up-to-now *since & for* **L** Love & relationship expressions Simple & compound adjectives describing personality Criticisms & generalisations: *can be (at times); tends to be* *get* to mean become **P** The schwa /ə/
4 Adrenalin Sports Risks page 32	Talking about frightening or exciting experiences Talking about sport **Anecdote:** telling stories **Game:** *The Adrenalin Game: Truth or Dare*	Web-page: www.deadmike.com – a skydiver's addiction to his sport Interview with Jane Couch, a female boxer People talking about past experiences People talking about sports Song: *River Deep Mountain High* by Ike and Tina Turner	**G** Past experiences: past simple for central events; present perfect with *Have you ever …* ; past continuous for background Comparison: comparative and superlative adjectives, *as … as* **L** Expressions about risk & excitement Gradable and absolute adjectives (*very good* vs *absolutely incredible*) Vocabulary of sport Time expressions **P** Using stress to express strong feelings
5 Kids Children Childhood memories page 42	Talking about the qualities of a good child & a good parent **Game:** *Definition Auction* **Anecdote:** childhood memories	Text: children's definitions of a mother Children's definitions of everyday things & concepts Extracts from Roald Dahl's autobiography, *Boy* Extract from Roald Dahl's autobiography, *Boy*	**G** Defining relative clauses Past time: *used to & would* **L** Vocabulary of education & childhood Guessing meaning from context **P** Syllable timed stress
6 News Paparazzi News stories page 50	Talking about celebrity gossip & privacy Talking about past experiences Exchanging personal news Showing interest & empathising Writing a letter to a friend giving news	Web-page: *Paparazzi* – views on the press intrusion News stories: *News in Brief* – short newspaper articles Radio news broadcasts Conversations giving personal news	**G** Passive voice Present perfect for recent events Irregular past tense verbs **L** Common verb collocations **P** Showing empathy
7 Party Festivals & parties Special occasions page 58	Talking about festivals **Game:** *Call My Bluff* Inviting people out, making excuses, making arrangements & stating intentions **Anecdote:** talking about parties Planning a party Writing a letter of invitation Writing a letter accepting or refusing a letter of invitation	Article: *Spain's Third City Sees Winter Off With a Bang* – the festival in Valencia Conversation about dates & boyfriends Conversation about the ingredients of a good party Questionnaire: *Are You a Party Animal Or a Party Pooper?* – how much do you really enjoy parties? Song: *It's My Party* by Lesley Gore	**G** Future forms: *will* for decisions and offers; *(be) going to* for intentions; present continuous for arrangements **L** Phrasal verbs Socialising expressions **P** Short vowels: /ɪ/ /e/ /ɒ/ /æ/ /ə/ /ʊ/ /ʌ/
8 Review 1 page 67			

Units & topics	Speaking & writing	Reading & listening texts	Grammar, Lexis & Pronunciation
9 Soap An American soap opera Family relations page 72	Talking about family relationships Talking about the characters in *Pacific Heights* Reporting conversations Making predictions Writing a TV preview	Who's who in *Pacific Heights* Scene 1 of *Pacific Heights* Who's who in *Pacific Heights*: Scenes 2–4 Scenes 2–4 of *Pacific Heights*	**G** Reported speech & thought Modals: *will ('ll)* simple, continuous perfect forms **L** Family relationships Describing people *say, tell & ask* Phrasal verbs Everyday expressions (*I see what you mean.*)
10 Time Time management Work page 82	Comparing sayings about time Talking about rules & regulations Talking about work places Writing a business letter Writing a letter of application	Radio discussion on attitudes to time Someone talking about dates that are important to them Article: *Time-Saving Tips* – advice on how to make lists and manage your time People talking about their work place	**G** Modals: *must(n't); should(n't); can('t)* for obligation, prohibition & permission – plus *(don't) have to;* **L** Sayings about time Time prepositions & expressions Business & time management expressions **P** Sounds: /s/ /z/ /θ/ /ð/
11 Journey Travel Holidays page 92	Talking about reasons for travelling Describing places **Anecdote:** talking about a perfect weekend **Anecdote:** a journey Writing holiday postcards Writing narratives: making stories more vivid & detailed	Extract from *The Beach* by Alex Garland Conversation about a round-the-world trip Interview with people talking about their perfect weekend Article: account of a motorbike trip across the United States Article: a pilot's mistake	**G** Modals: (1) *must; could; may; can't* for deduction; (2) *would* for unreal situations Past perfect **L** Geographical location Describing places
12 Basics Restaurants Food Sleep page 100	Talking about eating habits Using formal & informal register **Anecdote:** eating out Talking about unusual food Designing a meal Writing up the results of a survey	Conversation at a restaurant on a first date Interview about eating unusual food Report on sleep habits	**G** Quantifiers Countable & uncountable nouns **L** Restaurant language Social register Vocabulary of food, tastes & ways of cooking
13 Communication Telephoning Men & women page 108	Making phone calls Talking about male/female stereotypes Talking about different generations Writing a report based on statistics	Useful website addresses & telephone numbers Messages on an answering machine Phone conversation: Richard phones his girlfriend, the bank & his mum Questionnaire on what men & women really think	**G** Real conditionals, eg: first conditional; zero conditional; conditional imperative **L** Telephone, e-mail and website addresses Telephone language *Make & do*
14 Style Fashion Clothes Appearance page 116	Talking about getting ready to go out Talking about tastes in clothes **Anecdote:** clothes & accessories Describing people Talking about wishes Writing descriptions of people	People talking about their favourite clothes Extract from *Come Together* by Josie Lloyd & Emlyn Rees Song: *Ugly* by Jon Bon Jovi Interview with Jon Bon Jovi	**G** *I wish* + past simple Unreal conditionals, eg: second conditional **L** Verbs & verb phrases: clothes (*put on, get dressed, suit, fit,* etc) Clothes & materials Adjective order Clothes idioms **P** Pure vowels and diphthongs
15 Age Regrets Age Dilemmas page 126	Talking about regrets Talking about age limits **Game:** *Unreal: The Conditional Game* Talking about different ages in life Asking questions politely	Poem: *If …* – from Harley Davidson advertisement Article: *Ageism Turned Her into a Liar* – a woman lies about her age Conversation between the woman & her boyfriend in the article Text on uncomfortable situations & dilemmas People talking about the best age to be	**G** *I wish & If only* + past perfect Unreal conditionals, eg: third conditional; mixed conditionals Indirect questions **L** Vocabulary of age & regrets
16 Review 2 page 134			

• *Additional material* page 139 • *Verb structures* page 144 • *Grammar glossary* page 146 • *Phonetic symbols* page 146 • *Irregular verbs* page 147
• *Tapescripts* page 148 • *Preparation materials for the level III examination of the Escuelas Oficiales de Idiomas* page 161

1 Friends

1 Write down the names of three people who are important to you: a friend, a relative and somebody famous. Azuor, Roualdo, Beckam

> 1 Marisol
> 2 Andreas
> 3 Madonna

2 Ask other people in the class about their lists. Find out as much as you can.

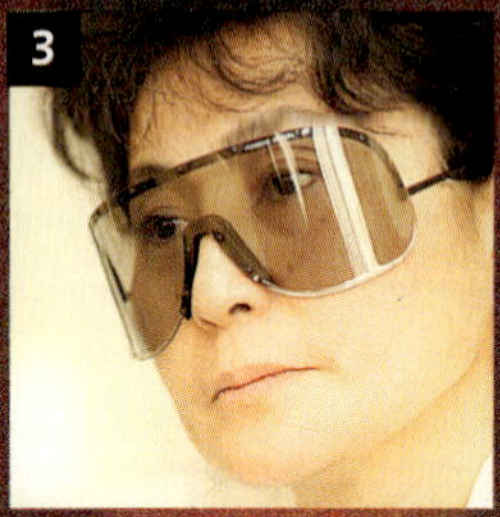

Fame

1 Discuss these questions:

 a) Who are the five most famous people in your country?
 b) Who do you think is the most famous man in the world?
 c) Who do you think is the most famous woman in the world?

2 Look at photographs 1–6.

 a) Do you know who these people are?
 b) What do you know about them? about him / about her

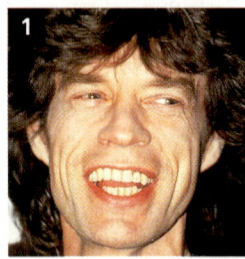

LANGUAGE TOOLBOX

He/She looks like …
This one could be …
Perhaps it's (Bob Marley)'s son/daughter/mother
Maybe it's …
It's difficult to say, but …

3 Each of the famous people in the photographs in 2 is related to one of the people below. Match each of the famous people to their relation and say how they are related.

– He could be Arantxa's father

Test your questions

1 These are the answers from an interview with a celebrity. Write the questions.

a) I was born in London, but I've got dual nationality because my mother's from Nicaragua. *Where were you born?*

b) No, I'm living in Ibiza now. *Are you living in London now?*

c) Not long. I moved from London with my two daughters, Assisi and Amba, about six months ago. *When did you move from London to Ibiza?*

d) Yeah, very happy. We love the outdoor life. Also, my mother's a Spanish speaker and I feel more comfortable in a Latin country. *Are you happy there?*

e) Yeah, I've made lots of new friends here. A few English, but my two best friends are Argentinian and Spanish. *Have you met a lot of people?*

f) I'm a painter, but I've recently started a jewellery business with a friend, and that takes up most of my time. I also do some modelling when I need the cash! *What do you do for a living?*

g) Well, with a business and two young children I don't have much free time, but I love reading and listening to music. *What do you do in your free time?*

h) All sorts: pop music and classical. *What sort of music do you like?*

i) No, never, but don't tell my father. *Do you ever listen the Rolling Stone?*

j) Not very often. My mother's in New York and my father's often on tour. But we all love big family get-togethers. *How often do you see your parents?*

k) That's a difficult question because I've been to so many amazing places, but I think Brazil is my favourite. The children love it there too. *What's your favorite place in the word to live?*

l) I think my father chose it: my mother wanted me to have a Spanish name. *Who chose your name?*

HANDICAP → Discapacitados (people)

2 🔊 01 Listen to the interview. Are your questions the same as the ones on the recording?

Pronunciation

1 🔊 02 Look at tapescript 02 and listen to the questions. <u>Underline</u> the strongest stress in each question. (página 148)

For example:
Where were you <u>born</u>?

2 Work with someone you don't know very well. Use questions from the interview and the following prompts to find out as much as you can about each other.

Have you …?   What's your favourite …?   Who …?   Do you enjoy …?
Are you good at …?   Can you …?   How long have you …?   Do you ever …?
Are you interested in …?

Friends   UNIT 1   5

Close up

Question forms

Work with a partner and discuss the following:

a) In each of the following questions, which word is the *subject*? Which is the *auxiliary*? Which is the *main verb*?

1. Has she been to Paris?
2. Did you have a good flight?
3. Is John staying at the George V?
4. What do you do?

b) In a question, does the subject usually come before or after the auxiliary?

c) What tenses are used in a)?

d) Match the tenses to the auxiliaries.

continuous tenses — have/has/had
perfect tenses — do/does/did
simple tenses — am/is/are/was/were

[Language Reference p8]

e) There are *nine modal auxiliaries*. Three of them are *can, could* and *would*. What are the other six?

f) *Which, when* and *how* are question words. There are five other important question words. What are they?

g) Where does a question word usually go in a question?

Subject questions

1. Which person is the *subject* and which is the *object* in this sentence?

> Mark Chapman shot John Lennon in December 1980.

2. What are the answers to these two questions?

   1. Who did Mark Chapman shoot?
   2. Who shot John Lennon?

   a) Is *who* the subject or the object of each question?
   b) Which question uses an auxiliary?

3. The words in these sentences have been mixed up. Put the words in the correct order. Add *did* when necessary.

   a) who Arantxa Sánchez trains?
   b) band play Bob Marley which with?
   c) Mick Jagger with songs who writes?
   d) marry Yoko Ono who?
   e) appear $1 million advert Claudia Schiffer in who car a paid to?
   f) for the World Ronaldo play in Cup who 1998?

   Match the questions to the answers in the box.

   > John Lennon   Keith Richards   The Wailers   Citroën   Brazil   Her father

4. Use the words in the box to make five true sentences.

a)	Elton John	died	Evita in the film of the same name.
b)	Madonna	wrote	*Candle in the Wind* at Princess Diana's funeral.
c)	Edith Piaf	played	*La Traviata* in 1853.
d)	Frank Sinatra	sang	*Je Ne Regrette Rien*.
e)	Verdi	performed	in 1998.

UNIT 1 *Friends*

TO BOTHER → Molestar

5 Write two questions for each of the sentences in 4.

For example:
a) Who performed …   Who performed 'Candle in the Wind' at Princess Diana's funeral?
   Which song …   Which song did Elton John perform at Princess Diana's funeral?

b) Who …   Which part …
c) Who …   Which famous song …
d) When …   Which American singer …
e) When …   Who …

Prepositions

1 Sentences in English can end with a preposition, for example: *Where do you come from?* Which prepositions are missing from these questions?

a) Who do you usually have lunch _____ ?
b) What are you learning English _____ ?
c) What do you spend most money _____ ?
d) Who does your teacher remind you _____ ?
e) When you go out with your friends what do you talk _____ ?
f) What kind of music do you like listening _____ ?

2 Work with a partner. Ask your partner the questions in 1.

Using questions

1 Many questions are formed using the same few structures. Match the questions to the most appropriate answers.

request → petición

Have you got …?	a) Have you got any children? (información)	d) Yes, plenty, thank you.
	b) Have you got a pen? (petición)	c) Sure. What do you want?
	c) Have you got a moment? (")	b) Yes, here you are.
	d) Have you got enough potatoes? (oferta)	a) Yes, three.
Is that …?	a) Is that your father?	c) Yes, I'm sorry. Is he bothering you?
	b) Is that my pen?	d) We'd better get a taxi. → Mejor cogemos un taxi.
	c) Is that your dog?	b) Yes, it is. I'm sorry, it looks just like mine.
	d) Is that the time?	a) Yes. That's the day he joined the army.
Would you like to …?	a) Would you like to go out for a coffee?	c) It's always been my dream to do that.
	b) Would you like to call me tomorrow?	d) Certainly. Is it OK if I smoke?
	c) Would you like to live in the country?	b) OK. What time would be good for you?
	d) Would you like to wait here for a moment?	a) Good idea. Where shall we go?

Language Reference p8

2 Which of the questions are *asking for information*? What are the others doing? Imagine the situations.   HAVE YOU GOT …? , IS THAT?

Noughts & Crosses

1 Work in two teams. Team A look at page 140.
                      Team B look at page 143.

2 Use the questions to play *Noughts and Crosses*. The aim of the game is to get a line of noughts or crosses before the other team.

a) Draw a Noughts and Crosses grid on a separate piece of paper.
b) Decide whether your team is noughts (0) or crosses (X).
c) Take it in turns to ask and answer questions. When a team answers a question correctly, they choose a square on the grid and mark a nought or a cross.

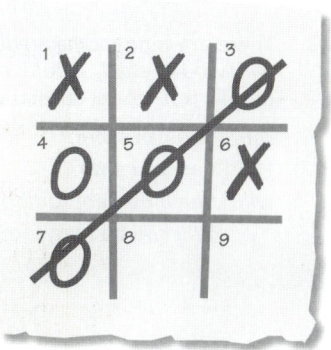

Friends UNIT 1

Language reference: questions

Question forms have many uses. Here are a few examples:

Asking for information:	Where's the nearest post office?
Asking for permission:	Is it OK if I leave work early tonight?
Making requests:	Could you pass me the salt?
Making offers:	Can I help?
Making invitations:	Would you like to go out for dinner?
Making suggestions:	Shall we go to the cinema?
Showing friendly interest:	How are your children?

Yes/No questions

1 When *be* is the only verb in the sentence, you put it before the subject in the question.

   Affirmative: **You were** in my class last year.
   Question: **Were you** in my class last year?

2 You usually put the auxiliary before the subject of the sentence.

   Present continuous
   You're working for IBM.
   Are you working for IBM?

   Past continuous
   You were thinking about Jack again.
   Were you thinking about Jack again?

   Present perfect
   She's been to Paris recently.
   Has she been to Paris recently?

   Past perfect
   He'd already left when she arrived.
   Had he already left when she arrived?

   Present simple
   He speaks English very well.
   Does he speak English?

   Past simple
   She played football yesterday.
   Did she play football yesterday?

   Note: Because there is no auxiliary in the affirmative of simple tenses, you use the auxiliary *do* to form questions.

3 There are nine *modal auxiliary verbs: can, could, will, would, shall, should, may, might, must*. You usually put modal auxiliaries before the subject.

   can   **You can** swim.
         Can you swim?
   will **She'll be** here tomorrow.
         Will she be here tomorrow?

Open questions

Open questions use question words: *when, where, who, why, how, which, what* and *whose*. You usually put the question word at the beginning of a question.

Do you smoke?	**How much** do you smoke?
Are you going?	**When** are you going?
Has he gone?	**Where** has he gone?
Are you tired?	**Why** are you tired?

Subject questions

When the question word is the subject of the sentence you do not use *do, does* or *did*:

Affirmative: *Mark Chapman shot John Lennon in 1980.*
Subject question: ***Who shot*** *John Lennon?*

This happens most often with *who*, but can also happen with *which* and *what*.
Which *company* ***bought*** *Rolls Royce in 1998?*
What happened *next?*

Questions ending with prepositions

Many verbs can be followed by a *dependent preposition*. You usually put the preposition at the end of a question.
*He spent all his money **on** whisky and beer.*
*What did he spend all his money **on**?*

Friends for life

1. Tina and Will met when they were both studying at the same university. Three years later, a student magazine contacted them and asked them to take part in a survey to find out how many people had stayed friends.
   Look at the photographs of Tina and Will. Do you think the following statements are true or false?

   a) Tina and Will had similar interests when they were at university.
   b) They chose similar careers when they finished their studies.
   c) They have similar lifestyles now.

2. Read what they both say about their friendship and find out if you were right.

That was then this is now

TINA I first met Will when I was looking for someone to share the house I was renting. I put an advertisement in the local student newspaper and he was one of the people who answered it. When we met, we hit it off straightaway and I told him he could move in.

Living with Will was fun. We soon found out that we had a lot in common and quickly
5 became close friends. We always had really good discussions about everything that was important to us at the time: politics, the environment, literature and other less important things like cooking. We also liked the same music and that's important when you're sharing a house. We fell out a couple of times about the housework. Will thinks I'm untidy but I think life's too short to worry about things like that.

10 When we graduated three years ago, we went our separate ways and since then our lives have been very different. I went back to my home town and got a job as a production assistant for art exhibitions. I like my job because I'm helping young people to get involved in the arts. I'm living with my parents because I'm not earning very much. Will thinks I'm crazy because money is very important to him now, but I get a lot of personal satisfaction
15 from my job. He's earning a lot of money, but he doesn't have time to spend with his family and his friends. I don't see him very often now. When he comes down for the weekend we have a laugh, but our lifestyles are so different now that we don't have very much to talk about.

WILL Tina and I got on very well together at university. When we first met, we clicked
20 straightaway and we ended up sharing a house for nearly three years. We had the same attitude to the important things in life and the only thing we argued about was the housework. I'm a Virgo so I'm very tidy whereas Tina's the opposite. I don't think she ever found out where we kept the vacuum cleaner!

When I left university, I moved to London and got a job in a finance company. I have to
25 work long hours and I don't really enjoy what I'm doing but I earn a very good salary. I'm very ambitious and I want to get to the top of my profession. I enjoy spending money on CDs, clothes, a nice car and going out to good restaurants. Tina's working really hard as well, but she's not earning much. I don't understand why she's doing it. I think she's having a holiday – it seems very idealistic to me. Anyway, it means that our lifestyles are
30 very different now so we've drifted apart. We haven't fallen out or anything. We still talk on the phone and when I go down to visit her, we have a laugh. I know she'll always be there for me.

(Adapted from *The Independent*, 9 April 1998)

Together at University — Tina now — Will now

Friends **UNIT 1**

DRIFT → "arrastrar"
TO GAMBLE → jugar en el casino.

Lexis 1 Tina and Will use several expressions to talk about their friendship. Complete as many of these expressions as you can from memory. Compare them with a partner. Then look at the article again to check.

(1) We met in the casino, they were working.
(2) They don't have much in common.
(3) They are like sisters.
(4) She's pretty, blonde long hair...
(5) She's full-time mum / housewife.
(6) She has a son.

a) Two expressions that mean 'we liked one another immediately'.
We clicked straightaway. We hit it off straightaway

b) An expression that means 'we had similar interests'.
We had a lot in common

c) An expression that means 'we enjoyed one another's company'.
We got on very well

d) An expression that means 'we got to know one another very well'.
We became close friends

e) An expression that means 'we argued'.
We fell out

f) Two expressions that mean 'we became more distant from one another'.
We went our separate ways We drifted apart

g) An expression that means 'I know I can count on her when I need a friend'.
She'll always be there for me

2 The following is a summary of Tina and Will's friendship. Put the lines of the summary in the correct order.

(3) met. They became close
(7) separate ways and they've drifted
(4) friends and got on
(1) Tina and Will hit it
(6) in common. Now they have gone their

(2) off immediately when they first
(9) out and they say that they are still
(10) there for one another. el uno para
(8) apart. They haven't fallen el otro.
(5) well together. They had a lot

Anecdote 1 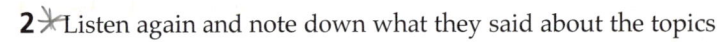 03 Listen to Balvir telling Tim about a close friend. Which of the following topics do they talk about? Cuando no se sabe si es una chica o un chico se usa THEY.

☑ How did you first meet? (1) ✓
☐ What was your first impression of them?
☐ What do you like about them?
☐ What don't you like about them?
☑ What do you have in common? ✓
☑ How do you differ? (2)
☑ Why did you become such (3) close friends?
☐ Will you be friends for life?

☑ What do they look like? (4) (she)
☐ What are they like as a person? ✓
☐ What special talents and abilities do they have?
☐ What kind of clothes do they wear?
☑ What's their job? (5)
☑ What's their family like? (6)
☑ What are their hobbies and interests? ✓
☐ What do you do and what do you talk about when you're together?

Balvir and Tim

2 Listen again and note down what they said about the topics.

3 Think about a close friend. You are going to tell a partner about him or her. Choose from the list in 1 the things you want to talk about. Think about what you will say and what language you will need. We were wet when we ...

4 Tell your partner about your friend.

10 UNIT 1 Friends

You've got a friend

Vowel sounds

1 Vowels in English can be *long*, as in 'feel' /fi:l/, or *short*, as in 'fill' /fɪl/. Look at the list of words. Think about the underlined sounds. Which are long vowels and which are short vowels? Divide them into two groups.

   a) call
   b) come
   c) darkest
   d) friend
   e) good
   f) got
   g) hurt
   h) need
   i) soon
   j) winter
   k) thank
   l) think

2 04 Listen to the words, then match the sounds to the phonetic symbols.

   Long: /ɑ:/ /i:/ /u:/ /ɜ:/ /ɔ:/
   Short: /æ/ /e/ /ɪ/ /ə/ /ʌ/ /ʊ/ /ɒ/

   For example: c<u>a</u>ll – /ɔ:/

3 Think of other words for each sound. Check them in your dictionary.

4 05 You are going to listen to the song *You've Got a Friend*. Tick the words from 1 as you hear them. Which word isn't in the song?

The Brand New Heavies entered the London club scene in the 1980s. Their music is influenced by 70s funk, soul music and American rap. They recorded their version of *You've Got a Friend* in 1997 on their album *Shelter*.

Carole King wrote *You've Got a Friend* in 1971

Friends UNIT 1

5 Look at the lyrics. The lines have been cut in half. In Column A the lines are in the correct order but in Column B they are mixed up. Listen and match the two halves of each line.

		A	B
VERSE 1	1)	When you're down	2) loving care
	2)	And you need some	6) even your darkest night
	3)	And nothing, no,	4) and think of me
	4)	Close your eyes	1) and troubled
	5)	Oh, and soon	3) is going right
	6)	To brighten up	5) I will be there
CHORUS	1)	You just call out	6) be there, yes I will
	2)	And you know	4) summer or fall *otoño*
	3)	I'll come running,	5) is call
	4)	Don't you know that winter, spring,	2) wherever I am
	5)	All you've got to do	7) a friend
	6)	And I'll	3) yeah, to see you again
	7)	You've got	1) my name
VERSE 2	1)	Ain't it good to know that	4) if you let them
	2)	People can	2) be so cold
	3)	They'll hurt you	5) let them
	4)	Take your very soul *alma*	1) you've got a friend
	5)	So don't	3) and desert you *abandonar*

Lexis

1 One of the lines is 'Ain't it good to know that you've got a friend'. What does *ain't* mean? Is it correct English?

2 Read the following lines from different pop songs. Rewrite the underlined words in more formal English.

 a) I <u>wanna</u> hold your hand.
 b) The sun's <u>gonna</u> shine on everything you do.
 c) It <u>ain't</u> me you're looking for, babe.
 d) The way I'm feeling, <u>yeah</u>, it just <u>don't</u> feel right.
 e) I can't get <u>no</u> satisfaction.
 f) You <u>gotta</u> roll with it.

3 Try to match the singer or band in the box with the lines of the songs in 2.

> Oasis   the Beatles   Bob Dylan   All Saints   the Rolling Stones   Lighthouse Family

Check your answers on page 141.

4 Collect other examples of 'pop song English' and bring them to class.

Noel and Liam Gallagher of Oasis

UNIT 1 *Friends*

You've got mail

1 These e-mail messages were sent to a magazine for English language students.
   a) Which ones do you think are the most and least interesting? Why?
   b) Are there any messages that you would be interested in answering?

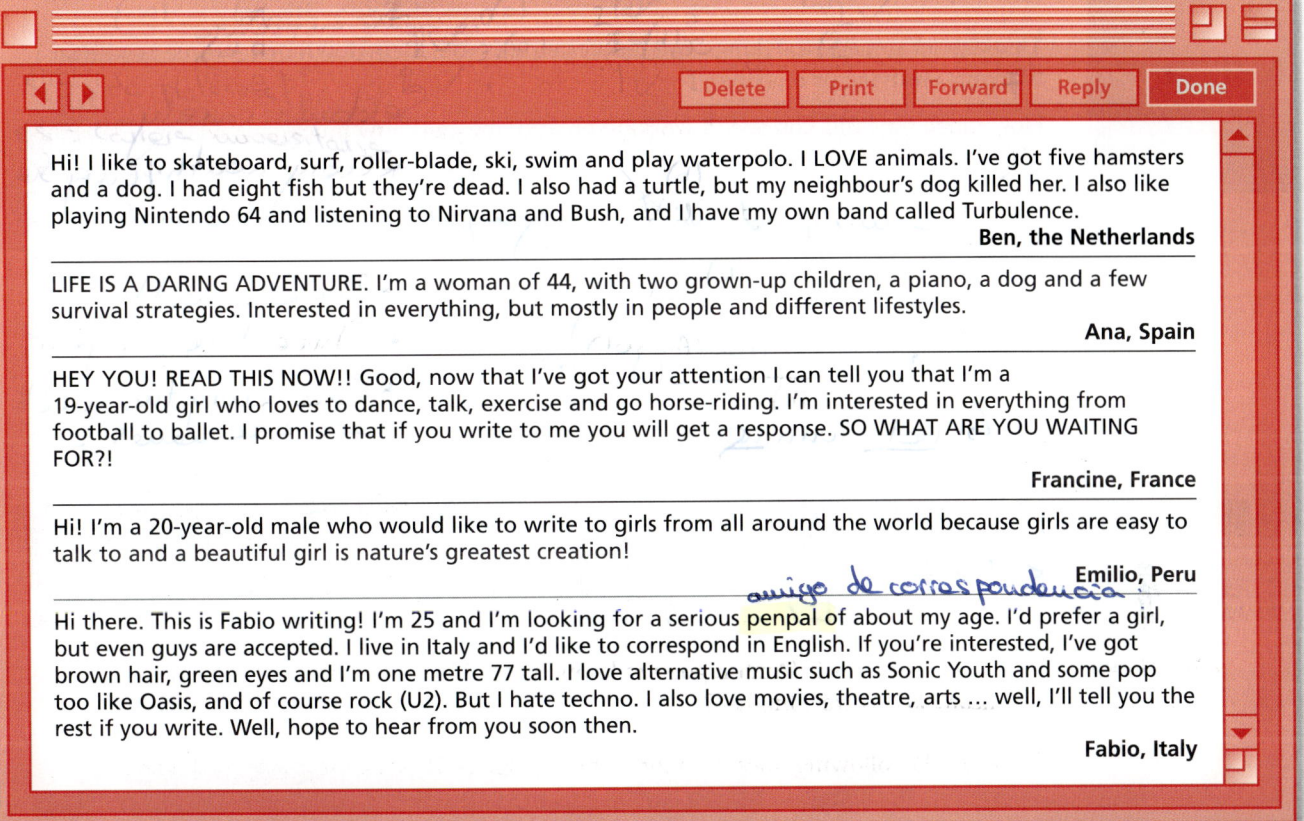

Hi! I like to skateboard, surf, roller-blade, ski, swim and play waterpolo. I LOVE animals. I've got five hamsters and a dog. I had eight fish but they're dead. I also had a turtle, but my neighbour's dog killed her. I also like playing Nintendo 64 and listening to Nirvana and Bush, and I have my own band called Turbulence.
Ben, the Netherlands

LIFE IS A DARING ADVENTURE. I'm a woman of 44, with two grown-up children, a piano, a dog and a few survival strategies. Interested in everything, but mostly in people and different lifestyles.
Ana, Spain

HEY YOU! READ THIS NOW!! Good, now that I've got your attention I can tell you that I'm a 19-year-old girl who loves to dance, talk, exercise and go horse-riding. I'm interested in everything from football to ballet. I promise that if you write to me you will get a response. SO WHAT ARE YOU WAITING FOR?!
Francine, France

Hi! I'm a 20-year-old male who would like to write to girls from all around the world because girls are easy to talk to and a beautiful girl is nature's greatest creation!
Emilio, Peru

Hi there. This is Fabio writing! I'm 25 and I'm looking for a serious penpal of about my age. I'd prefer a girl, but even guys are accepted. I live in Italy and I'd like to correspond in English. If you're interested, I've got brown hair, green eyes and I'm one metre 77 tall. I love alternative music such as Sonic Youth and some pop too like Oasis, and of course rock (U2). But I hate techno. I also love movies, theatre, arts … well, I'll tell you the rest if you write. Well, hope to hear from you soon then.
Fabio, Italy

2 Write an e-mail with a message about yourself.

3 This is a letter written by one of the people in 1. Read it and decide who wrote it.

Dear ....
Thank you for your e-mail message and your adress. I am writting to you to tell you more about myself and also to send you a photograph. That's me on the left. The one in the middle is my older brother, Olivier, and that's my sister Sonia on the right. I get on very well with my sister, but my brother and I have nothing in common — he's very serious and borring. He just spends all his time on the computer and never goes out.

I like going out — especially to dance. On Saturday nights I dance in a nightclub to earn some money because I'm a student. I'm studying English and Spanish at university, but I'm not sure why. I mean, I don't know what I want to do when I leave university.

Anyway, I love travaling and languages will be usefull for that. Last summer I studyed English at a school in Chicago (my parents are divorced and my dad lives there now) and next summer I want to go to Spain to learn flamenco and go horse-riding on the beach.

What else can I tell you? I'm single. I had a boyfriend for six months, but we split up because he was too jealous. I want to get maried and have children one day, but not yet!

As I told you in the e-mail, I'm interested in just about everything — even football! How about you? Please write soon and tell me what you're interested in. Appologies for my bad spelling.
Love …

4 Find ten spelling mistakes and ten missing capital letters and write the words correctly.

5 Write a letter introducing yourself to a penpal.

2 Relax

Think about some of the things you did yesterday. Note them down under three headings: working, studying or relaxing.

How much time did you spend working or studying, and how much time relaxing? Was this a typical day? Compare with a partner.

The Little Book of Calm

1   Look at the photograph. How do you think the woman is feeling? Look at the book she's reading. What do you think it's about?

The Little Book of Calm is only 10cm x 10cm. It contains only 1,000 words but has sold over two million copies and has made its author into a multi-millionaire.

Sally

Barbara

Robert

Peter

2 According to *The Little Book of Calm*, a relaxed person:

a) spends time alone.
b) has a short nap during the day.
c) goes for a walk in the country or in a park.
d) does some physical exercise.
e) goes running.
f) floats in water.
g) has a leisurely hot bath.
h) takes a different route to work or college.
i) drinks hot water.
j) has a massage.
k) goes dancing.
l) drinks milk.
m) changes their routine.

The four people in the photos read *The Little Book of Calm*. Do you think they liked it? Why/Why not?

3 🔲 06 Listen to each speaker. Were you right? What activities from 2 did each one mention?

Close up

Adverbs of frequency

1 Listen again and read tapescript 06. <u>Underline</u> all the words and expressions that tell you how often people do things.

For example:
… I <u>never</u> have time for a nap during the day. I have a massage <u>from time to time</u>, but I <u>hardly ever</u> have a leisurely bath …

2 Work with a partner. Match each of the words and expressions you have underlined in the tapescript with the word or expression below that has the most similar meaning.

| often   regularly   sometimes   not very often   don't ever |

3 Ask your partner questions to find out how often they do any of the things recommended by *The Little Book of Calm*. Do they do any other relaxing activities?

| Do you ever …?   Yes. Every day/often /once a week /sometimes …
                   Yes, but not very often/hardly ever/No, never … |

Relax UNIT 2 15

4 Where would you put *often* and where would you put *every morning* in this sentence?

Bob [a] walks to work [b].

Language Reference p16

5 Do the adverbs below usually go in position (a) or position (b)?

frequently from time to time always hardly ever never now and again occasionally once a month usually once in a blue moon rarely sometimes twice a year normally once every two weeks

6 Put the adverbs in **bold** into these sentences.

a) I eat out in restaurants. **once in a blue moon**
b) I go to the hairdresser's. **once every six weeks**
c) I argue with my brothers and sisters. **hardly ever**
d) I check my e-mails. **every day**
e) I listen to classical music. **now and again**
f) I forget where I've put my keys. **sometimes**
g) I'm late for appointments. **often**
h) I go for a run. **once or twice a week**

7 Do you think these sentences are true for your partner? Rewrite them changing the adverbs as necessary.

For example:
Mikel eats out in restaurants two or three times a week.

Now ask your partner questions to check if the sentences you have written are true.

For example:
How often do you go to the hairdresser's?
Do you ever listen to classical music?

8 Work with a partner. Ask your partner questions to find out how similar or different you are.

How often do you Do you ever	receive letters or e-mails dream in colour go to the gym surf the Internet rent videos get headaches look at yourself in the mirror write letters go to the theatre

Language reference: adverbs of frequency

Adverbs

always, often, frequently, usually, normally, generally, sometimes, occasionally, rarely, not often, hardly ever, never

The most usual positions are:
Before the main verb:
I **sometimes** have time for a nap.
I **rarely** read the paper.

After the verb *to be*:
He's **always** late.
She's **hardly ever** in when I call.

After the first auxiliary:
I've **often** wondered why he hates her so much.
He's **never** been sent a Valentine's card.

Adverb phrases

two or three times a week, every morning, once a month, from time to time, now and again, once in a blue moon, etc.

The most usual position is at the beginning or end of a clause.
I have a massage **from time to time**.
I have an English lesson **twice a week**.
Once a month I go dancing with my friends.

Note: always, usually and normally are not used on their own to tell you 'how often' something happens.
How often do you go out? ~~Always.~~ ✗
                        Every night. ✔
Do you ever play tennis? ~~Yes, usually.~~ ✗
                        Yes, once or twice a week. ✔
Do you often get headaches? ~~Yes, normally.~~ ✗
                        Yes, frequently. ✔

Sally sees herself as she really is

1 Read the article and find out:
   a) how Sally changes her mind about how she sees herself.
   b) what she thinks of *The Little Book of Calm*.

(Adapted from *The Weekend Telegraph*, 15 November 1997)

I was under the impression that I was quite a relaxed sort of person until I watched the video of my sister's wedding. As I watched myself, I realised that I am not the cool, calm, sophisticated woman I thought I was. In fact I'm the opposite. I fidget. I talk non-stop, fiddle with my hair, scratch my nose, wave my hands around like a lunatic, bite my nails, and I never sit back and relax on a seat, I sit on the edge of it, ready to jump up and go somewhere else.

So it was no surprise when a friend gave me *The Little Book of Calm* for my last birthday.

I read the blurb on the back cover. 'Feeling stressed?' it asked. 'Need some help to regain balance in your life? *The Little Book of Calm* is full of advice to follow and thoughts to inspire. Open it at any page and you will find a path to inner peace.'

So I opened it at any page and read the advice: 'Wear white.' Wear white! I haven't worn white since my first child was born. This is not good advice for someone who has to deal with young children and their dirty fingers every day.

I turned to another page. 'Take a lesson in calmness from children. Watch how children live every moment for the pleasure of the moment.' Do you know my children? When one of them is screaming, 'Aargh! he's pulling my hair!' and the other is screaming, 'She's taken my sweets!', the feeling I get is not calmness.

'Make an appointment with yourself to deal with worries at a specific time in the future.' Make an appointment! I've already got too many appointments. I don't need another appointment to worry about.

'Get up early and watch the sunrise.' Well that's nothing new. I wake up at the crack of dawn every day, thanks to the children. I haven't had a lie-in for years.

'For every ninety minutes of work, take a twenty-minute break.' Yes, I like that. But there's a problem. Who's going to tell my children 'Don't disturb Mummy now, she's having a break.'?

'Use a soft voice.' With fighting children? I don't think so. In fact, my voice is getting louder every day.

I decided to try once more. 'Rediscover milk.' No problem. I love milk and I drink it all the time … with a shot of strong Italian espresso coffee in it, of course. ■

2 Are these sentences true or false?
   a) Before seeing the video, Sally thought she was a calm sort of person.
   b) She wasn't surprised when she saw herself on video.
   c) She discovered that she's the sort of person who never keeps still.
   d) She read *The Little Book of Calm* from cover to cover.
   e) The advice in *The Little Book of Calm* changed her life.

3 Have you ever seen yourself on video? What were the circumstances? Were you surprised at how you looked? How did you feel about it? Ask a partner.

Lexis

1 Find expressions in the article with a similar meaning to the underlined words. Compare with a partner. Then look back at the article to check.

a) I never stop moving. (line 6)
b) I talk constantly. (line 6)
c) I touch my hair. (lines 6–7)
d) Arrange a time to give your attention to your worries. (lines 29–30)
e) I wake up very early in the morning. (line 34)
f) I never sleep late in the mornings. (line 35)
g) For every ninety minutes of work, rest for twenty minutes. (line 36–37)

2 Complete these sentences with words and expressions from 1 above. Sometimes you will need to change the grammar of the expressions.

a) Nobody can ever get a word in because you …
b) Don't phone me before eleven tomorrow morning. I want to …
c) Did you remember to ring the dentist and …
d) You look tired. Why don't you …
e) Sit still! Stop …
f) Carla, you'll break that if you keep on …
g) In this job you'll have a lot of new problems to …
h) Our flight leaves at 8.05 so we need to get up …

3 How well do you know your partner? Read the questionnaire on the right and choose A) or B) according to which you think is true for your partner.

4 The more B) answers you have, the more relaxed you are. Find out who's the most relaxed person in the class.

Close up

Present tenses

1 The article *Sally sees herself as she really is* uses three different present tense structures: the present simple, the present continuous and the present perfect. Look at the extracts below. Which tense is each one in?

a) I bite my nails and I never sit back and relax on a seat.
b) I haven't worn white since my first child was born.
c) 'Aargh! he's pulling my hair!'
d) 'She's taken my sweets!'
e) I wake up at the crack of dawn every day.
f) I haven't had a lie-in for years.
g) My voice is getting louder every day.
h) Don't disturb Mummy now, she's having a break.
i) I love milk and I drink it all the time.

HOW RELAXED ARE YOU?

1	A	I start worrying about Monday on Friday evening.
	B	I find it easy to switch off from work and relax at the weekend.
2	A	I'm always fidgeting.
	B	I find it easy to keep still.
3	A	When I visit people's homes, I sit on the edge of the seat for the first hour.
	B	When I visit people's homes, I sit back and relax straightaway.
4	A	I'm always fiddling with something.
	B	I don't need to have something in my hands.
5	A	I bite my nails.
	B	I never, or almost never, bite my nails.
6	A	I worry all the time.
	B	If I have a problem, I deal with it. If I can't do anything, I don't worry about it.
7	A	When I make an appointment, I start worrying that I'm going to forget it.
	B	When I make an appointment, I write it down.
8	A	I hate waiting in queues, I'm too impatient. If I can I push in.
	B	I accept waiting in queues because it's fair.
9	A	I lose my temper two or three times a week.
	B	I hardly ever lose my temper.
10	A	I usually arrive at appointments too early or too late.
	B	I usually arrive at appointments on time.

Why are you sitting on the edge of your chair?

I'm preparing myself in case someone should suddenly take it away…

Language Reference p19

2 Work with a partner. Look at the extracts from 1 and match each one to one of the following uses:
- shows that a situation is true all the time (present simple)
- shows that an activity is in progress and is temporary (present continuous)
- shows that something which started or happened in the past is important now (present perfect)

She's taken my sweets! → ejemplo típico.

3 Look at the four paragraphs below. Put the verbs in brackets in an appropriate present tense. Who or what are the paragraphs about? present simple, cont. o perfect

A
I (1) _wake up_ (wake up) three or four times every night. I (2) _'m giving up_ (give up) smoking and I (3) _haven't go_ (not/go) to the pub for two weeks. I (4) _don't want_ (not/want) to go to work and I (5) _hurry_ (hurry) home every evening. I'm the happiest man in the world.

＊ A NEW FATHER

B
I (1) _sleep_ (sleep) a lot during the day and often (2) _go out_ (go out) all night. I (3) _visit_ (visit) all the neighbours' gardens but I (4) _walk_ (walk) softly so nobody (5) _hear_ (hear) me. I (6) _wash_ (wash) at least twice a day and I (7) _eat_ (eat) as often as I can. I (8) _use up_ (use up) several of my nine lives already.

＊ A CAT

C
I (1) _'ve finished_ (finish) university but I (2) _don't know_ (not/ know) what I really (3) _want_ (want) to do so I (4) _'m working_ (work) here until I decide. I (5) _____ (wear) a uniform and a very silly hat. I sometimes (6) _serve_ (serve) 100 people in one day and at the end of the day I (7) _smell_ (smell) of chips. I (8) _'ve worked_ (work) here for less than a week and I'm already absolutely exhausted.

＊ A FAST FOOD RESTAURANT

D
I'm 28 and so I (1) _'m getting_ (get) old for this job but I (2) _'m making_ (make) a lot of money and I (3) _'m investing_ (invest) it wisely. I (4) _'ve travelled_ (travel) to some very exotic locations since I started 12 years ago and I (5) _'ve worked_ (work) in at least ten capital cities including Paris, Rome, London and Tokyo. I (6) _eat_ (eat) very healthily and I (7) _drink_ (drink) a lot of water. In fact, I (8) _'ve been_ (be) on a diet for 12 years.

＊ A MODEL

4 On a piece of paper write three true sentences about yourself. Use a different present tense for each one. Fold the piece of paper and give it to your teacher. Then take another student's piece of paper and guess who it belongs to.

Language reference: present tense structures

The present simple
You use the present simple mainly to talk about things which are true all the time.

1 Habits and routines
   I **bite** my nails and I never **sit** back and **relax** on a seat.
   I **play** football with my friends every Sunday.

2 Facts and situations we see as more or less permanent
   I **love** milk.
   The sun **is** 96 million miles from the earth.

The present continuous
You use the present continuous to talk about present situations which you see as temporary.

1 Activities in progress
   Don't disturb Mummy, she's **having** a break.
   I'm **learning** two foreign languages at the moment.

2 Changing situations
   My voice **is getting** louder every day.
   I'm **starting** to understand English much better now.

The present perfect
You can use the present perfect to talk about a present situation which is connected with the past.

1 A present situation which started in the past
   I **haven't worn** white since my first child was born.
   I've **worked** here for less than a week.

2 A past event which caused a present situation
   I can't finish the work. My computer **has crashed**.
   Where's my mobile phone? Oh, no, I've **left** it in the taxi.

Relax UNIT 2 19

Books, films & music

1 Find out how many people in the class:

- are reading a novel at the moment.
- enjoy reading biographies and autobiographies.
- still listen to the first records, tapes or CDs they bought.
- have a favourite place to read.
- prefer watching a film to reading a book.
- have been to a concert recently.
- have seen a film they didn't enjoy recently.

2 🔊 07 Listen to seven dialogues. What are the people talking about in each one: a book, a film or a piece of music?

3 Listen again. Which words and expressions helped you? Note them down under three headings: books, films, and music.

4 Find words connected with books, films and music and add them to the three lists.

reggaestorylinepaperbackhithiphopbluesnovelopera
shortstorypremierplotdancemusicalsciencefictionhorror
classicalsubtitlesstereosystembandorchestrasoundtrackdirector

5 🔊 08 Listen to these extracts from film soundtracks. What type of film do you think they go with? Choose from the list below.

| romantic comedy | gangster | action | thriller | science fiction |
| horror | western | love story | war | comedy |

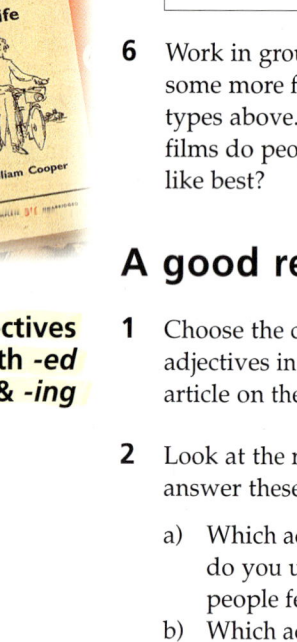

6 Work in groups. Think of some more films of each of the types above. Which types of films do people in your group like best?

A good read

Adjectives with -ed & -ing

1 Choose the correct form of the adjectives in bold in the article on the right.

2 Look at the replies in 1 and answer these questions:

a) Which adjective ending do you use to say how people feel?
b) Which adjective ending do you use to describe the people or thing that causes the feeling?

3 How do you choose a book?

We asked several people the question, 'How do you choose a book to read?'. Here are their replies:

1 'I judge the book by its cover. If the cover looks **interesting/interested**, I buy the book. Sometimes I'm lucky and the book is good, and sometimes I'm **disappointing/disappointed**.'

2 'I always read book reviews in newspapers and magazines and when I read about a book that sounds **interesting/interested**, I write it down in my diary.'

3 'I don't take any risks. I always read books by authors I know. I get really **exciting/excited** when one of my favourite authors brings out a new book and I buy it immediately. This way I'm never **disappointing/disappointed**.'

4 'I read the first page and if it's **boring/bored**, I don't buy the book. If I want to turn over the page and carry on reading, I buy the book.'

5 'It's easy. I never read fiction but I'm **fascinating/fascinated** by biographies of famous people. I find strong women in history particularly **inspiring/inspired**.'

6 'I tend to choose books written by women. They have a better feeling for characters and the relationships between them, and that's what I find **interesting/interested** in a book. Having said that, I've just finished a book by a man and it was brilliant!'

How are you feeling?

1 Tell your partner how you're feeling today. Explain why. Choose words from the box if appropriate.

> tired   happy   exhausted   excited   worried   cheerful
> relaxed   nervous   disappointed   confused   bored

2 Choose three other adjectives and say what makes you feel like this.

3 Choose three of the topics below and tell other students what you think about them. Use some of the words from 1.

For example:
I think the political situation in my country is very confusing.
I'm very worried about the political situation in my country.

- the political situation in your country
- the nightlife in your town
- winter
- karaoke
- English grammar
- motor-racing
- giving a speech
- jogging
- surfing the Internet
- finding out about other cultures
- travelling by air

Anecdote 4 Think about a film you have seen or a book you have read recently. You are going to tell a partner about it. Choose from one of the lists below the things you want to talk about. Think about what you will say and what language you will use.

☐ Where did you see the film? (at the cinema? at home? …)
☐ When did you see it?
☐ Why did you choose this film?
☐ What did you know about it beforehand?
☐ Who did you see it with?
☐ Do you know who directed the film?
☐ Who were the actors?
☐ What type of film was it?
☐ What was the main story?
☐ Did it have a happy ending?
☐ Did you enjoy the film more or less than you expected?
☐ Would you recommend this film?

☐ What was the last book you read?
☐ When did you read it?
☐ Why did you choose this book?
☐ Who wrote it?
☐ What did you know about it beforehand?
☐ Have you read any other books by the same author?
☐ Who were the main characters?
☐ What type of book was it?
☐ What was the main story?
☐ Did it have a happy ending?
☐ Did you enjoy the book more or less than you expected?
☐ Would you recommend this book?

5 Tell your partner about the film or the book.

Net reviews

1 Have you ever looked for information about a film on the Internet?

2 What do you think a film called *The Horse Whisperer* may be about?
Look at this web-page and match the headings to the information.

   a) cast
   b) keywords
   c) memorable quotes
   d) plot summary
   e) review
   f) type of film
   g) user rating
   h) title and main details

3 Read these comments made by Internet users about *The Horse Whisperer*. What rating out of ten do you think each person gave the film?

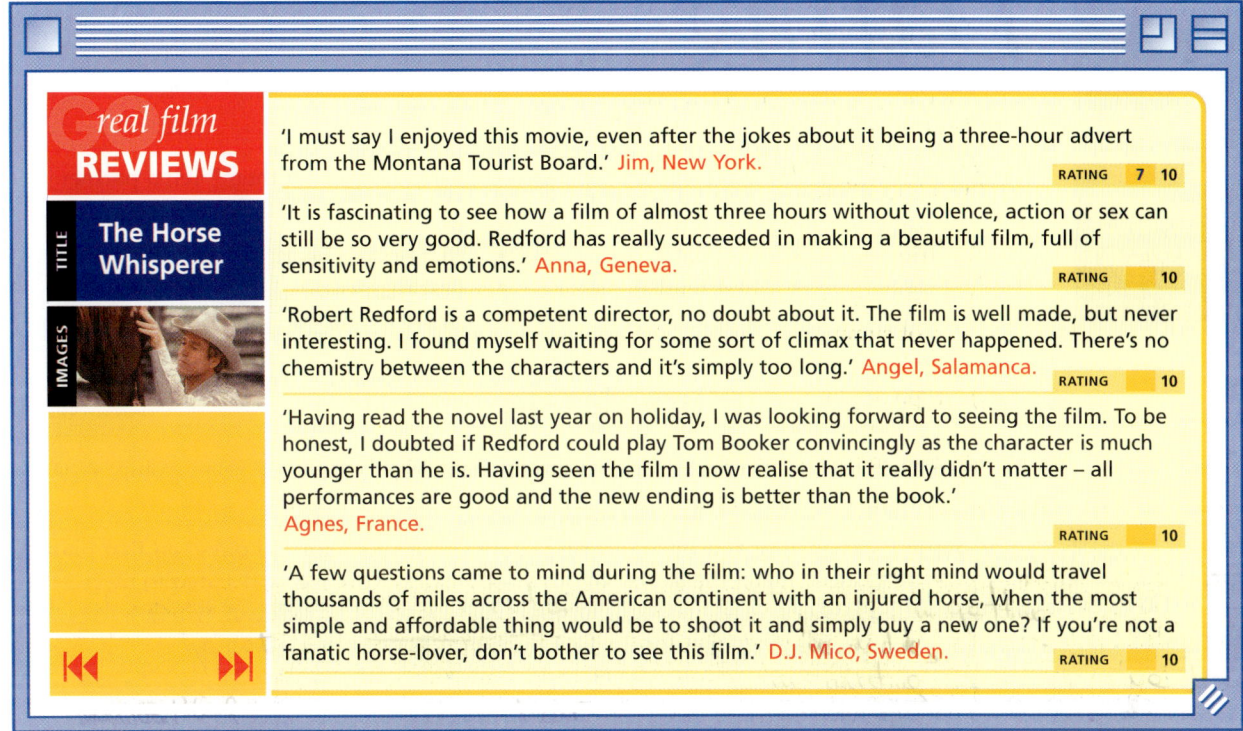

Great film **REVIEWS**

TITLE: **The Horse Whisperer**

'I must say I enjoyed this movie, even after the jokes about it being a three-hour advert from the Montana Tourist Board.' Jim, New York.
RATING 7 / 10

'It is fascinating to see how a film of almost three hours without violence, action or sex can still be so very good. Redford has really succeeded in making a beautiful film, full of sensitivity and emotions.' Anna, Geneva.
RATING __ / 10

'Robert Redford is a competent director, no doubt about it. The film is well made, but never interesting. I found myself waiting for some sort of climax that never happened. There's no chemistry between the characters and it's simply too long.' Angel, Salamanca.
RATING __ / 10

'Having read the novel last year on holiday, I was looking forward to seeing the film. To be honest, I doubted if Redford could play Tom Booker convincingly as the character is much younger than he is. Having seen the film I now realise that it really didn't matter – all performances are good and the new ending is better than the book.' Agnes, France.
RATING __ / 10

'A few questions came to mind during the film: who in their right mind would travel thousands of miles across the American continent with an injured horse, when the most simple and affordable thing would be to shoot it and simply buy a new one? If you're not a fanatic horse-lover, don't bother to see this film.' D.J. Mico, Sweden.
RATING __ / 10

A film review

Writing

THE HORSE WHISPERER

LANGUAGE TOOLBOX

It's directed by …
It's a romantic comedy/an action movie/a thriller …
It's based on a book by …
(Robert de Niro) plays the part of (Rocky Marciano)…
The film takes place in/ was filmed in …
What I liked/didn't like about it was …

Write a review of a film you have seen. Include the following information:

- the title of the film
- the type of film
- the name of the director (if you can remember)
- any other information such as whether it is based on a book, where it was filmed, etc
- the main actors and which characters they play
- a summary of the plot (in the present tense)
- what you particularly liked or didn't like about the film

3 Dating

Choose three or more of these 'firsts'. What do you remember about them? Tell a partner.

- first home
- first crush
- first holiday
- first friend
- first date
- first broken heart
- first hero
- first English lesson
- first regret
- first dance
- first kiss
- first trip abroad

Twenty-first century dating

1 Read these extracts from an article on how two couples began their relationship. What do you think happened before they first met or spoke to each other?

Couple 1 'Then Tom and I had our first "date" – we spoke for 11 hours and that phone call changed the course of our relationship. Now we've decided to meet.'

Couple 2 'It was love at first sight for Joel Emerson and Lisa Bunyan, which was lucky because they met for the first time on their wedding day!'

2 Work with a partner. Find out how the two couples met.

- Student A look at page 139 and read about couple 1.
- Student B look at page 140 and read about couple 2.

When you've finished reading, close your books and tell each other about the two 'dates'.

Lexis

1 Complete the sentences. Refer back to *Twenty-first century dating*, pages 139 and 140, if you need to.

a) I don't believe in _____ at first _____ .
b) Somewhere in the world there's a Mr or Miss _____ for everybody.
c) People don't usually marry the man or woman of their _____ .
d) _____ women enjoy their independence whereas _____ men tend to be keen to get married.
e) A man should _____ to a woman. It isn't natural for a woman to ask a man to marry her.
f) A marriage is more likely to succeed if both partners have had _____ before getting married.
g) If the bride and _____ are in love then it doesn't really matter what the parents think.
h) It's better to save the money than spend it on an expensive _____ in some exotic location.

2 Do you agree with the statements above? Discuss with your partner.

Listening

1 09 Listen to the two interviews about the relationships one year later. Have the relationships survived? What problems did each couple have? Listen and find out.

2 Listen again. Which of the following sentences belong to Tom and Kathy's story and which belong to Lisa and Joel's?

a) They arranged to meet at the airport.
b) She felt very nervous.
c) They've been married for a year now.
d) He looked just like his photo.
e) They've just celebrated their first wedding anniversary.
f) She went straight back home.
g) His mother hasn't spoken to him since the wedding.
h) They've moved away from their home town.
i) She hated his shoes.
j) They've been in their new home for about six months.

Close up

Present perfect & past simple

1 Look at these two sentences and answer the questions.

1 Kathy and Tom had an e-mail relationship for six months.
2 Joel and Lisa have been together for one year.

a) Do Kathy and Tom still communicate by e-mail?
b) Are Joel and Lisa still together?
c) Which tenses are the two sentences in?

2 Here is some more information about Tom, Kathy, Joel and Lisa. Look at the tenses of the verbs. Tick (✓) the situations which are still going on now.

a) Kathy has been single since she returned from Denver.
b) Tom went travelling in Europe for a few months.
c) Joel and Lisa haven't been back to their home town for six months.
d) Joel has been a marketing consultant since he left college.
e) Kathy has been looking for the man of her dreams for a long time.
f) Tom has had his own business manufacturing shoes since 1997.
g) Kathy hasn't used the Internet since she met Tom.
h) Lisa played the piano for ten years.

since & for

1 Complete the table on the right.

2 Write five sentences about yourself using the time expressions from the table: four that are true and one lie. Then read your sentences to your partner and see if they know which sentence is a lie.

since		for
yesterday	→	one day
1995	→	
	←	five minutes
my last birthday	→	
	←	ten years
I was born	→	
	←	two weeks
Christmas	→	
	←	an hour

Language reference: the past simple & the present perfect

The past simple

The past simple is used to fix events and situations in the past. You can use it to say when the event or situation happened.
I **saw** John in the supermarket.
He **lived** in Italy when he **was** a child.
Christina **went** to work on the bus until she **passed** her driving test.

The present perfect

The present perfect has several uses, but it always shows a connection between the past and now. In this unit, you use it to talk about situations which started in the past and which continue now.
We've **known** each other for 20 years.
I've **had** this watch since my 18th birthday.

since & for

Since is used to identify the point at which a period of time began. You normally use it with perfect tenses.
They've been married **since** 1999.
I haven't seen him **since** April.
She's lived in Chester **since** she was 18.

For is used with periods of time.
They've been married **for** five years.
He was in the army **for** 18 months.
I'll be at work **for** another hour if you want to call me.

'Remember our first meal together, when we sat on soap-boxes and ate off a tea-chest?'

How we met

1. Read Karen's account of how she met David and answer the questions.

   a) When did they meet?
   b) When did fate bring them together again?
   c) Where did she see him again?
   d) How long have they been together?

David and Karen

A KAREN, 18, AND DAVID, 21

I met him on a train last summer. He was gorgeous. We chatted and when I got off, he helped me with my luggage. Unfortunately, I was too shy to ask him for his phone number. But fate brought us together again. A few months ago, I saw him again at a party and he recognised me at once. The attraction was magnetic and now we've been together for three months, two weeks and three days.

2. Read Emma's account of how she met Paul. Complete the account with appropriate time expressions.

Paul and Emma

B EMMA, 32, AND PAUL, 35

(1) _____ , I went to the police station to report a burglary. I was really upset and the policeman who interviewed me was very kind and understanding. He calmed me down, gave me a cup of coffee and then drove me home. (2) _____ , he rang me up and asked me out and now we have been together (3) _____ .

3. Read about Sukwinder and Rajvir. Put the verbs in brackets in the correct form.

Rajvir and Sukwinder

C SUKWINDER, 63, AND RAJVIR, 70

I first (1) _____ (see) Rajvir near our house in Simla, India when I was 16. I (2) _____ (like) him but we didn't really talk. I told my father that I liked him and he (3) _____ (go) to visit his family. Then we (4) _____ (get) engaged. We couldn't get to know one another before we were married, so the first time I was alone with my husband was after the marriage. We (5) _____ (be) married for 43 years now and we (6) _____ (not/have) an argument yet.

4. Read about Elena and Basil and complete the account with appropriate verbs. What do you think happened to Basil's letters?

Elena and Basil

D ELENA, 86, AND BASIL, 87

I (1) _____ Basil when I was 23 and it (2) _____ love at first sight. We (3) _____ out together for over a year. We (4) _____ to get married, but my mother was against it because Basil is a Christian Scientist so I (5) _____ seeing him. I (not) (6) _____ from Basil for a long time, although he says he (7) _____ lots of letters. I (8) _____ other boyfriends, but I never got married. I (not) (9) _____ anyone else. It was 60 years later, when all my other boyfriends had died, that I (10) _____ to wonder if Basil was still alive. So I (11) _____ to Evergreen, a magazine for retired people. Four days after my letter was published, I (12) _____ a letter from Basil. He came to see me and after two days he (13) _____ . We (14) _____ married when Basil was 85 and I was 84 and we (15) _____ happily married for two years. I (not) (16) _____ at another man since the day Basil came back into my life.

5. Which of these stories do you think is the most romantic?

6. Think about couples you know: friends or family. What do you know about how they met? Tell your partner.

Dream date

The schwa The schwa is the commonest sound in English. Its phonetic symbol is /ə/. You hear it in words like: dinn<u>e</u>r /dɪnə/, cin<u>e</u>ma /sɪnəmə/, <u>a</u>round /əraʊnd/, stud<u>e</u>nt /stjudənt/. It is never stressed.

1 ▶ 10 Listen to the 'chat-up lines' below. All the schwas have been marked.

a) What's ə nice girl like you doing in ə place like this?
b) You know, I'm not just ən interesting persən, I have ə body too.
c) I'm in advətising. Would you like tə be in our next photo shoot?
d) Do you believe in love ət first sight or do I have tə walk past you əgain?
e) A: Do yə have ə boyfriend?
   B: Yes.
   A: Want ənothə one?
f) Your fathə must be ə thief, because he's stolən thə stars frəm thə sky ənd put thəm in your eyes.
g) I've just moved next door ənd I wəs wondering if you could recəmmend ə good restərant nearby. Would you like tə join me?

2 Work with a partner. Which chat-up lines do you like best? Which ones do you like least? Choose four chat-up lines and practise them.

3 Do you know any chat-up lines in your own language? Translate them into English and mark the schwas.

Lexis

1 What qualities do you look for in your ideal partner? Choose the six most important qualities from the list below.

> good-looking modest reliable generous broad-minded witty cheerful
> sincere rich intelligent hardworking outgoing easygoing faithful kind

Find someone else in the class who has chosen the same qualities.

2 Read the descriptions of different types of people below.

The sort of person who:
a) only thinks of their own needs and never thinks about other people.
b) thinks they know everything.
c) refuses to consider new ideas or other people's opinions.
d) is not up-to-date with modern ideas and values.
e) says they believe one thing and then behave in a way that shows they are not sincere.
f) forgets things, often because they are thinking about something else.
g) is easily offended.

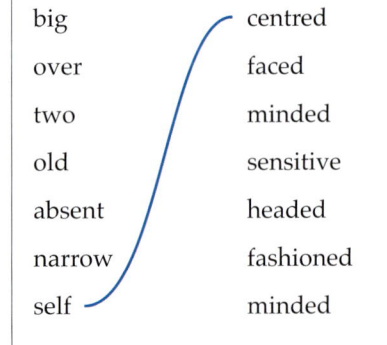

Match words from the two lists to form compound adjectives which fit the descriptions.

3 Many people believe that the identity of their ideal partner is written in the stars. You are going to read an article about an ancient Chinese form of astrology which divides people into nine personality types.

Read the article once and decide which description best describes you.

UNIT 3 Dating

KI ASTROLOGY

According to the ancient Chinese, everything goes round in nine-year cycles.

There are nine *Ki* personality numbers and each one is associated with an element: water, soil, fire, tree or metal.

1 (water)
You appear to be friendly and outgoing but you also have a very private side to your personality. You're a deep thinker and you enjoy your own company. Your cool manner is attractive, but it can frighten people off and leave you feeling a bit isolated.
You don't enter into relationships lightly and when you do you take them very seriously. You're not the romantic type, but you can be very passionate.
Famous ones: Johnny Depp, Quentin Tarantino
Compatible signs: 3, 4, 6, 7

2 (soil)
You love helping people and it's important to you that others are happy. You would give your neighbour the shirt off your back if they needed it. You hate arguments and you tend to avoid confrontation. You're best in groups rather than alone.
You're capable of great unconditional love, but you tend to choose partners who will take advantage of your generous nature.
Famous twos: Tom Cruise, Marilyn Monroe
Compatible signs: 6, 7, 9

3 (tree)
You're loud, talkative, active and fun. However, you're easily bored and tend to flit from one thing to the next. Some people think you're too honest and you frequently offend people.
Your dynamic nature makes you attractive to the opposite sex. You want exciting relationships, but you also need your independence.
Famous threes: Robert De Niro, Eddie Murphy
Compatible signs: 1, 9

4 (tree)
You're a good listener and you have a good understanding of other people's problems. However, you're not very good at making decisions about your own life and you tend to change your mind easily. You appear to be easygoing, but you can be stubborn and impulsive at times. On the one hand you're an idealist who is looking for true love, and on the other, you're often attracted to partners for exterior qualities like power or status.
Famous fours: Yoko Ono, Marlon Brando
Compatible signs: 1, 9

5 (soil)
You have a strong personality and people often turn to you for advice. You like to be the centre of attention and it is important for you to succeed in everything you do. But you don't always think before you act and you don't always learn from your mistakes.
In relationships you're caring and committed. However, because you like to experiment, you can be unfaithful.
Famous fives: Elizabeth Taylor, Bob Dylan
Compatible signs: 6, 7, 9

6 (metal)
You're a born leader who loves to be in control. You work hard to achieve your ambitions and you usually succeed. You are active and sociable, but you hate to be criticised. You're a good speaker and very charismatic.
You're faithful in relationships, but you like to be the boss. You tend to be attracted to softer partners.
Famous sixes: Madonna, Michael Jackson
Compatible signs: 1, 2, 5, 8

7 (metal)
You always seem to be happy. You're witty and good with words, but a good listener too. People enjoy your company and you make people feel at ease. Sometimes you say what people want to hear, even if it is not what you really think.
You love the excitement of romance. However, you tend to get bored quickly and your relationships do not always last very long.
Famous sevens: Michelle Pfeiffer, Melanie Griffith, Tina Turner
Compatible signs: 1, 2, 5, 8

8 (soil)
You are rather old-fashioned and do not like change. You tend to be very private and difficult to get close to. You have a strong sense of right and wrong and when you decide to do something, nothing can stop you.
Once you find someone, you tend to put all your energy into making the relationship work. You have a strong sense of family and commitment.
Famous eights: Steven Spielberg, Jackie Onassis
Compatible signs: 6, 7, 9

9 (fire)
People are attracted to your magnetic personality. You appear strong and in control, but underneath you're easily hurt. You can be over-sensitive at times. You need time on your own and you can't stand routine.
You're attractive to the opposite sex and when you're in love you're passionate, romantic and giving.
Famous nines: Jack Nicholson, Eva Peron
Compatible signs: 2, 3, 4, 5, 8

Now turn to page 141 and follow the instructions to calculate your *Ki* astrology sign. Did you guess correctly?

Criticisms & generalisations

1. How are the following ideas expressed in the article?
   a) You often scare people. (Personality 1)
   b) You usually choose partners who treat you badly. (Personality 2)
   c) You often lose interest in things and give up. (Personality 3)
   d) Sometimes you won't listen to reason. (Personality 4)
   e) You sometimes have affairs behind your partners back. (Personality 5)
   f) You usually choose partners who do what you tell them to do. (Personality 6)
   g) You usually abandon your partners when you lose interest in them. (Personality 7)
   h) You don't usually share your feelings. (Personality 8)
   i) You are sometimes too sensitive. (Personality 9)

2. Rewrite the following sentences using *tend(s) to be* or *can be*. Do you agree with the statements?
   a) Women are more sensitive than men.
   b) People of the older generation are narrow-minded.
   c) Very good-looking people are big-headed.
   d) Women are more faithful in relationships than men.
   e) People from hot countries are more outgoing than people from cooler climates.

Language Reference p30

I don't fancy yours much

1. 🔊 11 Meg and Rose are sisters. Meg met Rose's new boyfriend, Jake, for the first time yesterday. Listen to the conversation. What did Meg think of Rose's new boyfriend?

2. Listen again and read the conversation at the same time. <u>Underline</u> anything which is different from the recording.

Meg and Rose

Rose: What do you think of Jake?
Meg: He's all right.
Rose: You don't like him, do you?
Meg: Well, he was unfriendly.
Rose: Oh, he's just shy, that's all.
Meg: Shy? You must be joking – five minutes after meeting me he asked me to buy him a drink! That's not what I call shy!
Rose: OK, that was rude, but he's broke.
Meg: Huh, I'm poor myself and I'm trying to save up for my holiday.
Rose: All right, all right, I'll pay you back. He's good-looking, though, isn't he?
Meg: Yes, I suppose so – but he knows it. I think he's really big-headed.
Rose: You're just jealous.
Meg: No, I'm not. I don't want him. He's mean, big-headed and stupid.
Rose: What do you mean stupid? You're stupid too.
Meg: Shut up!
Rose: No, you shut up!
Meg: Mum!

3. What expressions do the two sisters use to avoid saying things directly? Refer to tapescript 11 if necessary.

[Language Reference p30]

4. Make the following critical comments less direct.

For example:
He's short-tempered. *He isn't particularly patient.*

a) She's insensitive.
b) He's big-headed.
c) They're stupid.
d) She's lazy.
e) She's mean.
f) They're narrow-minded.

Language reference: criticisms & generalisations

When you need to say something critical there are certain expressions you can use which make you sound more diplomatic. You can use the same expressions to make generalisations.

can be ... (at times)
You appear to be easygoing, but you **can be** stubborn and impulsive **at times**.
Because you like to experiment, you **can be** unfaithful.
You **can be** over-sensitive **at times**.

a little, rather & a bit
You can use *a little*, *rather* or, more informally, *a bit* to make the adjective less absolute.
You **can be** *a bit* stubborn at times.

tend(s) to ...
You hate arguments and you **tend to** avoid confrontation.
You **tend to** be attracted to softer partners.
You're not very good at making decisions about your own life and you **tend to** change your mind too easily.

not particularly/exactly ...
- He was unfriendly. → He **wasn't exactly** friendly.
- He's poor. → He's **not particularly** well-off.
- She's lazy. → She's **not particularly** hard-working.

You can sometimes use *not exactly* to express sarcasm.
You're **not exactly** Miss Einstein yourself.

UNIT 3 *Dating*

A boyfriend's worst nightmare

1. Work in groups. What could a boyfriend's worst nightmare be? Note down as many possible circumstances as you can think of. Now read the article.

My girlfriend has had a Canadian penpal called Eddie since she was in her early teens. That's OK. I also exchanged letters with Monique from France and Shauna from Australia until I went to university. But then I got involved in the excitement of university life and lost touch with them.

But my girlfriend is more loyal to hers. Or maybe her little penpal has a special place in her heart.

As they got older, their lives changed but they still continued writing to one another. She's a successful journalist now and he's got a very good job at the University of Vancouver. He is one metre 85, tall, dark and handsome. I am not one metre 85. Or dark. And I'm not particularly handsome. I know what he looks like because my girlfriend talks about him … a lot.

I also know that he's 27, he's an academic and he plays ice hockey. So he's both sporty and extremely intelligent. And tall, dark and handsome as I said before.

Several years ago, before I got together with my girlfriend, he was passing through London and stopped for a visit. When my girlfriend's mother met him, she liked him so much that she decided he was the ideal husband for her daughter.

So, bearing all this in mind, when my girlfriend ran towards me the other week with a letter from him in her hand and said, 'Guess what … Eddie's got a job in London for three years,' I wasn't exactly over the moon.

As the day of his arrival got nearer, I got more and more jealous. My girlfriend asked me, 'Why are you getting so stressed out about him? Yes, he's good-looking, interesting, intelligent and sporty. But it's you I love and it's you I'm with.' Believe it or not, this didn't make me feel any better.

Finally, the day arrived when I was to meet the famous penpal. My first thought when I saw him was, 'Tall, yes. Dark, yes. Handsome, yes. Intelligent, definitely. Charming, probably. It can't get any worse than this.'

(Adapted from *The Independent on Sunday,* 12 October 1997)

2. What do you think happened next? Write the last paragraph of the story.

3. Turn to page 143 and read the end of the story.

4. How does the ending compare with your version? When was the last time you had a weight lifted from your mind?

Lexis

1. Refer to the text and answer these two questions:
   a) Why did the writer stop writing to his penfriends? What happened?
   b) What happened to his feelings as the day of Eddie's arrival got nearer?

2. Here are some more examples of this use of *get*. Invent ways to complete the sentences and then compare with another student.

   For example:
   I got angry because *he kept me waiting for half an hour.*

   a) I got depressed because …
   b) I got bored because …
   c) I got confused because …
   d) I got upset because …
   e) I got involved in crime because …

3. Read the ends of the expressions - the parts you invented - to other students. See if they can guess which sentences they belong to.

Dating UNIT 3 31

4 Adrenalin

1 Which of the following would make you feel:

- angry?
- excited?
- scared?
- nothing?

> talking to someone you are really attracted to / taking an exam / climbing to a high point and then looking down / taking off in an aeroplane / riding on the back of a motorbike at high speed / being stuck in a traffic jam / giving a speech in front of an audience / going on a roller-coaster at the fair / finding out that you have been robbed / galloping on a horse / watching your national football team / being stopped by the police

2 Tell your partner about any of the situations you have experienced personally. Which experience has given you the biggest 'adrenalin rush'?

My name is Mike & I'm a skydiver

1 Have you ever done a parachute jump? Would you consider doing a jump?

- Yes, for charity.
- Yes, for fun.
- Yes, for money.
- No way!

---

adrenalin [ədrenəlin]; also spelt **adrenaline**. **Adrenalin** is a substance which your body produces when you are angry, scared or excited. It makes your heart beat faster and gives you more energy. *That was my first big game in months and the adrenalin was going.*

(Collins Cobuild English Dictionary)

2 Read about Mike and answer these questions:

a) Why did he start skydiving?
b) How did he feel on his first jump?
c) What caused his accident and why has he continued skydiving?

www.deadmike.com

I've just done my first jump since the accident that nearly killed me just over a year ago. As I was lying in hospital, thinking that I would never skydive again, I wasn't feeling glad to be alive. Instead, I was wondering how I could possibly live without it.

It all started one evening after another typical nine to five day. I was sitting at home thinking, 'There has to be more to life than this,' when an ad came on the television: 'Try skydiving,' it said.

The next day, I called my local skydiving centre and booked my first jump.

I spent a day training and then I was ready for my first jump. Or almost. First, I had to sign a document to say that I understood that I was taking part in an activity that could end in serious injury. At that moment I realised that I was about to do something voluntarily that would put my life at risk and as I signed, I wondered if I was completely mad.

I will never forget my first jump. Five of us walked to the runway and got into a plane barely big enough to hold three people. I was beginning to feel nervous, but the others were chatting and joking and I started to feel more relaxed. It was a beautiful, cloudless day and the sun was just going down. It took us about 20 minutes to get to 11,000 feet and then the trainer opened the plane door – the view took my breath away. Suddenly, it was time to jump and as I pushed myself away from the plane, I don't know what I was thinking, my mind went blank.

Words cannot describe the rush of adrenalin I experienced while I was free-falling.

At 5,500 feet I pulled the cord and the parachute opened immediately. Suddenly, everything was silent and peaceful. Twice I shouted, 'This is absolutely incredible,' though I knew there was nobody to hear me. It was the most amazing four minutes of my life.

From the first jump, I was hooked. I started spending every free moment I had skydiving. At work, I sat in front of my computer and imagined ways of making more money so that I could jump more often. It became my reason for living and nothing else mattered. I was addicted to skydiving.

Things were going really well. I was spending every free moment I had skydiving.

Then disaster struck on my 1,040th jump. Another skydiver collided with my parachute at 80 feet. I fell and hit the ground at about 30 mph, face down. I broke both legs, my right foot, left elbow, right arm, my nose and my jaw. I lost 10 pints of blood, 19 teeth and 25 pounds of fat. I was lucky to survive.

People who have never experienced skydiving will find it hard to understand that my only motivation to get better was so that I could do it again. All I can say is that for me, skydiving is life and life is skydiving.

3 The sentences below summarise Mike's story. Correct the details that are wrong.

a) Mike was reading a newspaper one evening when he saw an ad for skydiving.
b) He phoned the skydiving centre immediately and booked a jump.
c) After a day's training, he was sure he was doing the right thing.
d) His first jump was unforgettable. It was a beautiful morning and he was feeling relaxed.
e) After an hour's flight, he jumped out of the plane and his parachute opened immediately.
f) After his first jump, he didn't think he would do it again.
g) During his free time, he thought about skydiving a lot.
h) On his 1,040th jump he had an accident when his parachute didn't open.
i) He nearly died and thought that his skydiving days were over.
j) The only reason he wanted to get better was so that he could skydive again.

Lexis

1 Complete as many of these questions as you can from memory. Look back at the text on page 33 to check.

a) What couldn't you l_____ without?

b) Why do you think people t_____ p_____ in dangerous sports?

c) Have you ever p_____ your life at r_____ voluntarily?

d) When was the last time a view t_____ your br_____ a_____ ?

e) Do you know anybody who is a_____ to a sport like Mike?

2 Work with a partner. Ask each other the questions.

Grading adjectives

1 Find pairs of adjectives in the box that have similar meanings.

For example:
angry   furious

| angry exhausted incredible awful hilarious bad brilliant |
| excited furious tired thrilled good funny strange |

2 Put the adjectives in 1 under these two headings: very or absolutely.

For example:
very   absolutely
angry   furious

Language reference: gradable & absolute adjectives

Gradable adjectives
Adjectives like *good*, *small* or *pleasant* can go with adverbs like *very*, *fairly* and *rather*.
For example: **very** *good*; **fairly** *small*; **rather** *pleasant*.
You cannot use adverbs like *absolutely* and *totally* with these adjectives.

Absolute adjectives
Strong adjectives like *incredible* can go with adverbs like *absolutely* and *totally*.
For example: **absolutely** *perfect*; **totally** *unique*.
When Mike did his first jump, he shouted, 'This is **absolutely** *incredible*.'

Intonation

1 🔊 12 Complete the following dialogues, then listen and check.

A
A: _____ _____ _____ _____ skydiving?
B: _____ , _____ have.
A: _____ _____ good?
B: **Good?** _____ _____ _____ incredible!

B
C: _____ _____ _____ _____ surfing?
D: _____ , _____ have.
C: _____ _____ scared?
D: **Scared?** _____ _____ _____ terrified!

2 Listen again and notice the pronunciation of the words in **bold**.

3 Practise the dialogues with a partner.

4 Work with a partner. Make up and practise a similar dialogue using gradable and absolute adjectives.

A sporting life

Lexis

1. Put the sports into groups according to what you think they have in common. Think of different groupings.

   For example:
   swimming, surfing, sailing and scuba diving are all water sports.

   aerobics athletics badminton
   baseball basketball bungee jumping
   climbing cycling football
   horse-riding ice hockey judo
   karate rugby sailing scuba-diving
   skating skydiving snow-boarding
   surfing swimming table-tennis
   tennis volleyball weightlifting
   windsurfing

2. What verbs would you use with each sports: *do, play* or *go*?

   For example:
   go *swimming*
   play *tennis*
   do *weightlifting*

3. Can you add any sports to the list in 1?

4. In small groups discuss the following questions:

   a) Which of these sports do you do or watch?
   b) Which of these sports are shown on television a lot?
   c) Do you think any of these sports are unsuitable for women? Why?

5. 13 Jane Couch made UK sporting history when she won the first official female boxing match in November 1998.

   Listen to the interview. Which of the questions on the right does the interviewer ask? Make notes about Jane's answers to the questions.

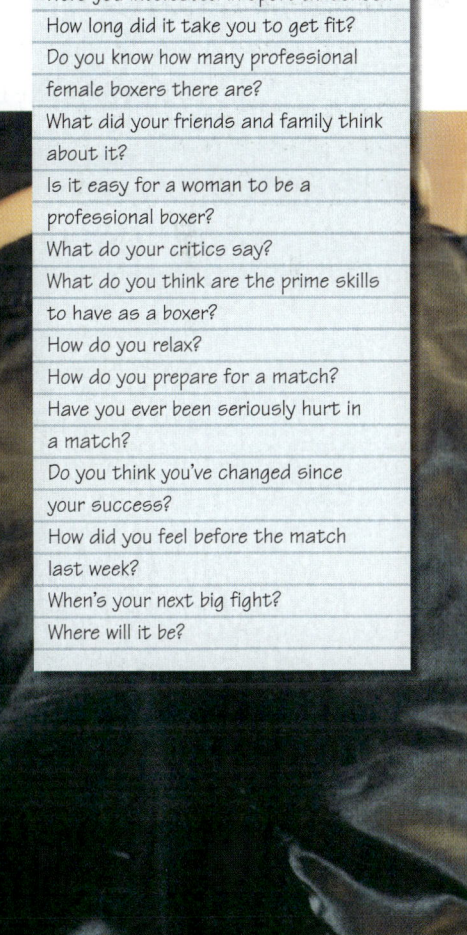

How did you get interested in boxing?
Were you interested in sport at school?
How long did it take you to get fit?
Do you know how many professional female boxers there are?
What did your friends and family think about it?
Is it easy for a woman to be a professional boxer?
What do your critics say?
What do you think are the prime skills to have as a boxer?
How do you relax?
How do you prepare for a match?
Have you ever been seriously hurt in a match?
Do you think you've changed since your success?
How did you feel before the match last week?
When's your next big fight?
Where will it be?

Adrenalin UNIT 4

Close up

Past experience

1 The grammar in the following sentences is correct, but the sentences don't make sense. The endings have been mixed up. Rearrange the sentences so that they make sense.

   a) Have you ever ridden a snake?
   b) Have you ever been asked to the top of a mountain?
   c) Have you ever met a desert?
   d) Have you ever driven a television programme?
   e) Have you ever been to make a speech?
   f) Have you ever crossed a famous person?
   g) Have you ever appeared on a Ferrari?
   h) Have you ever caught a horse on the beach?

2 Work with a partner. How do you think your partner would answer each question?

   a) Yes, I have.
   b) No, never … but I'd like to.
   c) No, never … and I wouldn't like to.

3 Discuss your answers. How well do you know each other? Ask more *Have you ever …?* questions.

4 ▶ 14 Listen to five people being interviewed about their past experiences and complete the table below.

Have you ever …	Y/N	What were you doing?	What happened?
a) had a sports injury?	_____	_____	_____
b) been in a dangerous situation?	_____	_____	_____
c) broken a bone?	_____	_____	_____
d) been really frightened?	_____	_____	_____
e) thought you were going to die?	_____	_____	_____

5 Work with a partner. Compare your notes then ask each other the questions from 4. Find out as much as you can.

6 Look at the questions in **bold** in 4. Three tenses are used: the past simple, the past continuous and the present perfect. Match the names of the tenses to the questions.

7 Look at tapescript 14. Find other examples of the three tenses.

   a) Which tense is the most useful for introducing a new topic of conversation?
   b) Which would you probably use if you wanted to say exactly when something happened?
   c) You want to tell a story. Which of these two beginnings do you prefer?

      1 It was late summer. People were sitting in street cafés, enjoying the sunshine and watching the world go by.
      2 It was late summer. People sat in street cafés, enjoyed the sunshine and watched the world go by.

Language Reference p38

8 The diagram below shows three timelines: one for each of the three tenses you're studying. Which timeline goes with which tense and why? Discuss with a partner.

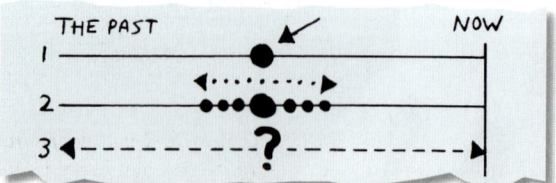

36 UNIT 4 *Adrenalin*

Language Reference p38

9 Complete these dialogues with the words in the brackets. Use the past simple, past continuous or present perfect. Sometimes more than one form is possible.

A
A: (1) _____ (you/read) *The Grapes of Wrath* by John Steinbeck?
B: Yes, (2) _____ (I/read) it last year when (3) _____ (I/travel) around the USA.
A: What (4) _____ (you/think) of it?
B: (5) _____ (I/love) it.

C
E: Nice car.
F: Thanks. (1) _____ (we/buy) it last week.
E: How much (2) _____ (it/be)?
F: £21,000. But (3) _____ (we/not/pay) for it yet.

B
C: So (1) _____ (you/lose) your laptop again.
D: Yes. Sorry. (2) _____ (I/leave) it in a taxi this morning.
C: (3) _____ (you/ring) the taxi company?
D: Yes, but they can't get hold of the driver.

D
G: What (1) _____ (you/do) at the time of the robbery?
H: (2) _____ (I/watch) television.
G: Which programmes (3) _____ (you/watch) that evening?
H: I don't remember.
G: No? (4) _____ (you/ever/be) in trouble with the law?
H: (5) _____ (that/be) a long time ago.
(6) _____ (I/change).

10 On a sheet of paper write six true sentences about yourself.

a) I haven't ... since ...
b) I ... for years
c) I didn't ... yesterday
d) I was ... + **ing** when ...
e) I've ... several times
f) I wasn't ... + **ing** when ...

11 Fold the paper and give it to your teacher. Then take another paper and guess which student it belongs to.

'Good news – first indications from the results of your tests suggest that you haven't gone permanently blind.'

Adrenalin UNIT 4

Language reference: talking about past experiences

The present perfect & the past simple

English often makes a distinction between *finished time* and *time-up-to-now*.
For example:

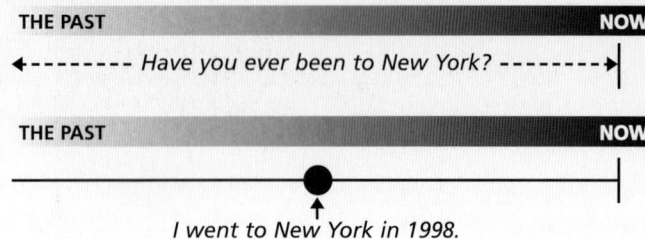

The present perfect is used to locate an action in time-up-to-now. The past simple is used to fix an action in finished time.

Time expressions

Choosing between the present perfect and the past simple is often a question of the *time expression* you need to use.

1 Some time expressions describe time-up-to-now: *this year; since I was six; this week; recently; ever; yet; for the last few days.* With these time expressions you use the present perfect.
2 Some time expressions describe fixed points in the past (finished time): *in 1984; when I was six; yesterday; before I left school; last week; at 6.00; two minutes ago; last term; at Christmas.* With these time expressions you use the past simple.

The present perfect as a conversation opener

You can use *Have + ever ...?* to establish the topic of a conversation or introduce a story.
Have you **ever been** to Tuscany?
Have I **ever told** you about the time I went skiing with my brother?
You will find more information about the present perfect in units 2, 3 and 6.

The past continuous & the past simple

The past continuous is almost always used in contrast with the past simple. You can use it to describe something which was in progress when the main events in the story happened. Here Mike talks about the first time he thought of trying skydiving.
*I **was sitting** at home when an ad **came on** the television.*

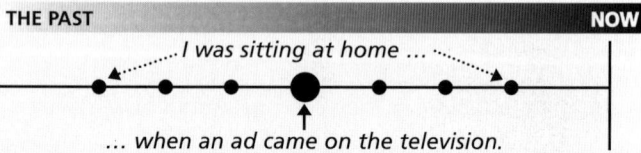

The past continuous and the past simple are also contrasted in more complex ways. Notice the way they are used together in this passage from the same text.
*I **was beginning** to feel nervous, but the others **were chatting** and **joking** and I **started** to feel more relaxed. It **was** a beautiful, cloudless day and the sun **was** just **going down**. It **took** us about 20 minutes to get to 11,000 feet and then the trainer **opened** the plane door – the view **took** my breath away. Suddenly, it **was** time to jump and as I **pushed** myself away from the plane, I don't know what I **was thinking**, my mind **went** blank.*

Anecdote

1 Think back to a moment when you felt a rush of adrenalin. You are going to tell your partner about it. Choose from the list below the things you want to talk about. Think about what you will say and what language you will need.

☐ Where were you? At home? In the car? At a sports event? In town?
☐ Did it happen recently? How old were you?
☐ Who were you with?
☐ What were you doing?
☐ What happened?
☐ How did you feel?
☐ What were the consequences?
☐ Would you like to have the same experience again?

2 Tell your partner the story. Give as much detail as possible.

LANGUAGE TOOLBOX

Stories are often told in five stages.

1 **Introduction**
Have I ever told you about the time I was attacked by a lion?

2 **Background**
I was on holiday with Jan ...
We were travelling around Africa on my Harley ...

3 **Problem**
Suddenly I heard a sound in the jungle ... The next moment I saw ... So there we were, up the tree ... We were beginning to feel rather nervous ...

4 **Resolution**
Then I had an idea ... In the end I managed to get the bike started ... I drove off at a hundred miles an hour ... I didn't stop till I got to Nairobi ...

5 **Comment**
I often wonder what happened to Jan ...

The Adrenalin Game: truth or dare?

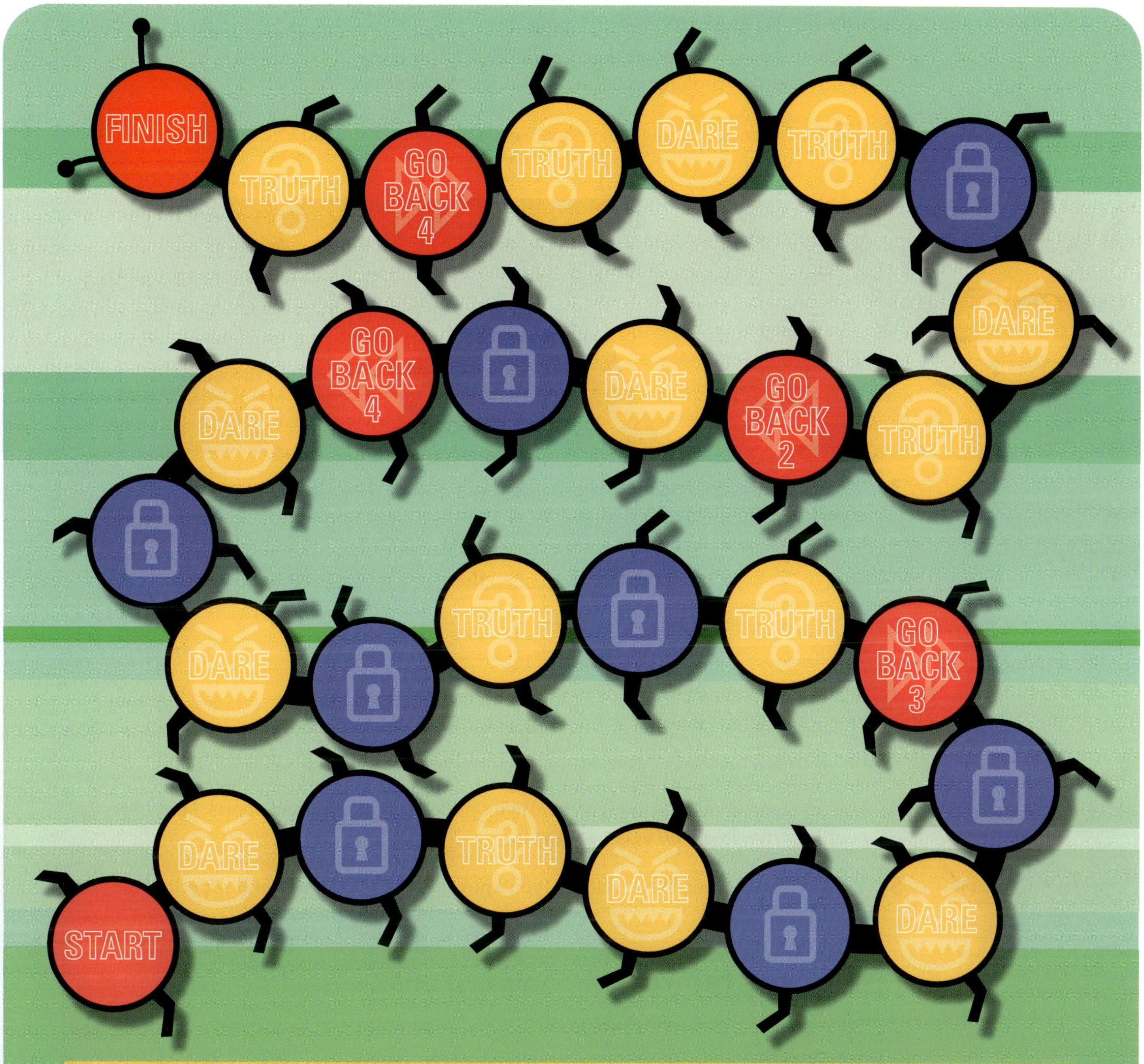

RULES OF THE GAME

Work in teams of three or four.

BEFORE THE GAME

Each team prepares ten 'TRUTH' questions and ten 'DARES'. Here are some suggestions:

TRUTH
Have you ever …?
Did you …?
When did you last …?
How many times have you …?
When did you first …?
What were you doing when …?

DARE
Sing a song in English.
Imitate a famous person.
Say the alphabet backwards.
Make three animal sounds.
Demonstrate disco dancing.
Show us everything in your pockets.

HOW TO PLAY

1 Each team throws the dice. The team with the highest score starts.
2 Teams take turns to throw the dice and move their counters round the board according to the number they throw.
3 When a team lands on a TRUTH or a DARE square, they nominate a team member, the 'victim', to answer a question, truthfully, or do a dare from the other team.
4 Teams must nominate a new victim each time until all team members have had a turn.
5 Teams cannot use the same TRUTH or DARE twice, unless they have used all their TRUTHS and DARES.
6 After hearing the TRUTH or the DARE, the victim can say 'change' and take a DARE instead of a TRUTH, or vice versa. After saying change, the victim cannot go back to the original TRUTH or DARE.
7 If the victim will not answer a TRUTH or do a DARE, the team loses its turn and moves its counter back to the square it was on at the beginning of the turn.
8 The winner of the game is the team that reaches the finish first.

Close up

Comparisons

1. Find the names of twelve sports.

   baseballboxingbungeejumpingcricketfootballformulaone
   skydivingrugbyrunningscubadivingskiingsnowboarding

2. 🔊 15 Listen and say which sports George, Katrina, Paul and Eva are talking about. Which key words helped you to identify the sports?

3. Listen again. Complete these sentences to summarise what the people say about their experiences. You may need more than one word for each gap. Read tapescript 15 again to check.

   a) _____ is slightly _____ than _____ . (George)
   b) _____ is just as _____ as _____ . (George)
   c) _____ was one of the _____ I've ever _____ . (Katrina)
   d) _____ are by far the _____ . (Paul)
   e) _____ is much _____ than _____ . (Eva)
   f) _____ isn't nearly as _____ as _____ . (Eva)

4. Use the same structures to give your own opinions about different sports. Find other people in the class who agree with you.

   Language Reference p40

5. Work with a partner. What rules do you know about comparative and superlative adjectives?

Language reference: comparisons

Comparative & superlative adjectives

1	fast	faster	the fastest
	cheap	cheaper	the cheapest
2	nice	nicer	the nicest
	safe	safer	the safest
3	big	bigger	the biggest
	hot	hotter	the hottest
4	slow	slower	the slowest
	few	fewer	the fewest
5	funny	funnier	the funniest
	easy	easier	the easiest
6	good	better	the best
	bad	worse	the worst

Comparative & superlative structures

useful → **more/less** useful → **the most/least** useful

exciting → **more/less** exciting → **the most/least** exciting

X **is/isn't as** fast/nice/big/slow/easy/good/ useful/exciting **as** Y.

Snowboarding is **similar to/like** skiing.

Modifiers

Football is **much/far/a lot** more popular than skydiving.
Skydiving isn't **nearly as** popular as football.
The Seikan tunnel in Japan is **a little bit/slightly** longer than the Channel tunnel.
Russia is **by far** the biggest country in Europe.
Harrison Ford is **one of** the most successful film stars of all time.

Adrenalin

River Deep Mountain High

1 Make lists of things which are:
- sweet
- deep
- strong
- high
- bright
- bigger than you

2 Work with a partner. Tell your partner about your list.

3 Complete the love letter.

4 🎧 16 Listen to the song *River Deep Mountain High*. How many of the images and comparisons in the song are the same as yours?

> Darling,
> When I was a little girl/boy I had a …
> Now I love you the way I loved my …
> You are sweeter than …
> And my love is stronger than …
> And it's deeper than …
> I love you like bees love …
> Like the sun loves …
> Like fish love …
> If I lost you I'd …
> I'm going to be as faithful as …
> I'll never …

Ike & Tina Turner
Ike and Tina Turner recorded **River Deep Mountain High** in 1966. It was produced by Phil Spector and Barry Greenwich

5 Kids

1 Note down the names of any children you know. Put them in the appropriate category.

- babies: 0–1 years old
- toddlers: 1–3 years old
- young children: 4–7 years old
- older children: 8–12 years old
- teenagers: 13+ years old

2 Tell your partner about them.

3 Divide into two groups: *parents* and *children*.

- Parents: discuss and list the qualities of a good child.
- Children: discuss and list the qualities of a good parent.

Then compare your list with the other group.

A child's point of view

1 Read these children's definitions of a mother and choose the one you like best.

A mum is a person who cares for you and tucks you in at night. When you've made a mistake she says it's all right.
Jan, age 13

Mothers are people who sit up worrying about you and when you come home they yell at you.
Gary, age 13

A mum is a woman who says 'go to bed' and when she says that, you stay very quiet and she forgets about you.
Aishling, age 9

A mother is a superwoman who can be in two places at once.
Judy, age 10

A mum is a person who cries when you do something bad, and cries even harder when you do something good.
Robin, age 14

A mum is someone who always knows when there is something wrong even if you don't tell her.
Lisa, age 14

Mothers are people who are angry when you're at home and sad when you're away.
Vinay, age 12

2 Write a similar definition for a father.

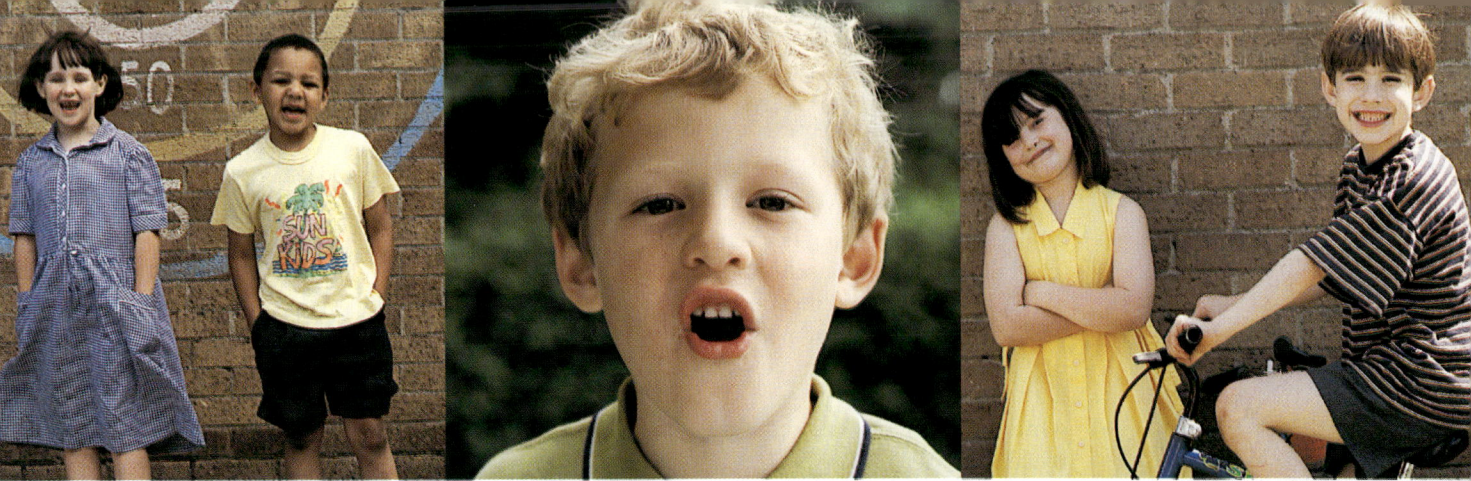

Children from St Thomas More School, Kidlington, Oxford

3 🔊 **17** You are going to listen to these children defining five things from the list below. Which things do they talk about and in what order?

a) God
b) a dinosaur
c) an iceberg
d) the Internet
e) the ozone layer
f) a vet
g) a police officer
h) a mobile phone
i) a robber
j) a museum
k) Autumn
l) a judge
m) a desert
n) a jungle
o) Christmas

4 Work with a partner. Imagine you are explaining other things from the list to a four-year-old child. Write down what you would say.

Close up

Defining relative clauses

1 Work with a partner.

a) Underline the relative clauses in the sentences on the right.
b) Which word is the relative pronoun in each case?
c) In each sentence, change the relative pronouns to either *who* or *which*.

1 It's something that lived a very long time ago. It looks very scary.

2 A person that helps people, in heaven.

3 It's something that crashes down on people.

4 A person that steals things at night.

2 Here are some typical children's jokes. Look at the pictures and complete the jokes with an appropriate word.

a) Q: What do you call an _____ that has a machine gun?
   A: Sir.

b) Q: What do you call a _____ who's very small?
   A: Minimum.

c) Q: What happened to the _____ who stole a calendar?
   A: He got twelve months.

d) Q: What do you call a _____ who's got no thumbs?
   A: Mr Justice Fingers.

e) Q: What prize did the man who invented the _____ win?
   A: The Nobel Prize.

Can you translate any of the jokes into your own language? Are they funny?

3 What do you know about education in the UK?
Complete these sentences using *who* or *which*:

a) A professor is a person ...
b) A secondary school is a school ...
c) Public schools are schools ...
d) A degree is a qualification ...
e) Undergraduates are people ...
f) A student grant is money ...

4 Write similar sentences about the education system in your country.

For example:
'Selectividad' is an examination which you take to get into university in Spain.

'You take the children's bath time too seriously, Norman ...'

Omitting relative pronouns

The relative pronoun is sometimes optional. For example, both of these sentences are correct:
He's the man that I saw.
He's the man I saw.

But in this sentence the relative pronoun is necessary:
He's the man that lives next door.

Language Reference p46

Read these sentences and cross out the relative pronouns which are optional.

a) Jill Bennett is the woman who you want to speak to.
b) She's seen the car which she wants.
c) It was the qualification in engineering that helped me get the job.
d) He's a man who likes his food.
e) It's a university which specialises in technical subjects.
f) What was the name of the film which you wanted to see?
g) The teacher that I liked best at school was Mr Stevens.
h) He's the teacher who taught us maths.

Where, when & whose

You can also make relative clauses with *where*, *when* or *whose*.

1 Complete these sentences with *where*, *when* and a relative clause so that they are true for you.

a) My schooldays were a time in my life ...
b) The town I grew up in is the kind of place ...
c) The best holiday I ever had with my parents was ...
d) I once had a fight with my brother/sister/best friend ...
e) We used to play in a place ...

Read one sentence to your partner and then tell them more about it.

2 Find out how many people in the class have these things in common with you and write down their names.

Find someone whose:

- car is the same make as yours.   _____
- birthday is in the same month as yours.   _____
- taste in music is the same as yours.   _____
- mother is the same age as yours.   _____
- shoe size is the same as yours.   _____
- favourite food is the same as yours.   _____

44 UNIT 5 *Kids*

Definition Auction

Rules of the game

1. Work in teams. The definitions are for sale in a public auction. Some of them are true and some of them are false. Each team decides which definitions they think are true.

2. Each team tries to buy the definitions that they think are true by bidding (offering) more money than all the other teams. You have a total of £10,000 to spend at the auction.

3. The winner of the game is the team that buys the highest number of true definitions.

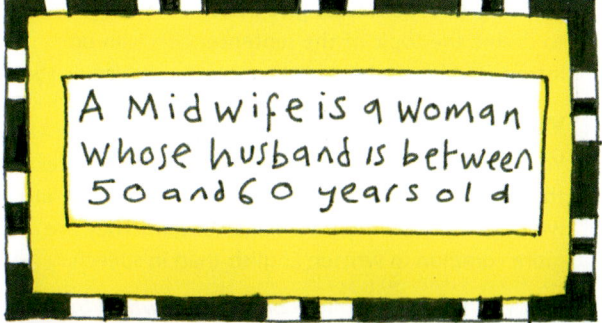
A Midwife is a woman whose husband is between 50 and 60 years old

A nappy is a child who is not happy

A truant is a school pupil who stays away from school without permission

A Mock exam is the exam you take when you want to go to university

A dummy is something you put in a baby's mouth to stop it crying

A bib is something that young children wear when they are eating

A bully is a field where young bulls are kept

A swot is a student who studies very hard

Kids UNIT 5 45

Language reference: defining relative clauses

Defining relative clauses give information which helps to define the topic of the sentence. They can be introduced by a relative pronoun: *who, which* or *that*.

who, which, that

You use *who* to refer to people, and *which* to refer to things or ideas. You can use *that* for either. *Who* and *which* are slightly more formal than *that*. They are more common in written English than in speech.

*An iceberg is an enormous block of ice **which/that** floats in the sea.*
*A judge is someone **who/that** decides how the law should be interpreted and applied.*

whom

Whom is sometimes used as a more formal alternative to *who* in sentences where it is the object.
Subject: *He did it.* → *He's the man **who** did it.*
Object: *I saw him.* → *He's the man **whom** I saw.*

Omitting relative pronouns

You can omit the relative pronoun when it is the object of the clause.

*He's **the man who(m)** I saw.*
→ *He's **the man** I saw.*

*She's **the woman who(m)** I helped.*
→ *She's **the woman** I helped.*

*That's **the company which** I worked for.*
→ *That's **the company** I worked for.*

when, where, whose

You can also use *when, where* and *whose* in relative clauses.

*Autumn is the time of year **when** leaves fall off the trees.*
*An art gallery is a place **where** paintings and sculptures are displayed to the public.*
*A widower is a man **whose** wife has died.*

Children's rhymes

Stress timing

1   ▭ 18 Look at this popular children's nursery rhyme and listen to the recording. The boxes show the stressed syllables.

2   Say the rhyme along with the recording. Follow the stress and speed of the recording. Try to finish at exactly the same time as the recording.

3   ▭ 19 Listen to another nursery rhyme. Work with a partner. Write the nursery rhyme. Use these words and any others you need. Then put boxes around the stressed syllables.

| again | in | shower | there | middle | stepped | Doctor |
| never | up | Foster | puddle | went | Gloucester | rain |

4   Listen to the rhyme again and practise saying it at the same speed.

5   Work with a partner. Make up a four-line rhyme with a simple rhythm, using words from the box below or your own words.

| Rome | home | comb | waiter | later | alligator | deliver | river | shiver |
| hat | fat | rat | far | car | wearing | sharing | staring | would | could | should |

46   UNIT 5   *Kids*

First memory: The Bicycle

1. You are going to read about one of Roald Dahl's childhood memories. Look at the picture and discuss the following:

   a) What year do you think it is?
   b) How old do you think the boys are?
   c) What are they wearing?
   d) How do you think their life was different from children's lives now?

Roald Dahl

Roald Dahl began writing after a 'monumental bash on the head', received when he was an RAF fighter pilot during the Second World War. He became one of the best-known and most successful of all children's writers.

2. Quickly read *First memory: The Bicycle* to find out Roald Dahl's 'greatest wish' at that moment in his life.

Between the age of seven and nine, only two moments remain clearly in my mind. The first lasted not more than five seconds, but I will never forget it.

It was my first term and I was walking home alone across the village green after school when suddenly one of the senior twelve-year-old boys came riding full speed down the road on his
5 bicycle about twenty yards away from me. The road was on a hill and the boy was going down the slope, and as he flashed by he started back-pedalling very quickly so that the free-wheeling mechanism of his bike made a loud whirring sound. At the same time, he took his hands off the handlebars and folded them casually across his chest. I stopped dead and stared after him. How wonderful he was! How swift and brave and graceful in his long trousers with bicycle-clips
10 around them and his scarlet school cap at a jaunty angle on his head! One day, I told myself, one glorious day I will have a bike like that and I will wear long trousers with bicycle-clips and my school cap will sit jaunty on my head and I will go whizzing down the hill pedalling backwards with no hands on the handlebars!

I promise you that if somebody had caught me by the shoulder at that moment and said to me,
15 'What is your greatest wish in life, little boy? What is your absolute ambition? To be a doctor? A fine musician? A painter? A writer? Or the Lord Chancellor?' I would have answered without hesitation that my only ambition, my hope, my longing was to have a bike like that and to go whizzing down the hill with no hands on the handlebars. It would be fabulous. It made me tremble just to think about it.

[Excerpt from *Boy* by Roald Dahl, 1984]

3. Read Roald Dahl's first memory again and find four differences between the picture and the extract.

Kids UNIT 5 47

Lexis

1. Roald Dahl uses exaggerated language to bring the scene alive. Find the actual words he uses to describe the following:

   a) The senior boy came riding <u>very fast</u> down the road.
   b) As he <u>passed me</u> he started back-pedalling.
   c) I <u>stopped</u> immediately and watched him.
   d) I will go <u>riding fast</u> down the hill.
   e) My <u>wish</u> was to have a bike like that.
   f) It would be <u>very nice</u>.

2. <u>Underline</u> all the words in Roald Dahl's first memory which you think are related to bicycles. Can you guess the meaning from the context? Compare with a partner.

Second memory: The Great Mouse Plot

1. 🎧 20 Read and listen to Roald Dahl's second memory. What was the terrible problem with the sweet shop?

> My second and only other memory of Llandaff Cathedral School is extremely bizarre. It happened a little over a year later, when I was just nine. By then I had made some friends and when I walked to school in the mornings I would start out alone but would pick up four other boys of my own age along the way. After school was over, the same four boys
> 5 and I would set out together across the village green and through the village itself, heading for home. On the way to school and on the way back we always passed the sweet-shop. No we didn't, we never passed it. We always stopped. The sweet-shop in Llandaff in the year 1923 was the very centre of our lives. To us, it was what a bar is to a drunk, or a church is to a Bishop. Without it, there would have been little to live for. But
> 10 it had one terrible drawback, this sweet-shop. The woman who owned it was a horror. We hated her and we had good reason for doing so.

2. Which of the following drawings is the most accurate illustration of the boys' routine?

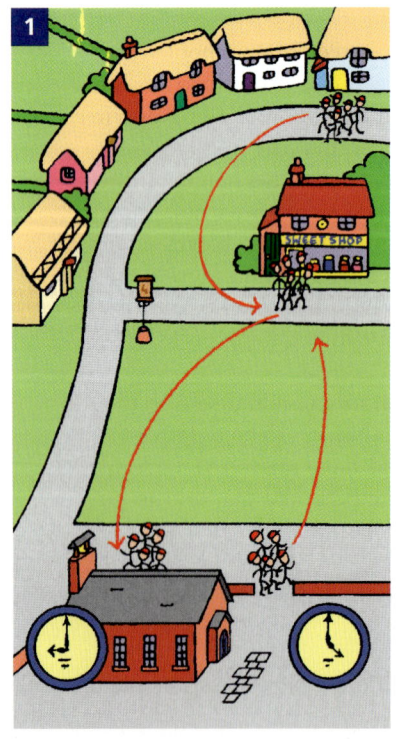 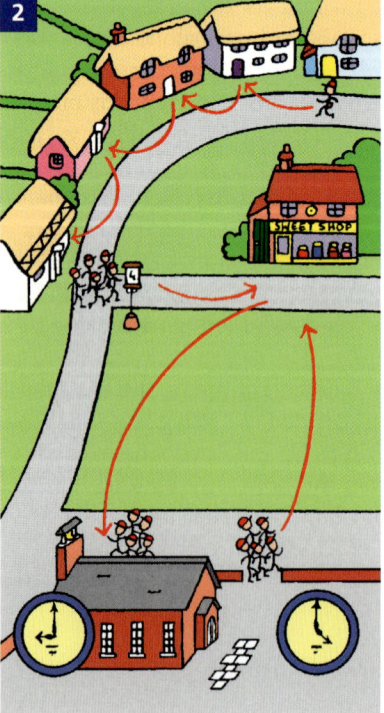 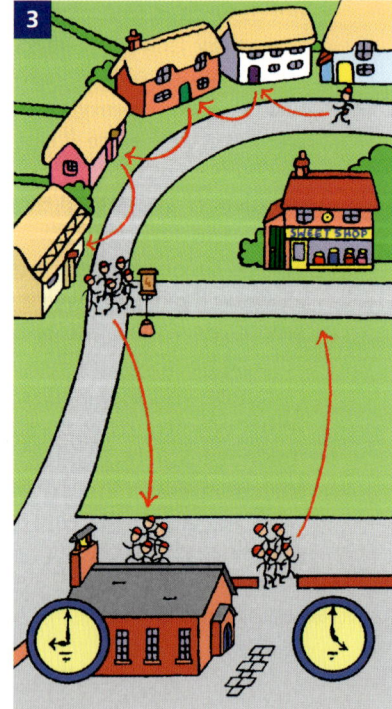

Close up

Would & used to

1 Complete the sentences below without looking back at the second memory.
   a) … I _____ start out alone but _____ pick up four other boys of my own age along the way.
   b) After school was over, the same four boys and I _____ set out together across the village … heading for home.

2 Do the sentences in 1 describe:
   a) repeated actions in the past?
   b) situations in the past?
   c) single events in the past?

(Language Reference p49)

3 The past simple, *would* + verb, and *used to* + verb are all possible ways to talk about the past.
The sentences below are all in the past simple. Read them and discuss these questions:

1 Which sentences could be changed to *would* + verb?
2 Which sentences could be changed to *used to* + verb?
3 What does this tell you about how to use these two structures?

When I was a child:
   a) I was afraid of the dark.
   b) I believed in ghosts.
   c) I went on holiday abroad three times.
   d) I broke my leg skiing.
   e) I sucked my thumb when I was tired.
   f) I started learning the piano.
   g) I had long hair.
   h) I didn't like vegetables.
   i) I went to church every Sunday.
   j) I lived right in the city centre.

Are the sentences true or false for you?

Anecdote

4 Think about your life at the age of eight. You are going to tell your partner about it. Choose from the list the things you want to talk about. Think about what you will say and the language you will need.

- [ ] Did your life use to be very different to how it is now?
- [ ] Where did you use to go to school? How did you get there?
- [ ] Do you remember any of your teachers?
- [ ] Were there any you particularly liked or disliked? Why?
- [ ] Who were your friends?
- [ ] What did you use to do before/after school or during the breaks?
- [ ] Did you ever do anything naughty? Were you caught and punished?
- [ ] What was your favourite game?
- [ ] What were your favourite sweets?
- [ ] Was there one of the older children you particularly admired?
- [ ] What was your greatest wish?

'My son, Eric, won't be coming to school today; he's in dreadful pain.'

5 ▭ **21** Why do the boys hate Mrs Pratchett, the sweet shop owner? If you would like to know what happens at the end of the story read tapescript 21 and listen to the recording.

Language reference: would & used to

would

You can use *would* … to talk about regular or repeated past actions. It sometimes suggests a feeling of nostalgia so is often used for personal reminiscences.

Every day my mates **would play** football after school.
I **would visit** my grandmother at weekends.
We **would go** skiing at the same resort every year.

You rarely use *would* with this meaning in the negative or question form.

used to

You can use *used to* like *would* for regular or repeated past actions, and also for past states or situations.

I **used to go** to church every Sunday.   I **would go** to church every Sunday. ✓
I **used to have** long hair.   I ~~would have~~ long hair. ✗

You can use *used to* in negative forms and in question forms.

Kids **didn't use to have** mobile phones. Now they do and I don't!
Did you use to like school?

6 News

Discuss these questions:

- What do you know about the people in these photographs?
- If you saw one of these photographs in a newspaper or magazine, would you read about it? Why/Why not?
- Who are the most photographed celebrities in your country?
- Is there any celebrity scandal in the news at the moment?

The hunters & the hunted

Read the web-page on page 51 and find the connections between:

Paparazzo   ➔   scooter
a photograph   ➔   a million dollars
Tom Cruise   ➔   a tunnel in Paris
Madonna   ➔   130 kph
Alec Baldwin   ➔   a black eye
George Clooney   ➔   a Vietnamese pot-bellied pig

PAPARAZZI

This page has been created to air concerns over the ever-growing problem of an aggressive breed of photographer known as the paparazzi.

The term 'paparazzi' comes from a character called Paparazzo in the Fellini film, *La Dolce Vita,* who rode around on a scooter taking photographs of the rich and famous. Modern day paparazzi take photographs of famous people, hoping to get them in an unflattering or compromising pose. The photograph is then sold for an enormous sum of money, sometimes close to a million dollars, to the tabloid press.

Some people say that celebrities are public property and that this invasion of privacy is to be expected – 'that's show business', they say. I think that this is true up to a point, but celebrities are being followed, harassed, chased, provoked and spied on in their own homes. That's not show business, that's criminal.

Unnecessary risks

- Tom Cruise has been pursued at high speed through the tunnel in Paris where Princess Diana was killed.
- When Madonna was promoting *Evita* in Rome, she had to drive away at 130 kph with her baby in the car because she was being chased. The paparazzi didn't even give her time to strap the baby into the car.

Invasion of privacy

- Alec Baldwin gave a paparazzo a black eye when he filmed him and his wife, Kim Basinger, returning to their Hollywood home with their new baby. Baldwin was arrested and charged with assault, but he was later acquitted.
- Cindy Crawford has been filmed in her bathroom from over a kilometre away with a huge telephoto lens.
- When Princess Diana's father died, a paparazzo was waiting outside her hotel – she tearfully begged him to leave her alone, but the pictures were printed in the national newspapers the next day.

Provocation

The paparazzi go out of their way to make people angry so that they can get a better picture. The American actor George Clooney was walking down the street with his girlfriend when a paparazzo shouted, 'Who's the fat girl?' The picture of Clooney's angry face was splashed all over the newspapers the next day. However, the actor got his revenge on the paparazzi when one of the photographers was hiding in his garden to get pictures of him and his girlfriend at home – the photographer was chased away by Clooney's pet Vietnamese pot-bellied pig.

The paparazzi are out of control. Some papers have recognised what is happening and have refused to buy pictures when it's obvious that a person's privacy has been invaded. Other papers must follow their example.

CLICK HERE TO VOICE YOUR OPINION

Lexis

1 Match words and phrases from the two columns to make seven expressions from the text on page 51. Do as many as you can from memory. Then look back at the text to check.

a) give (someone) a black eye
b) charge (someone) alone
c) follow (someone) angry
d) go (someone's) example
e) invade out of your way to do something
f) leave (someone's) privacy
g) make (someone) with assault

2 Complete the following sentences with expressions from 1. You will need to change the tenses of the expressions in some cases.

a) All I did was ask him to smile for the camera and he _____ .
b) His aggressive behaviour is unacceptable. He should be _____ .
c) I asked her why she was upset but she told me to _____ .
d) It really _____ when people don't stop at red lights.
e) Are you _____ annoy me? You know I hate it when you smoke in the kitchen.
f) David left school at sixteen and never went to college and now he's a millionaire. I should have _____ .
g) I regret asking my mother to stay. I feel that my _____ .

Discussion Discuss the following:

a) Celebrity gossip and scandal is boring.
b) Film and rock stars are paid too much.
c) Tabloid-type newspapers and magazines should be banned.
d) Information available over the Internet should be controlled.
e) The private lives of politicians and royalty should never be discussed by the press.
f) Highly paid film stars are public property.

LANGUAGE TOOLBOX

To interrupt
Sorry to interrupt, but …

To hold the floor
If you'd just let me finish …

To return to the subject
Yes, but as I was saying …

Close up

Irregular verbs

1 Test your irregular verbs. The irregular verbs below have been divided into five groups.

1	2	3	4	5
swim	break	let	grow	bring
drink	speak	set	fly	fight
ring	choose	cost	throw	catch

Why are they divided in this way? When you know the answer, add these words to the appropriate groups.

| steal | hit | know | begin | teach |

How many more verbs can you add to each group? Look at the irregular verb table on page 147.

2 Test your partner's knowledge of irregular verbs.

For example:
Student A: *Eat …?*
Student B: *Ate, eaten. Drink …?*
Student A: *Drank, drunk. Go …?*

The passive voice

NEWS IN BRIEF

POLICE THEFT
A television set (1) _____ from a Liverpool police station while officers were out fighting crime.

PLANE DRAMA
A drunk who tried to open an aeroplane door at 30,000 feet (2) _____ for the rest of a Denmark to Thailand flight.

CAMPER DIES
Camper John Barnes, 23, (3) _____ after a 200-metre fall into a rocky ravine with only a broken foot. Sadly he (4) _____ when he fell out of the ambulance on the way to the hospital in Perth, Scotland.

UNLUCKY BURGLAR
Burglar Frank Gort broke down and sobbed when he (5) _____ to seven years in jail, claiming it was his unlucky number. An understanding judge in San Antonio, Texas, took pity and gave him eight years instead.

WANTED MAN JAILED

Fugitive James Sanders, who escaped from jail in 1975, (6) _____ in Texas after ringing the FBI to check if he was still on its wanted list.

STABBED IN THE BACK
Mr Clarence Ramsey (7) _____ seriously _____ yesterday when a man came up behind him and stabbed him in the back. Turning round to face his attacker, Mr Ramsey was surprised to hear him say, 'Sorry. I thought you were somebody else.'

Language Reference p54

---

1 Complete the sentences below with the words and phrases in the box.

> a judge   a car crash   paparazzi   the police
> his pet Vietnamese pot-bellied pig

a) _____ arrested Baldwin and charged him with assault but _____ acquitted him.
b) _____ pursued Tom Cruise at high speed through the tunnel in Paris where _____ killed Princess Diana.
c) George Clooney got his revenge on the paparazzi when one of the photographers was hiding in his garden to get pictures of him and his girlfriend at home – _____ chased away a photographer.

2 Look at these extracts from the text on page 51. What verb structure do all the sentences use?

a) Baldwin was arrested and charged with assault, but he was later acquitted.
b) Tom Cruise has been pursued at high speed through the tunnel in Paris where Princess Diana was killed.
c) However the actor got his revenge on the paparazzi when one of the photographers was hiding in his garden to get pictures of him and his girlfriend at home – the photographer was chased away by Clooney's pet Vietnamese pot-bellied pig.

3 Discuss these questions.

a) How is the passive formed?
b) Only one of the sentences mentions the *agent*. Which one?
c) Which preposition is used with the agent?
d) What are the advantages of using the passive? Match these reasons to the three sentences in 2.

1 The agent is unknown.
2 The agent is obvious.
3 You want to keep the important information at the beginning of the sentence.

4 Complete the short newspaper stories on the left with a suitable verb from the box.

> steal   handcuff   rescue   sentence   arrest   injure   kill
> rob   damage   break   shoot   kill   find guilty   destroy

5 What are the experiences of the class? Ask questions to find someone who:

- has been searched by customs.
- has been stopped for speeding.
- has been let down by a friend.
- has been photographed by a local newspaper.
- has been mistaken for somebody else.
- has been injured playing a sport.
- has been given a present they didn't like.
- has been interviewed on radio or television.
- has been questioned by the police.

6 Work in groups of three. You are going to edit some short newspaper stories. Students A and B will each have three stories. The stories are the same, but the language used in them is different. Student C is the editor who will explain what you have to do.

Student A look at page 139.
Student B look at page 141.
Student C look at page 143.

Language reference: passives

There are various situations in which it is better to use the passive rather than the active.

The *agent* of a verb is the person, people or thing which performs the action. To include the agent in the sentence, you use *by*:

*A meeting was called **by** the marketing department.*

Passive without agent

1 The agent is unknown.
   *A bomb **was left** in the city centre last night.*
   *Her car **has been stolen**.*
2 You do not want to identify the agent.
   *The President admitted that mistakes **had been made**.*
3 You do not need to identify the agent.
   *The demonstrators **were charged** with disturbing the peace.*
4 You are not interested in the agent.
   *The acid **is** then **heated** to 100 degrees centigrade which causes it to react with the oxides.*

Passive with by + agent

When the agent is included you use the passive to put the most important information at the beginning of the sentence.
*The President is protected **by the CIA**.*
*Paper was invented **by the Chinese**.*

Headline news

1 Find the newspaper headlines for these four photographs. Which story would you read first? What are the news items about? Are there any stories like this in the news at the moment?

a **PEACE TALKS END IN ROW**

b **MINISTER QUITS IN MISSING CASH PROBE**

e **WEST TO AID SOMALIA**

c **FREAK STORM HITS HARVEST**

f **JOB FIGURES SOAR**

d **SCHOOL BARS NOSE-RING GIRL**

g **LOTTERY OCTOGENARIAN TO WED**

2 🎧 **22** Listen to the radio news broadcast from the same day as the headlines. What is the order of the four stories?

3 Listen again and answer these questions.

a) Who made an announcement?
b) Why was it made?
c) What is Robert Holmes' job?
d) What did the Prime Minister order?
e) Where is Robert Holmes right now?
f) What is Pauline Gates' problem?
g) What does Pauline have to do?
h) How old is Max Williams?
i) How much money does he have?
j) How old is Sally Lister?
k) How much did the ring cost?

4 Listen again and complete the text of the broadcast.

> And here are the news headlines.
>
> Following severe droughts in Africa, the President of the USA has announced _____ .
>
> Robert Holmes, Minister for the Environment, _____ . The Prime Minister _____ into the mysterious disappearance of a large sum of money. A spokesman for the minister told us that he was _____ and not available for comment.
>
> Schoolgirl Pauline Gates has _____ . According to headmistress Jean Bradley, _____ .
>
> And finally, to end on a happier note, wedding bells are ringing for _____ Max Williams, who won _____ in the lottery last month. He's going to marry _____ dancer Sally Lister. The happy couple posed for photographers outside the millionaire's luxury home in Essex and Sally held out her hand to show off her _____ engagement ring for the cameras.

5 Write a radio news broadcast based on these newspaper headlines and photographs. Invent any extra information you need.

a) BARRED FROM WORLD CUP FINAL

b) TEACHER QUITS IN EXAM ROW

c) HOLLYWOOD COUPLE TO SPLIT

6 'Broadcast' your news to the rest of the class.

Personal news

1 Read this dialogue and think about how it could be improved.

Ken: Hi, Steve. How are you?
Steve: Oh, not too bad. Actually, it's my wedding anniversary today.
Ken: Oh.
Steve: But um, I forgot and my wife was really upset.
Ken: Oh.
Steve: But I just rang Le Petit Blanc and they actually had a table free, so we're going out for dinner.
Ken: Oh.
Steve: Anyway, I must go.
Ken: Er, yeah, me too. See you!

2 23 Listen to the dialogue and note the differences.

3 Read the dialogues. In each case, choose an appropriate response from the box. More than one answer is possible in some cases.

> Congratulations!   Well done!   I'm sorry to hear that.   Oh, no!
> Lucky you!   That's terrible!   Excellent!   You idiot!

A
A: Have you heard about Chris and Shirley?
B: No … what about them?
A: They've split up.
B: _____ .

B
C: Hello. You're looking very pleased with yourself.
D: I am! I've just passed my driving test!
C: _____ . Can I have a lift?

C
E: Guess what. I've won a holiday to Florida.
F: _____ . Is it a holiday for two?
E: Yes, I'm taking my mum.
F: Oh.

D
G: I've just had some bad news.
H: What's happened?
G: I've failed my final exams.
H: _____ . Are you going to resit them?

E
I: Oh, no!
J: What's the matter?
I: I've left my bag on the bus.
J: _____ . What are you going to do?
I: I suppose I'd better ring the bus company.

F
K: Have a glass of champagne!
L: Thank you. What are you celebrating?
K: My wife's just had a baby.
L: _____ . Boy or a girl?

G
M: You don't usually take the bus!
N: No – my car's broken down again.
M: _____ .

H
O: I didn't know you had a car.
P: My parents have bought a new car and they've given me their old one.
O: _____ .

4 24 Listen to the dialogues and check your answers.

5 25 Listen to the responses. Practise the stress and intonation.

6 26 Listen to these ten sentences. How would you respond to each sentence?

7 Work with a partner. Choose five of the sentences below. Write five dialogues beginning with the sentences you have chosen. Act them out in class.

- ☐ You look happy!
- ☐ Why are you limping?
- ☐ Are you all right?
- ☐ That's a lovely watch. Is it new?
- ☐ You look upset – what's the matter?
- ☐ I hear you're leaving the company.
- ☐ Where are you going for your holidays?
- ☐ I haven't seen you in English lessons recently.

UNIT 6 *News*

A letter from Berlin

1 Read this letter from Pia to her friend Ian. Complete the letter with appropriate words. If you need help, look at the missing words in the box below. There is one word for each gap. They are not in the correct order.

> Anyway news but Well
> apparently feel soon
> hear what getting Apart
> pleased heard thing
> sorry forward applied
> loads embarrassing
> By the way

2 Work with a partner. Explain the relationships between Pia, Ian, Anna and Giorgio.

3 Answer each of the following questions with one or more of the above names.

a) Who lives in Berlin?
b) Who used to live in Berlin?
c) Whose mother has been ill?
d) Who's been promoted at work?
e) Who's got a new job?
f) Who's called off their wedding?
g) Who's gone back to Italy?
h) Whose parents have sent out wedding invitations?
i) Who's going on holiday in August?
j) Who's passed their driving test?

Berlin, 14th July

Dear Ian,
It was great to (1) _____ from you. I'm (2) _____ I haven't written sooner, (3) _____ my mother hasn't been very well, so I've been looking after her. She's a lot better now.

I was so (4) _____ to hear about your promotion. You deserve it – you've worked so hard at that job. (5) _____ done! I wish you were still living in Berlin so we could go out and celebrate.

Actually, I've got some good (6) _____ too – I've got a new job! You know I was fed up with my old job. Well, one day I was just looking through the ads in my local newspaper when I saw a job for an English school administrator. As you know, I've been looking for a job where I could use my English. So I (7) _____ for the job and got it. I'm really enjoying it and I've already learnt (8) _____ of new things. I have to answer the phone (sometimes in English!), send out information about the school and deal with any problems the students have. And the best (9) _____ is that I'm getting more money!

(10) _____, have you (11) _____ about Anna and Giorgio? They've called off the wedding. I've no idea why, but (12) _____ Giorgio's gone back to Italy and Anna's refusing to talk to anybody about it, even her old friends. I (13) _____ sorry for her parents – they've sent out all the invitations and now they've got to tell everybody that the wedding's cancelled. How (14) _____! I wonder if she's given him back that gorgeous ring?! (15) _____, I suppose it's better that they've split up now rather than after the wedding!

(16) _____ from that, everything's fine here in Berlin. It's getting hot and I'm looking (17) _____ to going on holiday in August. Don't forget that you're always welcome to come and stay – we'd love to see you.

Anyway, I must go now. Write (18) _____ and tell me how you're (19) _____ on.

Lots of love, Pia

PS Guess (20) _____! I've finally passed my driving test.

---

4 Ian answered Pia's letter. Use the expressions below to write his reply.

> Dear Pia,
> It was great ...
> I'm sorry ...
> I was so pleased ...
> Thank you for the invitation to come and stay, but actually, I've already made plans for the summer. I'm going ...
> By the way, Giorgio phoned me. Apparently, ...
> Apart from that, ...
> Anyway, ...
> Write soon.
> Lots of love,
> Ian
> PS Guess what!

News UNIT 6

7 Party

1 Think of a festival you know or have heard about. How much do you know about it?

a) What is the name of the festival?
b) When does it take place?
c) How long does it go on for?
d) What do you know about its history?
e) How do people celebrate?
f) How does the festival end?

2 Read this article about a big Spanish festival and find answers to the questions in 1.

SPAIN'S THIRD CITY SEES WINTER OFF WITH A BANG

It's March and I'm in Valencia, Spain's third largest city, with my new friend, José. It's 1 am. All around us, fireworks are going off and the streets are full of noisy revellers. 'Welcome to Las Fallas,' José grins. 'Here you're going to see how Valencians party!'

Seven hours later, I understood what he meant.

Las Fallas (the bonfire) explodes over Valencia every March from the 12th to the 19th. It takes the whole of the previous year to get organised and everybody joins in the preparations. The city buzzes with a festive vibe all week, but, like all good parties, it is at night when people really get down to some serious celebrating.

The tradition of Las Fallas began in the 18th century. At that time, craftsmen used special candles to light up the dark evenings while they were working. At the end of winter they celebrated by burning all their waste material in a ceremony that brought together people from all the neighbouring communities. Before burning the waste material, they made it into life-like statues, and then dressed them up to look like well-known but unpopular local characters.

Nowadays the statues, some of them over 30 metres tall, are made of cardboard and represent different aspects of modern Spanish society. The whole of the previous year is spent fund-raising, planning and constructing the monuments, some of which are worth over $200,000. But they all go up in flames with the maximum amount of fire and noise before the end of the festival.

The Valencians like their guests to enjoy themselves, but after one hour's sleep I am woken up by the sound of firecrackers and a brass band parading beneath my window. Valencia by day may be sleepier than Valencia by night, but during Las Fallas there's always something going on. From the outskirts of the city, 200,000 girls and boys, wearing traditional dress, march into the centre of town bringing flowers to decorate the statue of the Blessed Virgin.

The festival reaches its climax on 19th March, a public holiday and St Joseph's Day. This is the night when the cardboard statues are burnt. As midnight approaches, a feeling of anticipation rises up from the streets and hangs over the city. Firecrackers go off every second or two and midnight passes in a shower of explosions. The last statue burns down and ends Las Fallas. It is a sad moment, but the Valencians don't have time to mourn the end of this year's festival. After all, they're too busy planning for the next one.

(The Independent on Sunday 8 February 1998)

Glastonbury 1998

Phrasal verbs

1 Complete the sentences below with the correct endings from the box. All the sentences include phrasal verbs from the article on page 58.

   a) Don't sit around on your own: join …
   b) Half the town burnt …
   c) Even if I don't have an alarm clock, I always wake …
   d) It was a beautiful night with a full moon that lit …
   e) My cousin was injured when a firework went …
   f) We'll all miss you. The whole family's going to come to see you …
   g) We've wasted enough time. Let's get …
   h) What's going …
   i) You can't wear jeans to your brother's wedding: everybody will be dressing …

   > off at the airport.   up the whole bay.   up for the occasion.   up at six in the morning.
   > on here? It's way past your bedtime.   off in his hand and burnt him.   in the fun.
   > down to some serious work.   down in a fire in 1948.

2 Match the phrasal verbs in 1 to the meanings below.

   a) destroy completely by fire   f) illuminate
   b) wear special clothes   g) say goodbye before a journey
   c) explode   h) stop sleeping
   d) participate in an activity   i) begin seriously or enthusiastically
   e) happen

3 Complete these paragraphs with the same phrasal verbs. You may need to change the verb tenses to make them fit the sentences.

   A
   … They bribed a security guard to leave the briefcase in the house. But at about three in the morning the Prime Minister (1) _____ _____ . She couldn't get back to sleep so she went out for a walk. When the bomb (2) _____ _____ she was in an all-night café two kilometres away. The explosion was huge. It (3) _____ _____ the whole sky and the house was (4) _____ _____ .

   B
   John's leaving for his year in the USA next week so we're having a party to (5) _____ him _____ . It's going to be informal — you don't need to (6) _____ _____ or anything. Just come as you are and (7) _____ _____ some serious dancing. We've organised some party games, but if you don't want to (8) _____ _____ that's OK. There'll be lots of other things (9) _____ _____ .

4 *Call My Bluff*: Work in teams of three. Team A look at page 139. Team B look at page 143.

Pronunciation

1 The words in the box are from the article on page 58. They contain all the short vowel sounds in English. Work with a partner. Match the underlined sounds to the phonetic symbols.

   > around   band   busy   candle   city   different   festival
   > full   fund   good   guest   holiday   modern   public

2   27 Listen and check.

3 Add more examples of your own for each sound.

Close up

Future forms

1　🔊 28　Zoë and Sandy share a flat. Zoë comes home one evening to find Sandy looking miserable. Listen to their conversation and find out why Sandy's unhappy.

2　Look at tapescript 28 and find three different structures that refer to the future.

3　Which form is used:

　　a)　at the moment of making a decision?
　　b)　to talk about your intentions – what you've decided you want to do?
　　c)　to talk about fixed plans?

4　Read the conversations below to find out how the evening continued for Sandy and choose the most appropriate verb forms.

(Phone rings.)

Becky:　Hello.
Sandy:　Hi, Becky, it's Sandy.
Becky:　Hiya.
Sandy:　Becky, **will you do/are you doing** anything tonight?
Becky:　Yes. **I'll meet/I'm meeting** Alex and Suzy in about half an hour.
Sandy:　Where **will you go/are you going**?
Becky:　To the cinema. Would you like to come with us?
Sandy:　Yes, I'd love to. Where **will you meet/are you meeting**?
Becky:　At their house, but we could meet you in front of the cinema in George Street at half past eight.
Sandy:　OK, thanks. See you later. (Puts the phone down and calls out to Zoë.) **I'll go/I'm going** to the cinema with Becky.
Zoë:　Good idea.
Sandy:　And next time I see David, **I'm telling/I'm going to tell** him to get lost.
Zoë:　Hmm. **I'll believe/I'm believing** that when I see it.

(Phone rings.)

Zoë:　Hello.
David:　Is Sandy there, please?
Zoë:　Yes, hold on a moment – **I'll get/I'm going to get** her for you. (Whispers.) It's David.
Sandy:　(Coldly.) Oh, hello, David.
David:　Look, I'm really sorry I didn't call earlier, but I had to work late.

Sandy:　Oh, that's all right – I forgot you were going to ring anyway.
David:　Listen, I'm afraid I can't see you tonight, **I'll have/I'm having** dinner with my parents.
Sandy:　It doesn't matter – **I'll go/I'm going** to the cinema anyway.
David:　Oh, right. OK, well **I'll call/I'm going to call** you.
Sandy:　When? I mean, all right. Bye.
David:　Bye.

(Sandy puts the phone down.)

Zoë:　You didn't tell him to get lost.
Sandy:　Well, he apologised – and **he'll have/he's having** dinner with his parents. Anyway, I must go. See you later.

(Later, in front of the cinema.)

Sandy:　Hi, Alex. Hi, Becky. Where's Suzy?
Becky:　Oh, she changed her mind at the last minute. David phoned her and asked her to go for a meal at that new Japanese restaurant.
Sandy:　What?! Now **I'm definitely telling/I'm definitely going to tell** him to get lost!

Zoë and Sandy

5　🔊 29　Listen and check your answers.

Language Reference p61

6　Work with a partner and complete the replies. Use *will ('ll)*, *(be) going to* or the present continuous.

　　a)　There's no food in the house.
　　　　Don't worry …
　　b)　Can we meet for a drink on Tuesday?
　　　　I'd love to, but …
　　c)　Have you got your holiday organised?
　　　　Yes, we booked it last week. We …
　　d)　Are you ready to order, madam?
　　　　Yes, I think …
　　e)　Does Jack know we've changed the time of the meeting?
　　　　That's a good point. …
　　f)　The car needs a service.
　　　　Yes, I know …
　　g)　About your trip to Greece. Do you know there's a taxi strike next week in Athens?
　　　　Yes, Annie told me about it …
　　h)　Is there an agenda for the conference yet?
　　　　No, but …
　　i)　Your hair's getting long.
　　　　Yes, I know …

UNIT 7　*Party*

Invitations

1. Read tapescripts 28 and 29 again and find:
    a) two ways to ask somebody if they are free to go out.
    b) two ways to invite somebody to do something.
    c) two ways of refusing an invitation.
    d) the excuse David gives Sandy for not going out with her.

2. Use language from the tapescripts to write a dialogue based on the plan below.

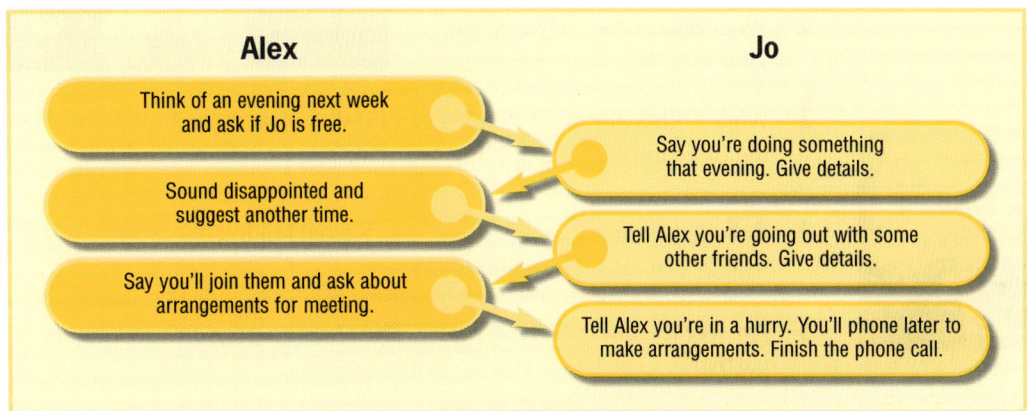

Alex
- Think of an evening next week and ask if Jo is free.
- Sound disappointed and suggest another time.
- Say you'll join them and ask about arrangements for meeting.

Jo
- Say you're doing something that evening. Give details.
- Tell Alex you're going out with some other friends. Give details.
- Tell Alex you're in a hurry. You'll phone later to make arrangements. Finish the phone call.

3. Practise the dialogue. Take it in turns to be Alex and Jo.

4. Work with a partner.

    Student A: you want to meet up with B and go somewhere.
    Student B: you don't want to go anywhere with A. Make excuses.

Language reference: future forms

The present continuous and the structures *will* (*'ll*) and *(be) going to* are three common ways to talk about the future. Each one tells us something different about what happened before the moment of speaking.

Will ('ll)

Form: *will* (*'ll*) + infinitive
Use: to state a new decision, to make promises and offers.
It's cold in here. I'll switch on the heating.
Don't worry. I'll call you tomorrow.
I'll help you carry your suitcase.

(be) going to

Form: *be + going to + infinitive*
Use: to talk about your intentions.
After university I'm going to travel for a year.
Next time I see him I'm going to tell him what I think.

Present continuous

Form: *be + present participle (-ing form)*
Use: to show that you are talking about your future arrangements, for example: appointments and organised events.
I'm playing tennis with Judy on Saturday.
We're having a party on Friday night. Would you like to come?
For other uses of these structures see unit 9.

Look at these three examples of different answers to the question:

Have you got any plans for the weekend?

1 Decision

No, I haven't. I think I'll call Jane and see if she's free.

2 Intention

TO DO
1 ~~Supermarket~~
2 ~~Take car to garage~~
3 Call Jane

Not yet. I'm going to call Jane and see if she's free.

3 Plan

FRIDAY

SATURDAY
1 pm – lunch date with Jane

Yes. I'm having lunch with Jane on Saturday.

Party UNIT 7

Parties

1 What sort of parties are these?
- housewarming
- leaving
- fancy dress
- 18th
- surprise
- Halloween

Masked Ball, Venice

2 What other types of party can you think of?

Alyson, Geoff & Rachel

3 Work with a partner. What do you think makes a good party? Write a list and agree on the three most important 'ingredients'.

4 ▶ 30 Listen to Alyson, Geoff and Rachel talking about the ingredients of a good party. Compare their ideas with yours.

5 Answer the questionnaire below. Then turn to page 142 and compare your score with a partner.

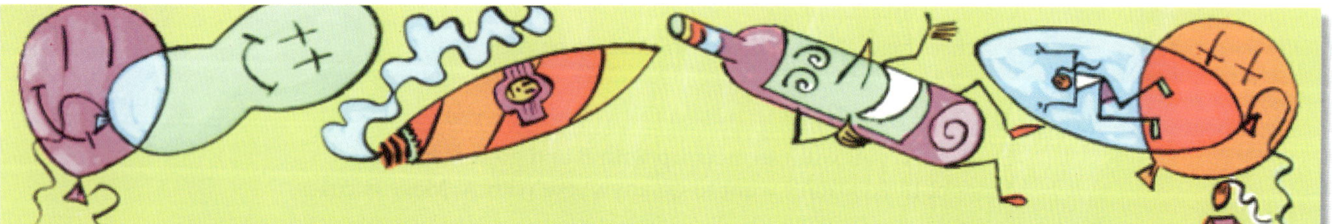

Are you a party animal or a party pooper?

1 You've been invited to a party but you're working the next morning. Do you …
a) think 'you only live once' and go and have a good time?
b) go to the party but leave at ten o'clock?
c) send your apologies and get an early night?

2 It's your birthday. Do you …
a) have a quiet family get-together, blow your candles out and go to bed early?
b) hope that nobody has remembered. You don't want to get older anyway?
c) have a big party and invite everybody you know?

3 You've been invited to a party by somebody you don't know very well. Do you …
a) go to the party and hope you'll meet lots of new people?
b) refuse the invitation. It's too scary?
c) go to the party but take a friend with you to make sure you'll have someone to talk to?

4 You arrive at a party and realise that the only person you know is the host. Do you …
a) panic and hide in the bathroom?
b) go and introduce yourself to anybody who looks interesting?
c) end up talking to the most boring person there because nobody else wants to talk to them?

5 Your favourite record comes on, but nobody else is dancing. Do you …
a) wait until a few other people are dancing and then join them?
b) stay where you are. You prefer to dance to your favourite record in the privacy of your own home?
c) start dancing on your own?

6 Somebody suggests playing party games. Do you …
a) suddenly remember a previous engagement?
b) feel embarrassed, but join in anyway?
c) suggest your favourite game and organise it?

Lexis 1 Complete as many of these sentences as you can from memory, using one word in each of the gaps. Compare your sentences with a partner. Then look back at the questionnaire to check your answers.

a) My philosophy is 'you only _____ once', so _____ sure you _____ good time'.

b) When I want to _____ an invitation, I sometimes say that I've got a _____ engagement, even if it's not true.

c) I'm not very good at going up to strangers and _____ myself.

d) Even when I'm not looking forward to going out, I usually end _____ enjoying myself.

e) From time to time, I really enjoy an evening at home _____ my own.

2 Are the sentences true for you? Discuss with a partner.

Let's party!

Anecdote 1 Think of a good party you've been to, or one that was a disaster. You are going to tell your partner about it. Choose from the list the things you want to talk about. Think about what you will say and what language you will need.

- ☐ Whose party was it?
- ☐ What was the occasion?
- ☐ Did you take a gift for the host?
- ☐ Who did you go with?
- ☐ Where was the party?
- ☐ Were there any decorations?
- ☐ Were there a lot of people there?
- ☐ Did you know most of the people there?
- ☐ What sort of food and drink did you have?
- ☐ What was the music like?
- ☐ Did you dance?
- ☐ Did you meet anybody nice there?
- ☐ What time did it finish?
- ☐ Did you stay to the end?

2 Tell your partner about the party.

3 Work in groups. You are going to take part in a competition to organise the best party. Decide on the following:

- budget
- date and time
- who to invite
- place
- formal or informal dress
- decorations
- entertainment (music, fireworks, etc)
- food and drink

4 Tell the rest of the class about your party. Try to convince them to come.

Manchester night life

It's my party ...

1 Look at the picture. What do you think the song is about?

2 ▭ 31 Listen to the song and see if you guessed correctly. Identify the following three people in the picture:

- the party hostess
- Johnny
- Judy

What is the relationship between them?

3 Listen to the song again and read the lyrics. In each line of the three verses there is an extra word. Find the word and cross it out.

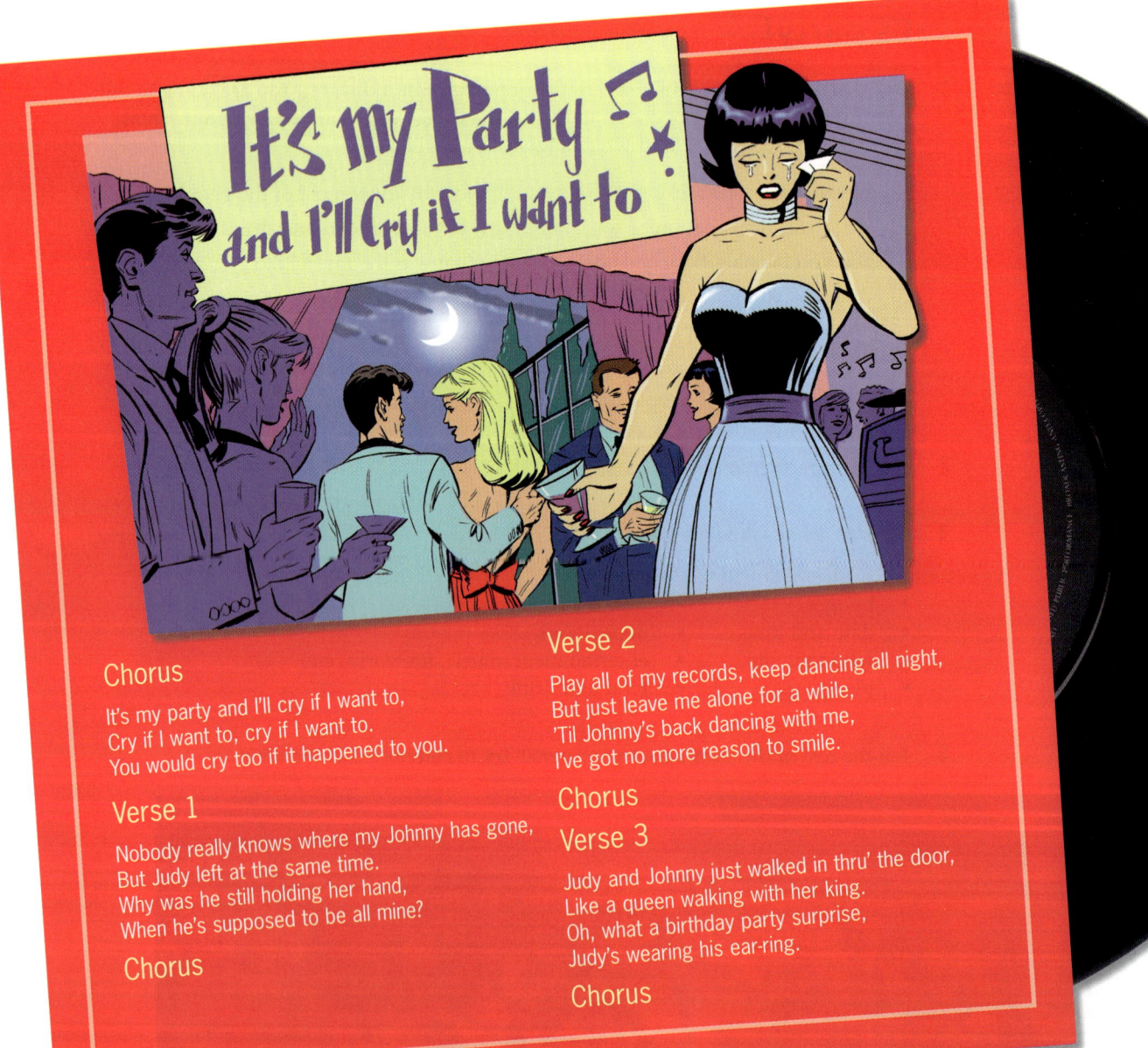

Chorus

It's my party and I'll cry if I want to,
Cry if I want to, cry if I want to.
You would cry too if it happened to you.

Verse 1

Nobody really knows where my Johnny has gone,
But Judy left at the same time.
Why was he still holding her hand,
When he's supposed to be all mine?

Chorus

Verse 2

Play all of my records, keep dancing all night,
But just leave me alone for a while,
'Til Johnny's back dancing with me,
I've got no more reason to smile.

Chorus

Verse 3

Judy and Johnny just walked in thru' the door,
Like a queen walking with her king.
Oh, what a birthday party surprise,
Judy's wearing his ear-ring.

Chorus

It's My Party was recorded by Lesley Gore in 1963.

It's My Party

It's My Party was Lesley Gore's first single in 1963, and became a number one hit within weeks. Although she recorded several top 40 hits during the 60s, it was her only number one song.

Special occasions

Writing **1** Match the letters of invitation to the replies.

1

Dear ...
Thanks for the invitation to dinner. I'd love to come. I haven't seen Brett and Alison for ages and your friend sounds really interesting. I'll bring some wine.
Look forward to seeing you on Saturday.

Love

2

Dear ...
It was great to hear from you. Sorry it's taken me a while to reply, but I've been up to my eyes in work recently. I'm pleased to hear that you're having such a good time at college and that you've made loads of new friends. David sounds nice. Three weeks? That must be a record for you!!
I'm writing to ask you what you're doing for the last weekend in May. I was wondering if you'd like to come down here and spend a few days by the sea. How about bringing David with you? (Can he cook?!) Please try to come. I'm really looking forward to seeing you.
Write soon and let me know.

Lots of love   xxx

3

Dear ...
Thank you for your kind invitation to your wedding anniversary. Unfortunately, I won't be able to join you as I'll be abroad on holiday. I hope the party goes well.
Best wishes for a happy anniversary on the 4th.
Love   x

PS Give my love to Uncle Ken.

4

Dear ...
Thank you for inviting me down for the weekend, but I'm afraid I've got exams the following week, so I won't be able to make it. I'd love to come another time, though. Maybe after my exams. I'll give you a ring and we'll fix a date.
Wish me luck for my exams.
Love

5

Dear ...
I hope you're well and that you're enjoying your new job. I'm writing to you because we would like you to join us for a small party to celebrate our 30th wedding anniversary on 4th September at the Ferncourt Hotel.
I do hope you can come. Please drop us a line to let us know.

Love

6

Dear ...
This is just a short note to ask you if you could come to dinner next Saturday. I'm sorry it's such short notice, but an old friend of mine phoned me yesterday to say she's coming for the weekend, and I'd love you to meet her. I think I've talked to you about her. Her name's Justy and she works for a film company in Spain. I'm going to ask Brett and Alison too. I do hope you can make it.

Love

2 Complete the following expressions so that they make sense. Then look back at the letters on the previous page to compare.

   a) We would like you to join us for a small party to …
   b) This is just a short note to ask you if you could …
   c) I do hope you …
   d) How about …
   e) Thank you for your kind invitation to your party. Unfortunately …
   f) I'm really looking forward …
   g) Thanks for the invitation to dinner. I'd love …
   h) Please try to …
   i) I was wondering if you'd like …
   j) Thank you for inviting me down for the weekend, but …

3 Label each sentence in 2 as follows:

   I for an invitation
   A for accepting an invitation
   R for refusing an invitation

   Underline the sentences which you consider to be the most formal. Compare your choice with a partner.

4 Work with a partner. Write a letter of invitation to another pair of students in the class. Include the date, the time and the place.

   Exchange your letters and write a reply accepting the invitation if you are free, or refusing it if you are not.

5 Match the greeting cards to the messages below. What is the occasion for each of these greetings?

   a) Congratulations. I hope you'll be very happy together.
   b) Congratulations. When's the big day?
   c) We're thinking of you and your family at this sad time.
   d) Congratulations. Hope she has her mother's looks and her father's talent for golf.
   e) Get well soon.
   f) We had a lovely evening. Don't forget to let me have that recipe.
   g) Many happy returns! Don't worry, you're only as old as you feel!
   h) Good luck. When's the housewarming party?
   i) All the best. We'll miss your smile around the office.
   j) Well done! Third time lucky.

8 Review 1

Test yourself

Here are some questions about units 1–7 of *Inside Out*. Find the grammar mistakes in the questions and correct them.

1. How Jane Couch did make history in November 1998?
2. Who did he write the book *Boy*?
3. When takes place Las Fallas in Valencia, Spain?
4. Which song Elton John sang at Diana's funeral?
5. Why did burglar Frank Gort got an extra year on his prison sentence?
6. How many words there are in *The Little Book of Calm*?
7. Where first met Australians Joel Emerson and Lisa Bunyan?

Can you answer the questions? Look back over units 1–7.

Once in a blue moon

Adverbs of frequency

1 Write questions with *How often do you …?*

a) How often do you go to the cinema?   b) _____   c) _____

d) _____   e) _____   f) _____

LANGUAGE TOOLBOX

hardly ever   often
every six months
occasionally
from time to time
twice a month
every morning
once in a blue moon
never   always
every other week
on Mondays
now and again
rarely   generally
usually

2 Ask other students the questions in 1. Who in the class does each activity the most and the least often?

Review 1 UNIT 8 67

Friends

Listening 1   ▷ 32 Each of the people below is friends with one of the others. Listen and write down any key words, (places, events, times, etc). Decide who is friends with whom.

| 1 Sue _____ | 2 Juan _____ | 3 Elisa _____ |
| 4 Enrico _____ | 5 Sindy _____ | 6 Hans _____ |

2   Have you got a friend that you met in an unusual way or in an unusual place?

Fancy going out?

Future forms 1   Choose the most appropriate form. In some cases there is more than one possibility.

Tomoko: Hi, Marie. (1) **Are you doing/Do you do/Will you do** anything tonight?
Marie: Yeah, I (2) **'ll see/'m going to see/'m seeing** a film with Peter and Berta. Do you fancy coming with us?
Tomoko: What (3) **are you going to see/are you seeing/will you see**?
Marie: We're not sure yet. We (4) **meet/'ll meet/'re meeting** at six thirty and then maybe we (5) **'re trying/'re going to try/'ll try** that new Indian restaurant before we go to the cinema.
Tomoko: Yeah, I (6) **'m coming/'ll come /'m going to come** along if you're sure it's OK.
Marie: Of course. We (7) **meet/'ll meet/'re meeting** outside school. Six thirty.
Tomoko: I (8) **give/'ll give/'m going to give** you a lift if you like. (9) **Will I call/Shall I call/Do I call** for you sometime after six?
Marie: Great. I (10) **'m seeing/'m going to see/'ll see** you later then.
Tomoko: Bye.

2   Work with a partner and improvise a similar conversation.

Sound & vision

Pronunciation 1   There are twelve pure vowel sounds in English. Think of three more words for each sound.

| /iː/ | /ɪ/ | /ʊ/ | /uː/ | /e/ | /ə/ | /ɜː/ | /ɔː/ | /æ/ | /ʌ/ | /ɑː/ | /ɒ/ |
| s<u>ee</u> | b<u>i</u>g | l<u>oo</u>k | bl<u>ue</u> | <u>e</u>gg | m<u>o</u>ther | w<u>or</u>d | m<u>ore</u> | c<u>a</u>t | c<u>u</u>p | st<u>ar</u>t | t<u>o</u>p |

2   Look at the picture on page 140. Which vowel sound is *not* in the picture? For example: *key* is /iː/.

Keep in touch

Tense review 1 Put the verbs in brackets into the most appropriate tenses.

Sydney,
15th May

Dear Lena,

Just a quick note (in English!!!) to say that I (1) _____ (have) a fantastic time here in Australia. I (2) _____ (be) here for over two weeks now! The course (3) _____ (be) really good and my English (4) _____ (get) better every day. I (5) _____ (meet) lots of interesting people and I (6) _____ (become) quite friendly with some of them.

Guess what! (7) _____ (you/remember) Miguel who we (8) _____ (meet) in Paris last year? Well, his brother (9) _____ (study) here, in the same class as me actually, and he (10) _____ (tell) me that Miguel (11) _____ (come) over here next month. He (12) _____ (spend) a few days here in Sydney on his way to Bali. I (13) _____ (hope) he (14) _____ (remember) me!

So, how's life for you? (15) _____ (you/miss) me? I (16) _____ (be) a bit homesick at first and I really (17) _____ (want) to see you, but I (18) _____ (feel) fine now. (19) _____ (you/see) Marcella recently? She (20) _____ (work) so hard for her exam when I last (21) _____ (see) her. The exam (22) _____ (be) next week, isn't it? (23) _____ (tell) her that I (24) _____ (think) of her.

Well, I (25) _____ (have got) a lesson in five minutes, so I (26) _____ (finish) now. I (27) _____ (write) again soon.

Take care and lots of love,

Virginia xxxx

2 Write a short letter to a friend telling them your news.

Do you know Paris?

Sentence stress 1 ▭ 33 Which do you think are the most strongly stressed words in this dialogue?

Val: Where do you live?
Tony: In Paris.
Val: Oh, really? Whereabouts?
Tony: Do you know Paris?
Val: Quite well. I've got a friend there.
Tony: Oh, right. Um, I'm right in the centre. Near the Champs-Elysées.
Val: Nice! Which street?
Tony: Rue Marbeuf. Do you know it?
Val: I think so. Is it just opposite that big café?
Tony: Yeah, that's right.
Val: Yeah, my friend lives in rue François, just round the corner.

Listen and check. Then work with a partner and practise the dialogue.

2 Write your own similar dialogue and practise it.

Did you know …?

Passive

Can you rearrange the information to make ten facts?

For example: 35,000 million bananas are harvested in Brazil every year.

a)	35,000 million bananas	use in the USA	every year.
b)	3,500 km² of the world's forest	rule by the House of Windsor	every day.
c)	The World Cup	invent	in 1928.
d)	25,000 litres of petrol	next see	in 2002.
e)	300 babies	eat in Japan	every year.
f)	Sliced bread	harvest in Brazil	since 1910.
g)	Great Britain	destroy	every week.
h)	Halley's comet	hold in Japan and South Korea	in 2061.
i)	20 people in India	born in the world	every minute.
j)	13,000 tonnes of fish	kill by falling coconuts	every second.

People & places

Relative clauses

1   Complete these questions with the missing words: *who, whose, which, that* or *where*.

Can you name:

a) the city __which__ was the birthplace of Marco Polo?
b) the pacifist _____ led India to independence?
c) the city _____ gave us the Beatles?
d) the French scientist _____ won the Nobel Prize in 1911?
e) the cosmonaut _____ was the first person in space?
f) the country _____ football legend Pele played for?
g) the singer _____ first number one was *Like a Virgin*?
h) the city _____ the prophet Mohammed was born?
i) the mountain _____ is home to the Greek gods?
j) the city _____ John F Kennedy was assassinated?
k) the only British monarch _____ ruled for over sixty years?
l) the explorer _____ was the first to reach the South Pole?
m) the country _____ Alexander the Great was born?

2   Work in small groups. The answers to the questions in 1 can be found in the box. There are more answers than questions. The group that answers the most questions correctly is the winner.

> Amundsen   Argentina   Armstrong   Brazil   Curie   Dallas   Egypt   Elizabeth
> Gagarin   Gandhi   Lennon   Liverpool   London   Macedonia   Mecca   Madonna
> New York   Olympus   Pasteur   Polo   Rome   Sting   Turkey   Venice   Victoria

3   For the answers that you didn't use write similar questions using 'Can you name …?'

Far, far away

Adjectives

1. Choose the correct alternative in bold in the text on the right.

2. Complete Anna's postcard to her friend with adjectives in an appropriate form.

> India captures the imagination. Colourful, **exciting/excited,** at times **exasperated/exasperating**, but never, ever dull. To some it is the most **fascinated/fascinating** place on earth and you are sure to be **captivated/captivating** from the moment you arrive. India's **amazed/amazing** diversity provides something for everyone. From the Himalayas, where you are dwarfed by some of the **most high/highest** mountains in the world, to the magical deserts and **charmed/charming** palaces of Rajasthan; from the **most busy/busiest** streets imaginable, where simply having a stroll can leave you absolutely **tired/exhausted**, to the hedonism of the palm-fringed beaches of Goa, where you'll feel a hundred per cent **relaxed/relaxing**. India is much more than a place you visit. India is an assault on the senses. A place you will never forget.

```
Hi M,
I'm having an absolutely (1) _____ time in Goa.
The weather is (2) _____ , the hotel is
(3) _____ and the food is really quite
(4) _____ . I've only been here a few days and
already I feel really (5) _____ . It's quite similar
to where we were last year, but this place is much
(6) _____ and not as (7) _____ . The local
sights round here are all pretty (8) _____ and all
in all I'd say the place is absolutely (9) _____ .
It's probably the (10) _____ place I've ever been
to. I've met loads of people – most of them are
(11) _____ , but a few are (12) _____ . In
fact, I met someone yesterday who's absolutely
(13) _____ . Wait 'til you see the photos! See
you in a couple of weeks. Miss you!
Anna xxxx

                                Mette Pedersen
                                Upperlandsgatan 118
                                Linköping
                                Sweden
```

3. Think of a holiday you've had or a place you've visited. Imagine you're there now. Write a postcard to a friend.

A letter to a friend

General revision

Here is Lena's reply to Virginia's letter which appeared on page 69. Find and correct the mistakes. There are at least 20 mistakes.

```
                                              Roskilde,
                                              23rd May
Dear Virginia,
   Thanks for your letter last week. It's great to hear that you have a good time in
Australia and I'm glad the school and the course are good.
   So, when Miguel is coming to Australia? Maybe I visit you at the same time! And what
is Miguel's brother like? Is he looking like him? Write soon and tell me all about it.
   Life here is fine, although we all miss you lots. We especially have missed you last
weekend. Juliette was having a party for her birthday. Everybody were there and I spent
most of the evening dancing.
   Remember the people which last month we met at the Superhead concert? Well, Juliette
was invited them to the party and we all got on really well. We had an absolutely good
time. Stefan and me really hit it off! In fact, I'll see him again tomorrow. He rung
me the day after the party to ask me out. I'm so exciting! I'll write soon and let you
know how it's all going.
   Marcella she say hello to you. Her exam has been yesterday. I don't speak to her
since then, but I'm sure she did fine.
   Me, Mum, Dad and Thomas are passing next week a few days with my grandparents in
Hamburg. As you know, we go usually there each year two times. I generally enjoy it,
but I'm glad always when it's time to come home. And this year it'll be more harder
than ever to be away!!!
Write again soon and have fun!

Love,

Lena xxxxxxx
```

Review 1 UNIT 8 71

9 Soap

1 Combine these words and part-words to form at least ten more family words.

mother	brother	nephew	second	-in-law
ex-	step-	single	sister	child
father	son	cousin	half-	parent
daughter	aunt	husband	niece	first
uncle	grand	great	wife	only

2 Use as many of the words as you can to describe yourself.

3 Draw a diagram to illustrate some of your own family relationships.

4
- Put (brackets) around the family members you live with.
- <u>Underline</u> the relatives that live nearest.
- ~~Cross out~~ the relatives you see least.
- (Circle) the relative you saw most recently.
- Put an asterisk (*) by the oldest relative and two asterisks (* *) by the youngest.
- Tick (✓) the relative you get on best with.

I'm Marie Lefarge's great granddaughter
I'm Jean Duval's daughter
Me
I'm Raquel Parmenter's niece
I'm Marc Duval's sister

5 Work with a partner. Compare your diagrams. Take it in turns to talk about some of the relatives you have identified. What are they like? What sort of lives do they live?

Pacific Heights

1 Read *Who's who in Pacific Heights*. Match the characters in **BOLD** to their photos in the family tree on page 73. Write the names of the characters above the photos.

Who's who in Pacific Heights

The series is set in Pacific Heights, California. **MAX DALTON** and **PHIL TURNER**, his son-in-law, run a large cosmetics corporation, DCC, which has been in the family for over 150 years. Max became managing director of Dalton Cosmetics Corporation five years ago when his father died and soon afterwards took Phil on as his junior partner. Together, they have transformed DCC from a small family business into a successful multinational company. They are in the process of negotiating a very important deal with a French distributor. The pressures of work are beginning to affect 60-year-old Max's health.

Max's second wife **SARAH** is a dynamic woman in her early fifties who runs her own business. She has always been an attractive woman and is the only member of the family with red hair. She insists that it is natural.

Max has two daughters by his first marriage. There's a big age gap between them: **PENNY** is in her late thirties and **LOU** is just 21. Lou has always wished that she was a boy (and looks like one with her long slim legs and short spiky hair). She's the baby of the family and Penny tends to mother her. Lou has never got over the death of her mother and she has a difficult relationship with Sarah. The two girls both take after their mother with their blonde hair and blue eyes.

As well as a daughter called Amy, Sarah has two sons from a previous marriage. Dave, 28, and his 27-year-old brother, **DANIEL**, look alike with their brown hair and dark brown eyes, but Daniel is more outgoing than his elder brother. Dave works as a sales manager for a computer company and is married to Clare. Daniel works as a sound engineer for a recording company and recently got engaged to Annick, whose father runs the French distribution company which is about to sign an important contract with DCC. Daniel met the beautiful young Frenchwoman soon after his ex-girlfriend, Katy, had left him for John, Daniel's best friend. At the time, Daniel was heartbroken.

Katy and Annick are both in their mid twenties, but apart from that they are very different. Annick is classically beautiful with her long thick dark hair and fine Mediterranean features, while Katy is attractive in a less conventional way: she's got long blonde hair with red and brown streaks, sparkling blue eyes and a flirtatious smile. Annick works for her father's company; Katy works as a set manager for a film company.

EDITH, Max's elderly mother, holds the whole family together. At the age of 78 she is still very active and everybody confides in her when they have a problem.

TV Gazette

2 Who are Annick, Katy and John? What is their relationship to Daniel?

Lexis **1** Refer to the Dalton family tree and the text and answer each of the following questions with one name:
  a) Who is Penny's grandmother?
  b) Who is Max's son-in-law?
  c) Who is Max's youngest step-son?
  d) Who is Daniel's ex-girlfriend?
  e) Who is Max and Sarah's future daughter-in-law?
  f) Who is Edith's daughter-in-law?
  g) Who is Edith's oldest granddaughter?

2 Write some similar questions and ask another student.

3 The mistakes in the following sentences have been ~~crossed out~~. Rewrite the sentences correctly.

  a) ~~In~~ the age of 52, Sarah is still an attractive woman.
  b) Lou ~~has 21 years~~.
  c) Katy has ~~blue big~~ eyes.
  d) Both Katy and Annick are in their ~~middle~~ twenties.
  e) Sarah's ~~red~~ curly hair makes her look young for her age.
  f) Edith is Max's elderly mother; ~~her age is~~ 78.
  g) Even though Edith is ~~at~~ her late seventies, she is still very fit for her age.
  h) Daniel is Dave's 27- ~~years~~ -old brother.
  i) Daniel is more outgoing ~~that~~ Dave.
  j) Most men ~~in~~ his age are not as hardworking as Max Dalton.

4 Think of your friends and family, or famous people, and complete these sentences in an appropriate way. Choose a different person for each sentence.

  a) _____ has got _____ hair.
  b) _____ is in his late/mid/early _____ .
  c) _____ has got _____ eyes.
  d) _____ is in her early _____ .
  e) _____ has a _____ .
  f) _____ looks _____ .

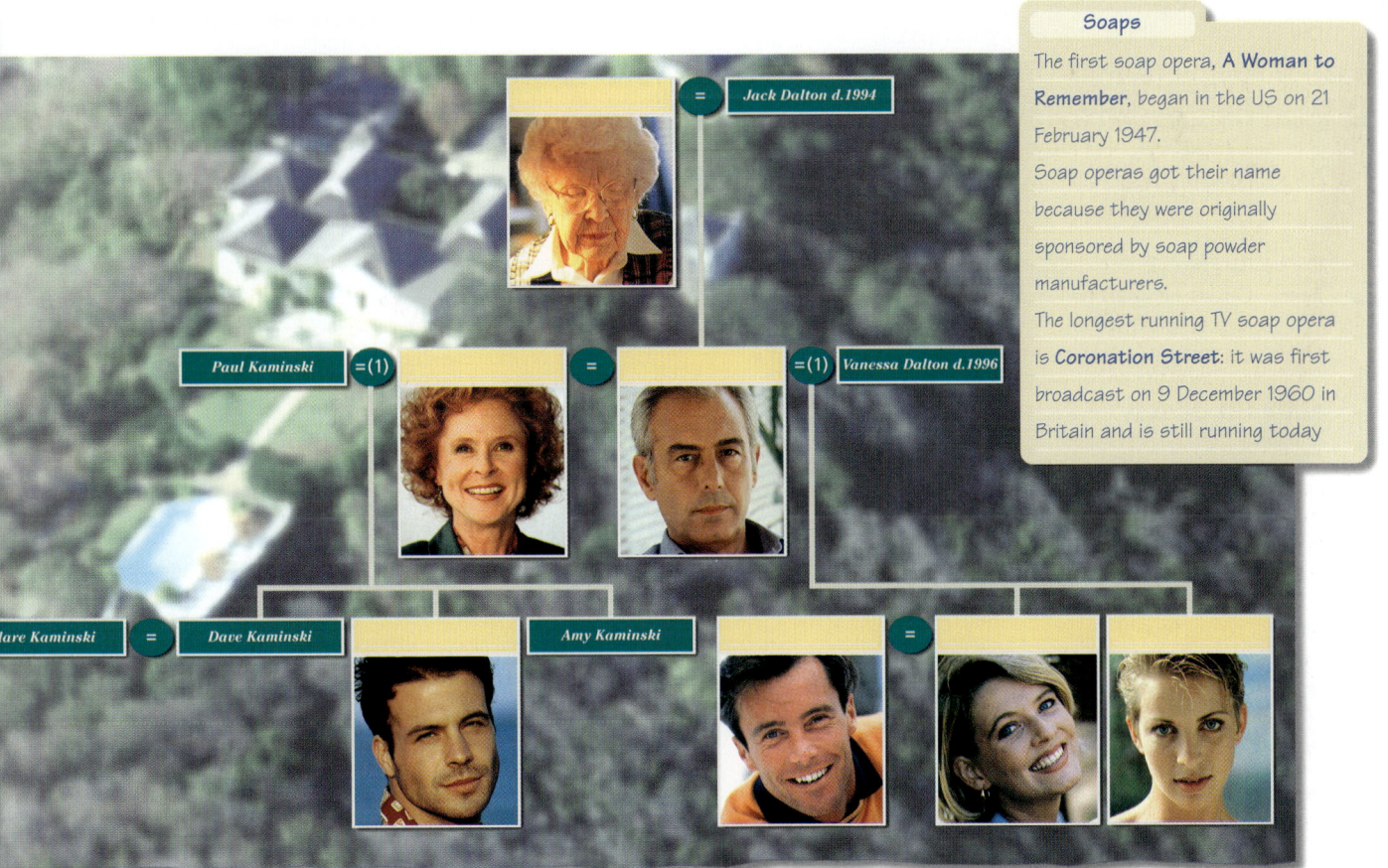

> **Soaps**
> The first soap opera, **A Woman to Remember**, began in the US on 21 February 1947.
> Soap operas got their name because they were originally sponsored by soap powder manufacturers.
> The longest running TV soap opera is **Coronation Street**: it was first broadcast on 9 December 1960 in Britain and is still running today

say/tell

1 Read *The story so far* and complete the gaps with *said* or *told*.

2 Who said:

a) 'It's all over between John and me.'
b) 'I'm not sure about me and Annick.'
c) 'You should have a rest.'
d) 'Don't say a word about this.'

3 Complete the following rule for *say* and *tell*.

- You _____ somebody.
- You _____ something.

The story so far:

Katy phoned Daniel and (1) _____ that she had split up with John. They arranged to meet and when he saw Katy, Daniel realized that he was still in love with her. Daniel (2) _____ Edith that he was having second thoughts about his engagement to Annick. Penny went shopping with Lou to buy her a bridesmaid's dress for the wedding. On the way back to the Daltons' house they saw Daniel with Katy. Penny (3) _____ Lou not to say anything.
Max went to the doctor with pains in his chest and the doctor (4) _____ him that he was suffering from overwork and stress. He (5) _____ that he should take it easy for a while.

TV Gazette

Pacific Heights: Scene 1

1 🔊 34 Scene 1 is divided into four parts. Listen to the scene and read the script. How does the story develop in each part? Listen for new information about the characters, their situations and their actions.

Scene 1
Part 1 Edith is in the kitchen at the Daltons'. Daniel arrives …

Daniel: Hi, Grandma.
Edith: Hello, dear. How's it going?
Daniel: Oh, don't ask.
Edith: Are you still thinking about Katy?
Daniel: Yes. I can't get her off my mind. I don't know what to do.
Edith: I thought you'd got over her.
Daniel: I had … until I saw her again. When she told me she'd broken up with John, all the old feelings came back.
Edith: But Daniel, what about Annick and the wedding?
Daniel: I know. I thought I loved Annick. When I asked her to marry me I meant it – but now I'm not sure how I feel.
Edith: Look, why don't you go away for a few days and think about it? How about going to stay with Dave and Clare – they'd love to see you.
Daniel: But I thought Dave was in Mexico.
Edith: Oh, yes, he is, isn't he? Oh, well, Clare's there – you could talk it through with her.
Daniel: Yes, that's not a bad idea. I'll go and see her tomorrow.

Part 2 Max and Sarah arrive back from work …

Max: What a day! The traffic was worse than ever.
Edith: Sit down, both of you. Do you want juice?
Sarah: Oh, thank you, Edith. I'm worn out.
Daniel: Why, have you had a busy day?
Sarah: Yes, I've been shopping with Annick. She asked me to help her choose her wedding dress.
Edith: Did you have any luck?
Sarah: Yes, finally. You should see her, Daniel. She looks gorgeous.
Daniel: Oh … good. I … I've got to go out. See you later.

Part 3 Edith, Max and Sarah in the kitchen …

Sarah: What did I say?
Edith: Listen, there's something you should know.

Max: What's the matter? Mom, are you all right?
Edith: Yes, I'm fine, dear. It's Daniel – he says he's having doubts about Annick.
Max: What! What does he mean?
Edith: He's seen Katy again.
Max: Katy? I thought she was married to somebody else. Anyway, it's too late to cancel the wedding now.
Sarah: Oh, but Max, if Daniel's still in love with Katy …
Max: I don't care who he's in love with, the wedding is going ahead.

Part 4 Lou and Penny arrive …

Penny: Oh, dear. What's going on here?
Max: Er, nothing – everything's fine.
Edith: Juice, dear?
Penny: Oh, yes, please. We've had a terrible day – we've been shopping to get Lou a bridesmaid's dress and she says she won't wear a dress.
Lou: Well, I hate dresses – it's not fair. Why can't I wear a suit?
Sarah: Because you're a bridesmaid and bridesmaids don't wear suits – it's only for one day.
Lou: Why don't you mind your own business?
Penny: Lou!
Max: How dare you speak to Sarah like that – I think you'd better apologize, young lady!
Lou: Don't call me young lady!
Max: Say you're sorry right now, or I'll …
Edith: Max, calm down. Remember what the doctor told you.
Lou: It doesn't look as if there's going to be a wedding anyway – I've just seen Daniel with Katy, and he had his arm around her.
Max: What! Wait till I get my hands on that boy.
Edith: Max, he's not a boy, he's a man. It's his life. Leave him alone.
Max: Leave him alone. I'll leave him alone if he messes this up for me. I'll never speak to him again. Annick's father is about to sign the biggest contract we've ever had and you tell me to leave him alone.
Sarah: Max, wait …

74 UNIT 9 *Soap*

2   Why are the following characters particularly worried about the wedding?

- Daniel
- Lou
- Max

3   Work with a partner. Talk about the characters in Scene 1 and explain how they feel about each other.

Lexis

1   Find phrasal verbs in the script with the following meanings:

a) to recover (from an unpleasant or unhappy experience or an illness) (Part 1)
b) to finish a relationship (with someone) (Part 1)
c) to discuss (something) thoroughly (Part 1)
d) to continue as planned (Part 3)
e) to happen, to continue (Part 4)
f) to spoil (something), to cause (it) to fail (Part 4)

2   Complete the following with phrasal verbs from 1.

a) A: I've got a problem I'd like to discuss.
   B: Sure, _____ .
b) A: Is Carmen still going out with John?
   B: No, _____ .
c) A: Are you still annoyed about losing in the semi-final?
   B: No, _____ .
d) A: How did your speech go?
   B: I'm afraid _____ .
e) A: What's _____ ?
   B: I don't know. I think there must have been an accident.
f) A: Do you think we'll get a game today? I mean, the pitch must be flooded by now.
   B: They said _____ .

3   Each of the following expressions from the script in Scene 1 has a word missing. Try to add the missing word from memory. Then look back at the script to check.

a) It's ___ fair! (Part 4)   e) I ___ worn out. (Part 2)
b) I ___ care. (Part 3)   f) Leave him ___. (Part 4)
c) How dare ___! (Part 4)   g) What's ___ matter? (Part 3)
d) What ___ day! (Part 2)   h) Mind your ___ business. (Part 4)

4   Work with a partner. Choose at least three expressions from 3 and write a dialogue using them.

5   Work in groups. You are going to act out a part from Scene 1. There are six characters in the scene:

Part 1: Daniel, Edith
Part 2: Daniel, Edith, Max, Sarah
Part 3: Edith, Max, Sarah
Part 4: Edith, Max, Sarah, Lou, Penny

- Decide which part of the scene and which character you will act out.
- Decide what mood your character is in.
- <u>Underline</u> the main stressed words.
- Practise the part by yourself and with other students.

Now act out your part in front of the rest of the class.

'It just didn't work out. She was a Gemini; I was a Libra. His girlfriend was a Taurus; my boyfriend was a Sagittarius; his wife was a Leo ...'

Close up

Reported speech

1	Present continuous (direct speech)	Past continuous (reported speech)
'I'm having second thoughts.'	He said that he was having second thoughts.
	He told Edith that he was having second thoughts.

What happens to these structures? Write some examples of your own to show how they backshift.

a) present simple
b) present perfect
c) past simple
d) will
e) can
f) must/have to
g) (be) going to

2 These two sentences are in the imperative. What happens to them in reported speech?

a) 'Go away!'   b) 'Don't do that!'

3 How many people have you talked to so far today? Write their names down in the order in which you saw them. Try to remember one thing you said to them and one thing they said to you. Now tell your partner.

4 Follow these instructions:

a) Write down the names of half the students in the class.
b) Think of a question you would like to ask each of the students.
c) Write down what you think their answers will be. If you don't know, write 'I've no idea.'
d) Ask them the questions and note down their answers.

5 Report what you thought the answer would be and what they really said.

For example:
I thought Hakim was going to go to the cinema with his girlfriend this evening, but he said/he told me he was going to stay at home and watch TV.

Language reference: reported speech

In conversation you often need to report something that someone said earlier. In its simplest form this is a sentence with two clauses using *say*, *tell* or *ask*.

Reporting verbs: say/tell/ask

say + something
He **says** he's almost ready.

tell + somebody
He **tells me** you're having problems with your car.

You can use *that* to join the two clauses.
He **says that** he's almost ready.
He **tells me that** he's almost ready.

ask + somebody
Ask is often used in the past form: *asked*.
You usually use a question word (*what*, *when*, etc) or *if* to join the clauses.
He **asked me what** I was doing.
She **asked me if** I'd made my decision.

Backshifting

Sometimes you use *said* or *told* and backshift the verb tenses.
'I **want** a juice.'
She said she **wanted** a juice.
'I'**m having** second thoughts.'
He told Edith that he **was having** second thoughts.
'I'**ve split up** with John.'
She told him that she **had split up** with John.
'I'**m going to stay** with Clare.'
He said he **was going to stay** with Clare.'

Note: You don't have to backshift the verb tenses if you are reporting something which is still true.
They say Argentina **has** an excellent teacher training system.
The Times says he's going to resign.

Thoughts

You use the same structures to report a thought.
Jack? I think he'**s gone** to pick Ben up from the airport.
You backshift the verb tenses to show that the thought you had was not correct.
Bill! Hi! I thought you **weren't coming**.

Pacific Heights: Scenes 2–4

1. How much can you remember about the characters in *Pacific Heights*? Complete these sentences.

   a) _____ is engaged to _____ .
   b) _____ is married to _____ .
   c) _____ broke _____ 's heart.
   d) _____ is _____ 's business partner.
   e) _____ has a difficult relationship with _____ .
   f) _____ confides in _____ .
   g) _____ has recently split up with _____ .

2. Read the background information about the characters in *Pacific Heights* Scenes 2–4 and complete the gaps with the names of the characters. There may be more than one answer.

   a) _____ is married to _____ .
   b) _____ is _____ 's girlfriend.
   c) _____ and _____ are identical twins.
   d) _____'s wife is older than him.
   e) _____ and _____ are involved with an Animal Rights group.

3. Think about your own friends and family. Can you complete any of the sentences in 1 and 2 with people you know personally? Tell your partner about them.

Who's who in *Pacific Heights* Scenes 2–4

Phil Turner is an ambitious man in his early forties and he is hoping to take over as Managing Director of DCC when Max Dalton retires. Max has a good working relationship with Phil, but is secretly jealous of his son-in-law's youthful energy and athletic good looks.

Phil and Penny have three children who have all inherited their father's dark hair and their mother's blue eyes: a stunning combination. Ella and Mara are identical twins and only their closest friends can tell them apart. Although they're only 16, they're very independent. Their 19-year-old brother, Charlie, is a surf champion whose good looks have made him extremely popular with women. One of Ella and Mara's friends, Becky, is his present girlfriend, but what Becky doesn't know is that Charlie is also having an affair with Clare, Dave's wife.

Clare, who is a therapist, has always liked younger men. Dave is 28, five years younger than her. As a sales manager for an international company, Dave often travels abroad on business.

At the age of 24, Amy is Sarah's youngest child. She lives with her boyfriend, 26-year-old Mark, and they have a three-year-old son, Jack. They are both part-time students and so they share the household chores and childcare. They also belong to an Animal Rights group whose latest campaign involves a demonstration against tests carried out on animals at DCC.

TV Gazette

Dave and Clare

Charlie

Ella and Mara

Listening   **1**   📼 **35** Look at the drawings from the director's sketchbook. Listen to scenes 2–4 and put the pictures in order.

Scene _____
Mark and Amy talk about the demonstration.

Scene _____
Ella and Mara talk to their parents, Phil and Penny.

Scene _____
Conversation between Ella and Mara.

2   Answer these questions:

     a) Where's Charlie's surfboard?
     b) What's Ella and Mara's problem?
     c) What's Becky's problem?
     d) What's Amy's problem?

Lexis   **1**   Complete these everyday expressions from Scenes 2–4 with the correct word.

     a) What have you been up **to/around/down**?
     b) It's **around/beneath/up** to you.
     c) I see what you **mean/say/feel**.
     d) I must have **made/done/said** a mistake.
     e) I've told you once and I'll tell you **instead/again/last**.
     f) She'll get **under/over/up** it.
     g) It serves him **wrong/left/right**.
     h) Have you any **belief/opinion/idea** what they do to them?

2   Match the expressions in 1 to these sentences.

     1   I realise now that I was wrong.   5   You should have listened to me before.
     2   I understand.   6   It's your decision.
     3   What have you been doing?   7   It's his own fault.
     4   Do you know what happens?   8   She'll recover.

3   Listen to Scenes 2–4 again and put the expressions in 1 in the order in which you hear them.

4   Complete the summary of Scenes 2–4.

Ella and Mara told their parents _____ . But Penny and Phil told them _____ .

Meanwhile Charlie arranged to go and spend the weekend with Clare while Dave was away in America. He told his parents _____ .

Mara told Ella _____ .

Amy said _____ . But Mark told her _____ .

78   UNIT 9   *Soap*

Pacific Heights: The next episode

1. Work in groups. Predict what will happen in the next episode of *Pacific Heights* based on the following information:

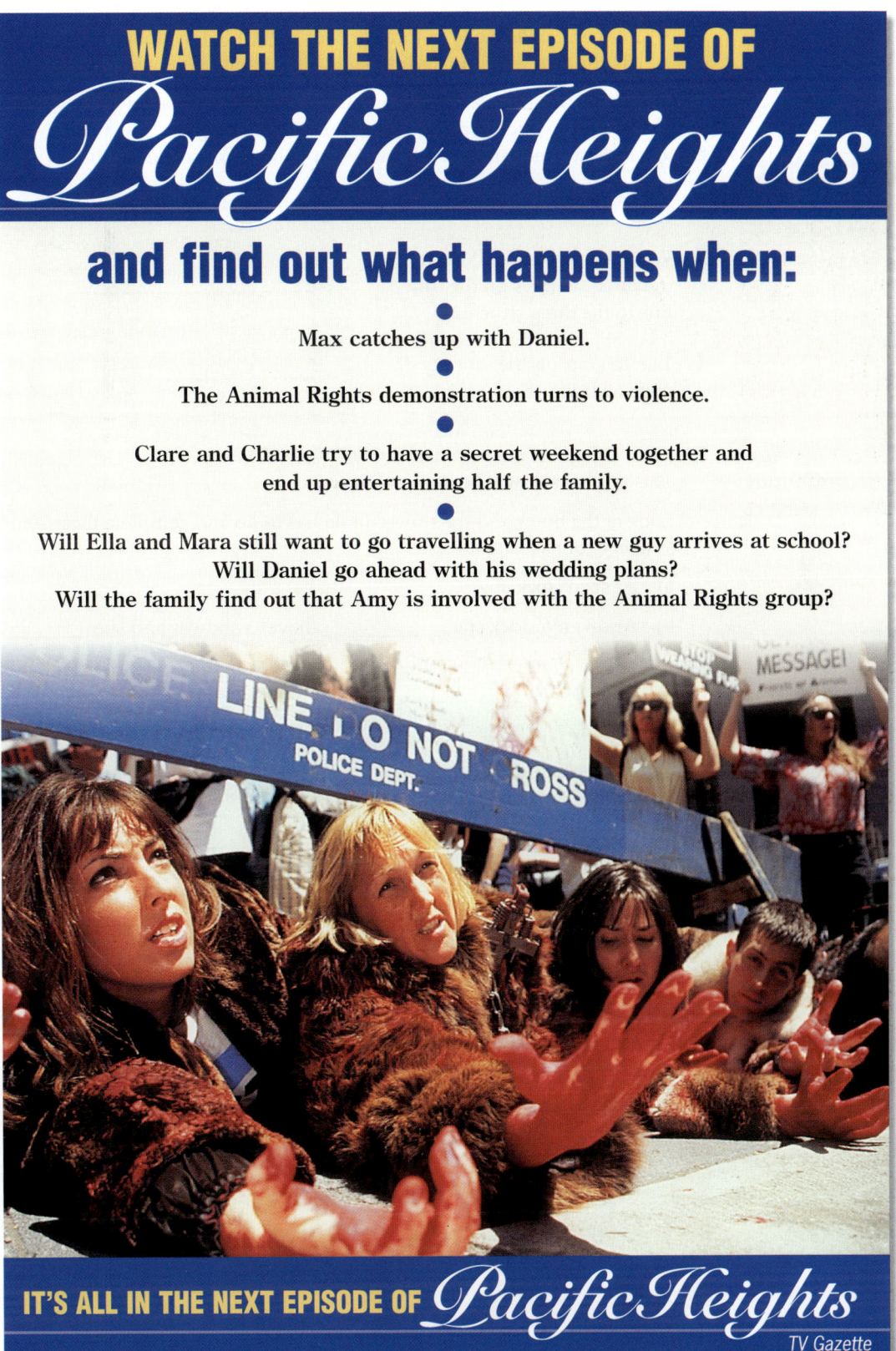

WATCH THE NEXT EPISODE OF *Pacific Heights* **and find out what happens when:**

- Max catches up with Daniel.
- The Animal Rights demonstration turns to violence.
- Clare and Charlie try to have a secret weekend together and end up entertaining half the family.

Will Ella and Mara still want to go travelling when a new guy arrives at school?
Will Daniel go ahead with his wedding plans?
Will the family find out that Amy is involved with the Animal Rights group?

IT'S ALL IN THE NEXT EPISODE OF *Pacific Heights*

TV Gazette

2. Write a similar TV preview to the one above for the episode *after* next.

3. Read what other groups have written and compare your predictions. Which version do you like best?

Close up

will for prediction

Language Reference p81

1. *2020 Vision.* In a recent report from the Henley Centre, UK, the following predictions were made about British family life:

   - In the year 2020 the divorce rate <u>will be</u> over 50%.
   - In the year 2020 one in three Britons <u>will be living</u> alone.
   - By the year 2020 the traditional nuclear family <u>will have become</u> a minority.

   a) In your opinion, are these predictions negative or positive?
   b) Are they valid predictions for your own country?
   c) If these predictions come true what will the consequences be?

LANGUAGE TOOLBOX

This time next year …
The next time you see me …
Sometime soon …
By the time I'm (forty) …
In (five) years' time …

2. What are the names of the <u>underlined</u> structures in the three predictions above?

3. Work with a partner. Match the three symbols on the time line to the three structures.

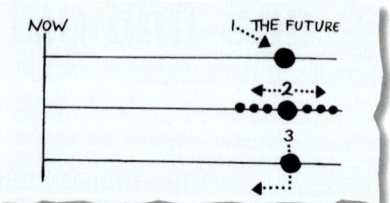

4. Talk to your partner about your own future.

will + continuous
will + perfect

1. Tania O'Donnel is an art dealer. She lives in Oxford. This is what she will be doing tomorrow.

   Look at the times and the things Tania has to do and complete these sentences using *will be (doing)* or *will have (done)*.

   a) At six o'clock she _____ (have) a shower.
   b) At seven o'clock she _____ (have) a shower and she _____ (eat) breakfast.
   c) At eight she _____ (drive) to London.
   d) At nine thirty she _____ (visit) the new de Kooning exhibition.
   e) At eleven thirty she _____ (leave) the de Kooning exhibition and she _____ (talk) Roland Hoff.
   f) At twelve thirty she _____ (finish) with Roland Hoff and she _____ (have) lunch with Dani.
   g) At two she _____ (have) lunch and she _____ (meet) her accountant.
   h) At five thirty she _____ (drive) back to Oxford.

80 UNIT 9 *Soap*

2 Write similar sentences about what you will be doing tomorrow.

3 Write three predictions: one about yourself, one about your partner and one about your country.

Language reference: will for the future

will ('ll)/won't + verb

Will as a future form has several important uses.

1 For prediction
 *In the year 2020 the divorce rate **will be** over 50%.*
2 For promises and offers
 *Don't worry, **I'll help** you.*
3 For refusals
 *It's no use asking. I **won't tell** you anything.*
4 For requests
 ***Will** you **marry** me?*

You will find more information about future forms in unit 7.

'You'll be hearing from my lawyer.'

will + continuous & perfect forms

1 Continuous
 will + be + -ing
 *In the year 2020 one in three Britons **will be living** alone.*
 *This time next week **we'll be lying** on the beach at Cancun.*

 You can use this structure for an action around a time in the future. The action starts before and finishes after a specific point.

 For example, imagine today is Tuesday. Next Tuesday you're going on holiday: you're going to the beach. It's not important to know exactly when you'll go to the beach or exactly when you'll return to the hotel.

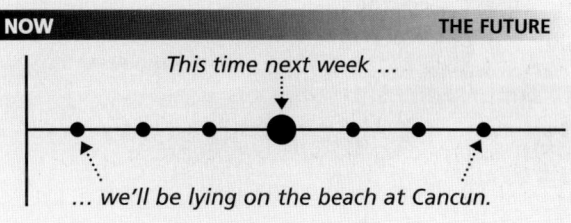

2 Perfect
 will + have + past participle
 *By the year 2020 the traditional nuclear family **will have become** a minority.*
 ***I'll have finished** the report by three, so we can meet after that.*

 You can use this structure to describe a future event from the point of view of a later time.

 For example, imagine you have to finish a report. You don't know exactly when you'll finish it, but you're sure it'll be before three o'clock.

 You can use the preposition *by*, meaning *not later than*, with this structure.

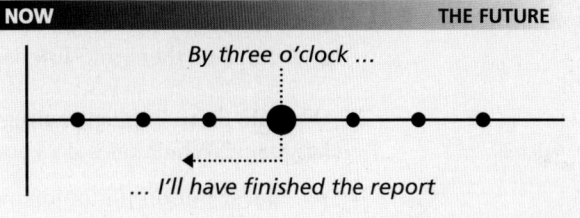

10 Time

Time

The earth is about 4,700 million years old. If the time scale is reduced so that the earth is one year old, humans would have appeared at 8.35 pm on 31st December.

1 Look at these three sayings about time:

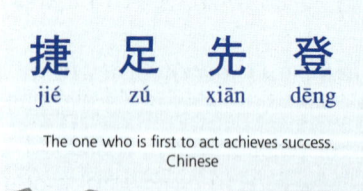

捷 足 先 登
jié zú xiān dēng

The one who is first to act achieves success.
Chinese

Время –
лучший врач

Time is the best doctor.
Russian

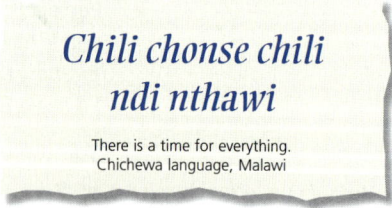

Chili chonse chili ndi nthawi

There is a time for everything.
Chichewa language, Malawi

How many sayings about time can you think of in your own language? Choose three and translate them into English.

2 What do these English sayings mean to you? Are they similar to any in your own language? Which ones do you like best?

- Never put off till tomorrow what you can do today.
- Better late than never.
- There's no time like the present.
- Tomorrow never comes.
- Today is the tomorrow we worried about yesterday.
- Time heals all wounds.
- Time is money.
- Time flies when you're having fun.

Punctuality

Discuss the following in small groups:

a) How punctual are you? Do you usually arrive late, early or on time? Think about some of these events:

- a first date
- an English lesson
- a job interview
- a wedding
- a film
- a football match
- a rock concert
- a family dinner

b) What about your friends and relatives? Are you typical of people in your country?

Listening 1 Read the questionnaire below and tick your answers. Then compare with a partner.

QUESTIONNAIRE

1 You have to attend a meeting which is scheduled to start at nine o'clock. Do you arrive …
a) exactly on time?
b) ten minutes early?
c) anything up to ten minutes late?

2 You've arranged to meet a friend in the centre of town. How long do you wait if your friend is late?
a) Five minutes.
b) Fifteen minutes.
c) Half an hour or more.

3 You're at home working on an important piece of work that has to be finished for tomorrow when a friend calls by unexpectedly. Do you …
a) invite the friend in and hope they won't stay too long?
b) invite the friend in but tell them that you haven't got much time to spare?
c) tell the friend you're busy and you'll call them when you've got more time?

4 You have to do a job that's difficult or unpleasant. Do you …
a) accept that you have to do it and do it straightaway so that you can forget about it?
b) put it off to another day?
c) leave it until the last minute because you need to feel the adrenalin rush produced by stress?

5 In your opinion, a hard-working person works …
a) eight hours a day.
b) eight to ten hours a day.
c) twelve or more hours a day.

'Now, write one hundred times: "I must not waste my time".'

2 🔊 36 Listen to the radio broadcast with Roberta Wilson, time management consultant, and Paul Roesch, the interviewer, discussing the same questions. Note down what they say about each one. Do you agree with them?

3 Work with a partner. Write down at least three activities you think are a waste of time.

Time UNIT 10 83

Pronunciation

1. Work with a partner. Say the words in the box. Then match the underlined sounds to the phonetic symbols on the left.

thirty	there	month	second
Thursday	Tuesday	weather	Wednesday
Saturday	weeks	first	third
hours	weekends	that	these

For example:
/θ/ thirty

2. ▶ 37 Listen and check.

Dates

1. Choose five dates that are important to you. Then dictate them to your partner. Say why you chose them.

2. ▶ 38 Listen to Julie talking about dates that are important to her. Write down the dates as you hear them and make notes on why they are important to Julie. Compare with a partner.

Prepositions

1. Test your prepositions. Complete these sentences with *on*, *in* or *at*.

   a) My mother was born _____ the 1950s.
   b) I work best _____ night.
   c) We always have a big family meal _____ New Year's Eve.
   d) I spend at least two weeks by the sea _____ the summer.
   e) I start work every morning _____ 9 am.
   f) I always try to get home from work _____ time to read my children a bedtime story.
   g) I never have a nap _____ the afternoon.
   h) I would like to have lived _____ the Middle Ages.
   i) My birthday is _____ March. In fact it's _____ 6th March.
   j) I started learning English _____ 1995.
   k) Nothing special happens in my family _____ Christmas.
   l) My boss never starts meetings _____ time. She's usually at least ten minutes late.
   m) I usually feel depressed _____ Monday mornings.
   n) I spend a lot of time with my friends _____ the weekend.
   o) I'm enjoying life _____ the moment.

2. Are the sentences in 1 true or false for you? Turn them into questions and ask your partner. Find out as much as you can.

For example:

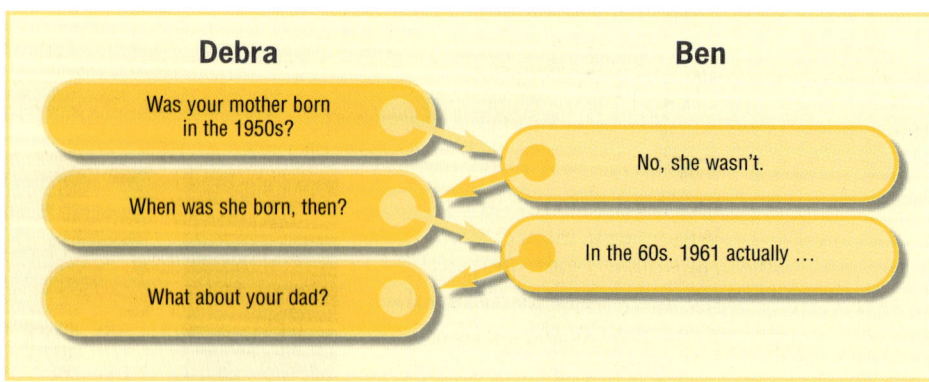

84 UNIT 10 *Time*

Time expressions

1 Look at the monthly planner and follow the instructions.

DECEMBER						
M	T	W	T	F	S	S
–	–	1	2	3	4	5
6	7	8	9	10	11	12
13	14	15 Today	16	17	18	19
20	21	22	23	24	25	26
27	28	29	30	31	–	–

a) ~~Cross out:~~

   Christmas Day
   New Year's Eve
   Boxing Day
   Christmas Eve

b) Imagine today is the 15th.

   Underline: Circle: Put in (brackets):

   the day before yesterday   tomorrow   in four days' time
   the weekend before last   next Saturday   in a fortnight's time
   the day after tomorrow   a week today   the whole of last week
   the Monday after next   a week tomorrow   two weeks ago

   Which dates are still free?

2 Use expressions in 1b to tell your partner about some of the things you've done recently and your future plans.

For example:
The weekend before last I went walking in the mountains with some friends.

3 Use the words in the box to describe the times shown.

| about   just before   just gone   just after   almost   around   XX-ish |

4 Work with a partner. Use the expressions in 3 to tell your partner about at least six things you have done so far today, and what time you did them.

Time UNIT 10

Things to do …

Look at the 'things to do' lists below.

- Are you the sort of person who makes lists?
- Are these the sort of lists you make?
- How many 'things to do' do you have on your list now?

1 Read the article on page 87 and match the four people mentioned to their list.

TIME-SAVING TIPS: LISTS

Making lists is relaxing. It makes you feel important – all those things to do. It dictates the shape of the immediate future; it calms you down (it's OK, it's on a list somewhere) and it makes you feel good when you cross something off (list-making is standard practice in therapy for depression). It might even help you to get things done too.

The world divides in two when it comes to listing. Type A makes orderly lists, prioritises and calmly sets to work on them. Type B waits until panic sets in, grabs the nearest envelope and scribbles all over it, sighs with relief and promptly loses it.

The more you have to do, the more you need a list and few people with high-powered jobs get by without them.

Barbara Vanilli, chief executive of a large chain of supermarkets, says, 'Before I go to bed, I have to write down everything that's going to stop me sleeping. I feel I won't forget anything I've written down, so my lists are a great comfort.'

Women always think they're better at lists than men. Men tend to have Tasks which they assemble into Action Plans whereas women just have lists of Things To Do. Jacqueline Maddocks, head of Maddocks Publishers, says, 'My male colleagues only make lists for work, whereas I have to make lists for work and for home too. It's essential to write things down. If you're constantly thinking, "I must remember this," it blocks your mind.'

James Oliver, psychologist, has created his own 'time management matrix'. He writes a list of things to do and then organises them into categories: things that have to be done straight away, other things that it would be good to do today, things that are important but haven't got to be done immediately and things that are less urgent but that he doesn't want to forget. 'Using categories to order the world is the way the human mind works,' he says. 'After that, you should put things into hierarchies of importance.' But he warns against the danger of Excessive List Syndrome. 'If people get obsessed with making lists, it doesn't work. They have too many categories and lose their capacity to prioritise.'

It's all a question of what works best for you, whether it's a tidy notebook, a forest of Post-it notes or the back of your hand. Having tried all these, student Kate Rollins relies on a computerised list, printed out each morning to be scribbled on during the day. 'My electronic organiser has changed my life,' she says. 'Up to now, I've always relied on my good memory, but now that I'm working and studying, I find I've got too much to keep in my head.'

So what are you waiting for? No, you're not too busy to make today the first day of your upgraded time-managed life. In fact, there's no better time than the present to get an upper hand on time and begin to take increased control of your work and life. So, get out your pencil and paper and make a list. ■

(*Weekend Telegraph*, Saturday December 13 1997.)

---

2 Talk about the article from memory using these prompts:

- good things about making lists
- type A/type B
- before bed
- women/men
- matrix
- categories
- excessive list syndrome
- electronic organiser
- what are you waiting for?

Collocation

1 Complete as many of these sentences as you can from memory to make collocations. Then look back at the article to check.

a) What do you plan to do in the _____ future? (line 5)

b) Is it _____ practice to wear smart clothes in your company or school? (line 8)

c) Do you know many people with _____ jobs? (line 21)

d) Is Bill Gates still _____ executive of Microsoft? (line 22)

e) Have you got a/an _____ organiser? (line 68)

2 Work with a partner. Ask each other the questions from 1.

3 Which of these words can combine with the underlined nouns from 1 to form new collocations? Check them in your dictionary and write some new sentences.

| low-paid | distant | senior | personal | normal |

List any more collocations to do with work or time that you know.

Close up

must & should

1 Look at James Oliver's time management matrix and match the following sentence beginnings to the squares on the matrix.

a) I *must* do it today ...
b) I *should* do it today ...
c) I *must* do it soon ...
d) I *should* do it soon ...

	URGENT	NOT URGENT
IMPORTANT	I	II
NOT IMPORTANT	III	IV

2 Complete the sentences in 1 with an appropriate ending.

1 ... but if I run out of time I can leave it until first thing tomorrow.
2 ... so I'll see if I've got time next week.
3 ... or there'll be trouble tomorrow.
4 ... so I'll do it next week.

3 Write your own 'things to do' list according to the matrix above. Use it to talk to your partner about your priorities for today/this week/this month.

(Language Reference p90)

4 Work with a partner. Match the following headings to the four sets of verbs and phrases in the table below: permission; no obligation; obligation; prohibition.

A
_____
have to
have got to
must
is/are supposed to

C
_____
don't have to
haven't got to

B
_____
can't
isn't/aren't allowed to
mustn't/isn't/aren't supposed to

D
_____
can
is/are allowed to

5 Think about the place where you work or study. Are there many rules and regulations? What are they?

UNIT 10 *Time*

Office cultures

1. Look at the people in their different work places.
   - Are the clothes the people are wearing formal or casual?
   - How do they compare to work places you know?
   - What sort of companies do you think they are? Why?

2. ▭ 39 Listen to the people in the photos talking about their companies. Did you guess correctly?

3. Listen again and correct the information below if necessary.

OFFICE 1
- Working hours are flexible.
- Women aren't allowed to wear trousers.
- You can smoke in the cafeteria.
- You're allowed to have your lunch at your desk.

OFFICE 2
- You can't smoke in the office unless you're working late.
- You have to go to the canteen if you're thirsty.
- You aren't supposed to have a break every two hours.
- You can wear jeans.

OFFICE 3
- You don't have to dress smartly.
- You're supposed to start work at eight o'clock.
- You can't smoke in the building.
- If you want a coffee, you have to go to the café next door.

4. Would you like to work in any of these offices?

Time UNIT 10

Language reference: obligation, prohibition & permission

Must, *should* and *can* are *modal auxiliaries*. All modals have certain special characteristics, for example:

1 They are used to modify the meaning of another verb.
2 They take the infinitive without *to*.
 *That's a terrible cough. You **should** see the doctor.*
3 They do not add an *s* in the third person.
 *He's putting on a lot of weight. He **should** go on a diet.*
4 You cannot use them with another auxiliary – even in questions and negatives.
 ***Must** you go? You **shouldn't** do that.*

Have to is similar to a modal verb in its meaning but not in its form.

1 It includes *to*.
 *I **have to** go to the dentist.*
2 It takes *s* in the third person in the present simple.
 *She's a diabetic, so she **has to** take insulin.*
3 Questions and negatives are formed with *do* in the present simple and *did* in the past simple.
 *This is a very informal office. You **don't have to** wear a tie.*

Modals are used to express a great range of meanings. The differences between them are sometimes subtle.

must & have to

The difference between *must* and *have to* is not great.

Must is often used to talk about personal obligations.
*I'm gaining weight. I **must** go on a diet.*
*I **must** phone my mother. I haven't seen her for ages.*

Have to is a little more impersonal.
*Everybody **has to** pay taxes.*
*I **have to** do an English exam next week.*

When you are not sure, use *have to*.

mustn't & don't have to

Mustn't and *don't have to* are very different from each other.

Mustn't is used for prohibition.
*You **mustn't** smoke in a petrol station.*
*It's a secret. You **mustn't** tell anyone.*

When you use *don't have to* it means there is no obligation, negative or positive.
*Teachers in the USA **don't have to** wear ties.*
*You **don't have to** leave yet. There's an all-night bus.*

can/can't

Can't is often used like *mustn't*.
*You **can't** smoke in a petrol station.*

Can tells you that an action is possible and/or permitted.
*You **can** leave now if you want to.*

must & should

Must is a simple, strong obligation. *Should* is weaker: a less important obligation, or one that is not respected.

*I **should** go to see the doctor, but I've got too many other things I have to do.*
*I **should** revise for the exam, but I'm going out with some friends instead.*

It can also be used for recommendations.
*You **should** stop smoking. You're killing yourself.*

Other expressions

There are many other expressions that are related to permission and obligation.

Be allowed to is similar to *can*.
*You **are allowed** to go home early on Friday if we've finished all our work.*

Supposed to is sometimes similar to *should*. It can imply that people do not follow the rules all the time.
*I'm **supposed to** wear a suit to work, but I sometimes come in jeans and a T-shirt.*

To whom it may concern

1 Choose two correct ways to start a business letter from Column A.

A	B
Dear Mr Peter,	Lots of love,
Dear Mr Peter Maggs,	Yours,
Dear Mr Maggs,	Best wishes,
Dear Mr or Mrs,	Yours sincerely,
Dear Sir or Madame,	Your friend,
Dear Sir or Madam,	Yours faithfully,

Match the ways of starting a business letter with appropriate endings from Column B.

Do you know any other ways of starting or ending business letters?

2 Here are some examples of phrases often used in business letters. Complete the sentences with the words in the box.

> apply   unfortunately   hearing   response   complain
> 16th May   confirm   enclose   grateful   pleased

a) Thank you for your letter of the _____ which I received this morning.

b) I would be _____ if you could send me some information about summer courses at your school.

c) I _____ my curriculum vitae for your attention.

d) _____ I am not available on the date you suggest in your letter.

e) I would be _____ to attend an interview at any time convenient to you.

f) I am writing to _____ about the damage caused by your company when they delivered a sofa to my home last week.

g) We look forward to _____ from you as soon as possible.

h) We would be grateful if you could _____ your reservation in writing.

i) I am writing in _____ to your advertisement in *The Guardian*.

j) I would like to _____ for the position of IT assistant in your school.

3 Match each of the phrases in 2 to one of the functions below. There are two phrases for function c.

a) asking for information
b) applying for a job
c) beginning a letter
d) closing a letter
e) giving bad news
f) giving good news
g) complaining
h) saying that you are sending something with the letter
i) asking for confirmation

4 Anthony Clifford is interested in applying for the post of flight attendant. Read his letter and decide whether you think he would be considered a suitable candidate. Why/Why not?

WORLDWIDE AIRLINES

FLIGHT ATTENDANTS

Worldwide Airlines are currently seeking friendly, service-oriented people who take pride in their performance and appearance.
Applicants must be over 20 years of age and have at least two years' post high school education or work experience.

- Physical requirements:
  able to lift, push and pull heavy articles as required.
  Minimum height 1m 60, maximum height 1m 85.
- Languages: able to read, write, speak and understand English. Other languages an advantage.

Interested candidates can write to the following address for an application form and additional information:
Worldwide Airlines Inc,
PO Box 2983, Chicago, USA.

1566b 49th East Street
Santa Barbara, CA

Worldwide Airlines Inc
PO Box 2983
Chicago
USA   5th February 2000

Dear Mr or Mrs,

Application for the post of flight attendant

I saw your advertisement in the *Morning Post* and I want to be a flight attendant.
I am 21 years old, and I have just graduated from university. I have put my c.v. with this letter so that you can see what I've done and I'd love to come for an interview any time you like.
How about sending me an application form and some more information about the job?
I can't wait to hear from you!

Lots of love,

Tony

5 Improve Anthony's letter by using some of the phrases in 1 and 2 above.

6 Look at a corrected version of the letter on page 141 and compare it to your own version.

11 Journey

1 Read this excerpt from a book called *The Beach* by Alex Garland. Why did the author go travelling?

> A few years ago I was going through the process of splitting up with my first serious girlfriend. She went away to Greece for the summer and when she came back she'd had a holiday romance with some Belgian guy. As if that wasn't enough, it seemed that the guy
> 5 in question was going to show up in London some time over the next few weeks. After three hellish days and nights, I realised that I was dangerously close to losing my head. I biked over to my dad's flat and emotionally blackmailed him into lending me enough cash to leave the country.
> 10 On that trip I learnt something very important. Escape through travel works. Almost from the moment I boarded my flight, life in England became meaningless. Seat-belt signs lit up, problems switched off. Broken armrests took precedence over broken hearts. By the time the plane was airborne I'd forgotten England even
> 15 existed.

split up (line 1): end a relationship
show up (line 5): arrive
lose (your) head (line 7): go mad
emotionally blackmail (line 8): use emotions to manipulate someone
take precedence over (line 13): become more important than

The Beach
The Beach is Alex Garland's first novel. It has now been made into a film starring Leonardo di Caprio.

2 Work with a partner. Have you ever travelled for any of these reasons? Tell your partner.

- to escape boredom
- to run away from a broken heart
- to broaden your experience of the world
- to learn languages
- to get a suntan
- to live out your dreams
- to take a break from your career
- to visit historical sites or travel along a historical route
- to raise money for charity

Can you think of any other reasons to go travelling?

3 Where have the class been? Ask other students in the class and make a list of countries, regions and famous cities. Try to find a place for every letter of the alphabet. You can include regions and cities in your own country.

4 Describe where five of the places in your list are using the expressions below. Say where the place you live is. Find as many ways to describe it as you can.

It's in the	north/south-west northern/south-western part	of (Poland) of (Argentina)
It's	on the coast in the mountains in (Lombardy)	to the north of (Los Angeles) not far from (Grenoble) between (Milan) and (Brescia)

Conrad's round-the-world trip

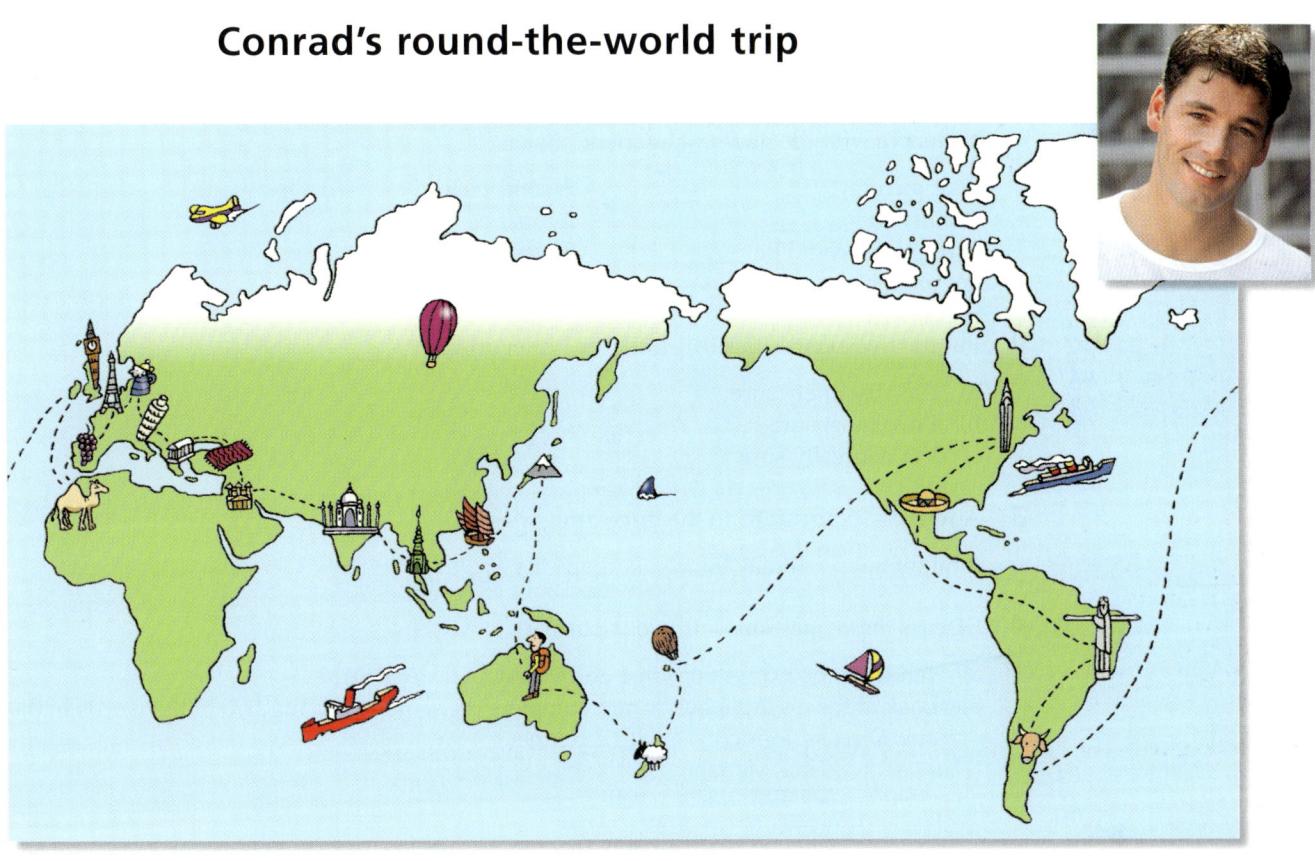

1. Look at the photos taken by Conrad on his round-the-world trip. Could any of them have been taken in your country? Where?

2. 🔊 40 Listen to Conrad showing his travel photos to a friend. He tries to get the friend to guess where the places are. Which two photos do they talk about?

3. Where do you think the remaining four photographs were taken? Discuss with your partner. Note down any places where a photo definitely couldn't have been taken.

   Check on page 140.

Journey UNIT 11

Close up

Speculating & deducing

1 Listen to the conversation between Conrad and his friend again. Complete these sentences with the guesses the friend makes:

First picture
It must be _____ .
I suppose it could be _____ .
It's probably _____ .

Second picture
It must be _____ .
It can't be _____ .
Maybe it's _____ .

2 Put the five expressions in 1 into three categories.

a) I'm absolutely sure
b) I'm almost sure
c) I'm not really sure

3 Add these expressions to the three categories in 2:

It might be … It may be … Perhaps it's …

4 Discuss these questions with your partner:

a) Which of the expressions in 1 and 3 contain a *modal verb*?
b) Look at the example below and complete the sentences using two of the words in the box. Discuss your choice with a partner.

| must mustn't can can't |

There's someone at the door.
It _____ be Carmen: she's working late tonight.
It _____ be John: he always comes home around this time.

Language Reference p94

5 Rearrange the sentences below so that they make sense without changing any of the words.

a) They can't be too short of money. You must be joking.
b) You've been driving all day. You must be delighted.
c) That hotel must be doing well. It's never got anybody in it.
d) I must be getting old. I've heard such a lot about you.
e) A new car? On my salary?! They go skiing every year.
f) The new restaurant can't be very good. It's always got the 'No Vacancies' sign up.
g) You must be Sarah's husband. I can't remember anything about last night.
h) Great news about your engagement. You must be absolutely exhausted.

Language reference: speculating and deducing

There are many ways to say how certain or uncertain you are about something. Here are some of them:

Modal auxiliary + infinitive

It **must be** …
It **may be** …/ It **could be** … / It **might be** …
It **may not be** … / It **might not be** …
It **can't be** …

Other phrases

It's **definitely** …
It's **probably** …
I **think** it's …
Perhaps it's … / **Maybe** it's …
I **don't think** it's …
It **probably isn't** …
It **definitely isn't** …

Notes:
In this context, the opposite of *must* is *can't*.
The keys **can't be** in my coat because I wasn't wearing it. They **must be** in your bag.
It must be means 'I'm sure it is', it can't be means 'I'm sure it isn't'.

There is no important difference between *may*, *could* and *might* in this context.

Wish you were here

1 These are three postcards Conrad wrote from places in the photos on page 93. Complete them with one of the words below. Use each word only once.

> fascinating   sandy   peaks   jams   breathtaking   overlooking   touristy
> spicy   friendly   gorgeous   palm   clear   breaking   paradise

Dear Brad,
This is a (1) _____ city, but you can't imagine the traffic (2) _____ and the noise. I'll never complain about the traffic at home again – or the food! The food's really (3) _____ here. It's quite a (4) _____ place but the people are very (5) _____ . I've met a (6) _____ American girl who's invited me to LA.
Conrad

Brad Goodwin
14 South Street
Tingalpa
Brisbane
Queensland
QLD 4173
Australia

Dear Paul,
I'm writing to you from my hotel (7) _____ the lake. The view is (8) _____ . In the distance I can see snowy mountain (9) _____ and down by the hotel pool I can see a lovely girl – must go.
Conrad

Paul Kelly
33b Container Street
Sutherland
NSW 1499
Australia

Dear John,
Yes, I'm in (10) _____ !
(11) _____ beaches stretch as far as the eye can see and the water is (12) _____ and warm. The only sound is the wind in the (13) _____ trees and the waves (14) _____ on the beach. The women are beautiful. I'm never coming home.
Conrad

John Pizzigallo
40 Ryan Drive
Sutherland
NSW 1499
Australia

2 Which places do you think he sent the postcards from?

3 Write postcards from two of the other places Conrad visited.

Anecdote

4 🎧 41 We asked the three people in the photograph to imagine they could spend a dream weekend anywhere in the world. Listen to their answers to the following questions. Each time there is a pause, guess where the person would like to go.

- ☐ Who would your ideal companion be?
- ☐ How would you get around?
- ☐ What would you wear?
- ☐ What would you buy?
- ☐ What would you eat and drink?
- ☐ What essential items would you take with you?
- ☐ Who would you most like to meet there?
- ☐ What sights would you want to see?
- ☐ Who would you send a postcard to?
- ☐ What would spoil your perfect weekend?

Liz, Rick and Cristina

5 Imagine your own dream weekend. You are going to tell a partner about it. Choose from the list in 4 the things you want to talk about. Think about what you will say and the language you will need.

6 Tell your partner about your dream weekend. Would you make good travelling companions?

Journey UNIT 11

Close up

would for unreal situations

1 Look at these four questions. <u>Underline</u> the auxiliary verbs.

   a) What did you do?
   b) What are you doing?
   c) What will you do?
   d) What would you do?

2 Add the following endings to the four questions in 1.

   ... when you finish university?   ... if you won the lottery?
   ... yesterday?   ... at the moment?

Language Reference p96

3 Which sentences refer to real situations?

4 Imagine you opened the door of the classroom and found you were in ...

   - Siberia
   - Hawaii
   - Scotland
   - the Kalahari desert
   - Cairo
   - the Amazon rainforest

   Work with a partner. Choose one place and discuss what it would be like.

   - What would it look like? What sounds and smells would there be? What would the buildings be like?
   - What would the weather be like?
   - What would the people look like? What would they be wearing?
   - What would you eat and drink?
   - What would you be able to do? What wouldn't you be able to do?
   - Would you have a good time?

Language reference: would for unreal conditionals

would (not) + infinitive

The contracted forms are *'d* and *wouldn't*.
I'd wear a hat on the beach.
I wouldn't go to the Sahara without sun block.
Would you **travel** alone to Thailand or **would** you **go** with friends?

Would is the past tense of *will*, but this does not really explain how you use it.

Imaginary or improbable situations

One of its main uses is to show that we are talking or writing about a situation that is *imaginary* or *improbable*. For example, imagine you opened the door of the classroom and found yourself in Iceland:

- *It would be cold.*
- *Everybody would be wearing warm clothes.*
- *You'd be able to visit hot springs.*
- *Most people would speak good English.*

Unreal conditionals

Would is often found in *unreal conditional sentences*.
If I had the money I'd buy a new car.

You will find more about conditional sentences in units 13, 14 and 15.

Note: You will find more information on *would* for past habits in unit 5.

UNIT 11 *Journey*

Coast to coast

1 Read this account of Nick Campbell's motorbike trip across the US. What problems did he have?

NICK CAMPBELL sat at the side of the road and wondered what to do next. He looked at the second-hand Harley Davidson he'd bought from a back-street garage back home in Miami at the beginning of his trip six weeks before.

For years he had dreamt of crossing the United States from east to west by motorbike and he'd finally decided that it was now or never. He'd given up his job, sold his car and set off for the journey of his dreams. He'd been lucky, or so he thought, to find this old Harley Davidson and had bought it for a very reasonable price – it had cost him just $600. But five kilometres from Atlanta, he had run out of luck. The motorbike had broken down.

He pushed the bike into town and found a garage. The young mechanic told him to leave the bike overnight and come back the next day. The following morning, to his surprise, the man asked if the bike was for sale. 'Certainly not,' he replied, paid his bill and hit the road.

When he got to Kansas the old machine ran out of steam again. This time Nick thought about selling it and buying something more reliable, but decided to carry on. When the bike was going well, he loved it.

However, in Denver, Colorado the bike broke down yet again so he decided to take it to a garage and offer it for sale. The mechanic told him to come back in the morning.

The next day, to his amazement, the man offered him $2,000. Realising the man must be soft in the head, but clearly not short of money, Nick asked for $3,000. The man agreed and they signed the papers. Then the mechanic started laughing. In fact it was several minutes before he could speak and when he could he said, 'That's the worst deal you'll ever make, boy.' He …

(Adapted from *The Independent on Sunday*, 22 February 1998)

2 Discuss the following in small groups.

a) How much did Nick pay for the bike?
b) How much did he sell it for?
c) How much money did he make from the sale?
d) Guess why the mechanic said, 'That's the worst deal you'll ever make, boy.'

3 Now read the real ending to the story on page 142. Do you think the mechanic was fair? How do you think Nick felt?

Anecdote

4 Think back to a journey you have been on. You are going to tell a partner about it. Choose from the list the things you want to talk about. Think about what you will say and what language you will need.

- ☐ Where was the journey from and where was it to?
- ☐ What form of transport did you use?
- ☐ Who did you go with?
- ☐ How much time did you spend preparing for it?
- ☐ What did you take with you?
- ☐ What was the weather like?
- ☐ How long did it take you?
- ☐ How many times did you stop en route? What for?
- ☐ Did anything unusual or unexpected happen?
- ☐ Would you go on the same journey again? Why/Why not?

5 Tell your partner about the journey. Give as much detail as possible.

Close up

Past perfect

1 Where was Nick Campbell at the beginning of the story?

2 What happened in Miami, Atlanta, Kansas and Denver?

3 Discuss the following with a partner:

a) Which events are described using:
   - the past perfect
   - the past simple

b) How is the past perfect formed?

c) Which of these three explanations best describes how we use the past perfect?
   - to look back at a past event
   - to look back at a past event from another point in the past
   - to look back at a past event from another, more recent, point in the past

4 Complete each of the following sentences using the past perfect.

a) Michael was looking forward to the trip to Moscow because …
b) He was late leaving his house because …
c) That morning the traffic was very slow from his house to the airport because …
d) At check-in he had to accept an aisle seat because …
e) He bought three new ties in duty-free because …
f) The departure was delayed because …
g) The connecting flight in Copenhagen was cancelled because …

5 Work with a partner. Write a similar set of sentences. Make sure each sentence uses a past perfect.

For example:
Vicky was looking forward to her dinner with Roy because …

Language reference: past perfect

You can use the past perfect to show clearly that one past event happened before another past event.

For example:
(1) *I lent her £5.* (2) *She forgot about it.*
→ *She forgot that I **had lent** her £5.*

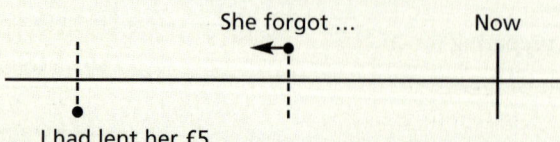

… I had lent her £5

The contracted forms *I'd*, *he'd*, etc and *hadn't* are used in speech and informal writing. The contraction of *had* is the same as the contraction of *would* (*'d*), but the context always makes it clear which one is intended.

Conjunctions

Conjunctions like *after*, *when*, *by the time* and *because* are often used to combine a past simple clause with a past perfect one.

*The film **had started** when I arrived.*
*By the time the plane was airborne **I'd forgotten** England even existed.*
*He had a puncture **because** he **hadn't checked** his tyres.*
*After **we'd signed** the contract we opened a bottle of champagne.*

Tell us a story

1 Read this true story and explain the significance of the following words and phrases.

a) microwave   b) anti-terrorist lock   c) Swiss army knife   d) Indian Ocean

A photographer called John was flying first class from London to Nairobi in Kenya when one of the co-pilots came out of the cockpit to make some coffee in the microwave. He couldn't make the machine work, so he asked his fellow pilot to help him. As the other pilot left the cockpit, he let the heavy metal door close behind him. The pilot started an urgent, whispered discussion with his colleague. The two pilots had locked themselves out of their cockpit and, as they told the photographer (who promised not to tell the other passengers) the door was fitted with an anti-terrorist lock. This meant that not even the pilots could open it from outside the cockpit. John remembered that he had put his Swiss army knife in his hand luggage. However, he couldn't remember where he had put his hand luggage and spent five minutes opening and closing overhead lockers until he found it. John and the pilots attacked the door with the knife, the lock started to come loose and when they broke into the cockpit, the plane was cruising eastwards over the Indian Ocean.

(Adapted from *Focus* January 1999)

2 Work in teams. Add adverbs from the three boxes below to the story. Add as many as you can.

A adverbs of attitude
unbelievably   naturally   unfortunately   sadly   fortunately   curiously

B adverbs of manner
carelessly   unexpectedly

C adverbs of time
immediately   a few months ago   gradually   eventually
after a while   finally   several weeks later   in the end

3 Discuss the following with your partner.

a) Do you think pilots often make this kind of mistake?
b) What do you think is the safest way to travel?
c) Do you prefer to travel by air, by road, by rail, or by sea? Why?

4 Work in groups and write a story.

a) Choose one of the story 'skeletons' on the right or invent one of your own.
b) Discuss each sentence and add as many details as you can think of.
For example:
Who were the people? What were they like? Where did they go on holiday?

c) Write the story and include the following:
   - at least two adverbs of *attitude* from box A
   - at least one adverb of *manner* from box B
   - at least three adverbs of *time* from box C
   - at least three *past perfect* sentences from box D below

D past perfect sentences
They hadn't gone far when the car broke down.
She had never met anybody like him before.
By the time the police arrived everybody had calmed down.
It was the most breathtaking view they had ever seen.
He had never felt like this before.
When they looked behind them they saw the damage they had done.

STORY SKELETON 1
A man went abroad on holiday.
He met a woman and they fell in love.
He asked her to marry him.
The man went home.

STORY SKELETON 2
Three friends went on holiday in a car.
They camped.
Things went wrong.
They got home safely.

5 Read each other's stories and vote for the best one.

12 Basics

1 Work with a partner. Read through the statements below and guess whether they are true or false for your partner.

Your partner:

- has eaten at a restaurant in the last week.
- has a healthy diet.
- drinks a lot of coffee.
- always has wine with meals.
- is a good cook.
- eats a big breakfast.
- often eats fast food.
- usually eats lunch alone.

2 Ask your partner questions to find out whether you were correct. How many did you guess right? Did you find out anything surprising?

First date

1 What sort of things can go wrong on a first date?

2  42 Listen to the first part of the conversation. How do you think the two people feel?

3 43 Listen to the next part of the conversation and find out what went wrong.

4 Listen to the whole conversation again and complete the sentences with an appropriate quantifier.

a) Would you like _____ wine?
b) Two glasses of red wine, please, and could we have _____ olives with that?
c) Oh, dear, I didn't know you were vegetarian. I don't think there are _____ vegetarian dishes on the menu.
d) Yes, there are. Look, there are _____ of things.
e) And could we have _____ French bread and a bottle of mineral water, please?
f) Oh dear, did it go on your skirt?
   Just _____ . It's OK.
g) Waiter, waiter! Can you bring a cloth? I've spilt _____ wine.
h) It's OK, honestly. Hardly _____ of it went on my skirt. Just a drop.

Close up

Quantity

1 Put the quantifiers from 4 on page 100 into these three categories:

countable nouns	uncountable	both countable & uncountable
a few	a little	some

2 Now add these quantifiers to the categories in 1.

> a lot of   not much   several   very few   not many   a couple of   lots of   very little

3 In each of the following sentences there are two words that are possible and one that isn't. ~~Cross out~~ the incorrect word in each sentence.

a) There wasn't **much/some/any** salt in her omelette.
b) There was **some/a bit of/a few** ham in her vegetarian salad.
c) **A few/Several/A little** of his chips were burnt.
d) There were **hardly any/little/not many** desserts they liked on the menu.
e) There were only **a couple of/a little/a few** flavours of ice-cream to choose from.
f) There were **no/very few/any** taxis outside when they left the restaurant.
g) He had never had **some/any/so many** problems in this restaurant before.
h) They had **anything/hardly anything/nothing** in common.

Countable & uncountable nouns

1 Test your countables and uncountables. Classify these words:

> car   mobile phone   computer   job   meat   love   travel   pasta   music   fridge
> passport   washing machine   money   humour   rice   nicotine   oxygen

2 Choose words from 1 to complete the sentences below. Compare with a partner.

I could live without …   I couldn't live without …
I could live without a …   I couldn't live without a …

3 Complete these grammar rules and give examples.

a) You can use numbers (one, two, three, etc) only with _____ nouns.
b) _____ nouns have a singular and a plural form.
c) _____ nouns only have one form (usually – but not always – singular).

4 Decide whether the following nouns are countable, uncountable, or both (countable/uncountable). There are three of each type.

> bread   Coca-Cola   food   glass   sandwich   lamb   pea   oyster   salt

5 Complete these sentences with three of the countable/uncountable nouns from 4. Use each noun twice, once as countable and once as uncountable.

a) The _____ are in the cupboard over the sink.
b) _____ is sold all over the world.
c) In spring there are _____ in all the fields around here.
d) Would you like another slice of _____ ?
e) I'm thirsty – I think I'll have a _____ .
f) _____ is one of the hardest materials there is.

6 Are the following nouns countable or uncountable?   > people   news   jeans   scissors

7 Choose the correct words, plural or singular, in these sentences.

a) I believe that most people **is/are** basically good.
b) The news **was/were** on when I got home.
c) **Those/That** jeans really **look/looks** good on you.
d) If you're looking for the scissors, **they're/it's** in the kitchen.

Language Reference p102

Basics   UNIT   12   101

Language reference: countable & uncountable nouns

Nouns are *countable* (C), *uncountable* (U) or both (C/U).

Countable nouns

Countable nouns have a singular and a plural form, and you can use numbers with them.
one idea → two ideas
one table → two tables
one man → two men
You can use *definite* and *indefinite* articles with them: **the** idea, **the** ideas, **an** idea.

Uncountable nouns

Uncountable nouns have only one form. Most of the time, this is singular.
Knowledge is power. (Popular saying)
Beauty is Truth. (John Keats)
When **hunger knocks** at the door, **love flies** out of the window. (Proverb)
Food comes first – morals later. (Bertolt Brecht)
You cannot use uncountable nouns with numbers and you can rarely use them with the indefinite article.

A few uncountable nouns only have a plural form.
These **clothes are** too small for me.
My **trousers need** dry-cleaning.
My **jeans are** ripped.
Other plural uncountables include *shorts, knickers, sunglasses, scissors*, etc.

Nouns which are both countable & uncountable

Many nouns have more than one meaning. They can be countable with one meaning and uncountable with another.
Glass is a useful material. (U) (glass as a material)
Can I have **a clean glass**? (C) (an individual object)

Partitives

Partitives are ways of counting uncountables.
an item of clothing
a piece of information
a carton of milk
Sometimes the partitive can be missed out.
Can I have **a coffee**? (= a cup of coffee)
Would you like **a Coke**? (= a glass, can or bottle of Coke)

Oddities

There are some oddities. Two of the most important are:
1 people (C) – singular form/grammatically plural:
 People are strange.
2 news (U) – plural form/grammatically singular:
 Hurry up: **the news is** on.

Quantifiers

Quantifiers are ways of talking about quantity other than by using exact numbers. You can use some with countable nouns, some with uncountable nouns and some with both.

Quantifiers for countable nouns include *a few* and *many*:
a few tables
How many men?

Quantifiers for uncountables include *a little* and *much*.
A little learning is a dang'rous thing. (Alexander Pope)
How much money?

You can use *a lot* and *some* with both countables and uncountables.
a lot of/some ice-cream
a lot of/some chips

Eating out

1 Match these waiter/waitress questions with an appropriate response.

a) Who's the fish?   Yes, thanks.
b) And to drink?   Over here.
c) Did you have a reservation?   'Non,' please.
d) Is everything OK?   No, that's everything.
e) Anything else?   Just some olive oil, please.
f) Smoking or non-smoking?   A bottle of house red, please.
g) Would you like dressing on that?   Yes, under 'Clinton'.

2 What would you say? Choose the appropriate word.

a) You're at the bar and you want to buy somebody a drink …
 'What can I **drink/get/pay** you?'
b) The waiter is taking the orders and you don't want a first course …
 '**Anything/Nothing/No** to start with, thanks.'
c) Somebody is offering you some more wine and you don't want very much …
 'Just a **bit/drop/small**, thanks.'
d) The waiter is offering you food and you don't want any more …
 'I'm **all right/very well/not interested**, thanks.'
e) There's a phone call for you just as the food arrives. You want your friends to start eating …
 'Don't **expect/wait for/stop** me.'

3 Read this conversation in a restaurant. What do you notice about it?

Waiter:	Did you phone us?	**Waiter:**	OK. And you?
Man:	Yes. There are two of us. The name is Jones.	**Man:**	Don't give me a starter. I just want the grilled salmon steak.
Waiter:	Go and sit over there by the window.	**Waiter:**	What do you want with it?
...		**Man:**	A side salad. Oh, and get us some house red and mineral water.
Waiter:	Haven't you decided yet?		
Woman:	No, we're not ready. Go away and get us some drinks.	**Waiter:**	All right.
		...	
Waiter:	What sort?	**Waiter:**	What did you think of the food?
Woman:	Two gin and tonics.	**Man:**	It was OK.
Waiter:	Right.	**Waiter:**	Do you want coffee now?
...			
Woman:	Oy! Come here.	**Woman:**	Yes, two. Black. And bring me the bill.
Waiter:	What do you want?	**Waiter:**	Yeah, OK.
Woman:	Give me the tomato salad and then the lamb.		

4 Work in groups of three. Imagine the conversation is taking place in an expensive restaurant. In groups of three:

a) Rewrite the conversation with more appropriate language.
b) Insert your own section where something terrible/funny/embarrassing happens.
c) Practise the conversation.
d) Perform your revised version for the rest of the class.

Anecdote

5 Think back to a restaurant where you have spent an enjoyable (or unenjoyable!) evening. You are going to tell a partner about it. Choose from the list the things you want to talk about. Think about what you will say and what language you will need.

- ☐ Where was the restaurant?
- ☐ What was it like?
- ☐ Was it full or empty when you walked in?
- ☐ And when you left?
- ☐ What sort of people were eating there?
- ☐ Was it noisy or quiet?
- ☐ Who were you with?
- ☐ What did you have to eat?
- ☐ What did you have to drink?
- ☐ Did you have to wait a long time for your food?
- ☐ Was the waiter or waitress helpful?
- ☐ Did you have a dessert?
- ☐ Did you enjoy your meal?
- ☐ Were there any problems?
- ☐ How long did you spend in the restaurant?
- ☐ Was the meal expensive?
- ☐ Who paid?
- ☐ Did you leave a tip?

6 Tell your partner about the restaurant. Give as much detail as possible.

What's for dinner?

1 Look at the photograph. How many items of food can you name?

2 Look at the following items of fresh food. Look up any words you don't know in your dictionary. Explain the use of the colours.

> aubergines   bacon   beans   cauliflower   celery   cod   courgettes
> cucumbers   figs   garlic   grapefruit   hake   leeks   lettuces
> limes   lobster   melons   mushrooms   mussels   olives   onions
> oranges   peaches   peppers   plums   prawns   raspberries
> salmon   sardines   sausages   spinach   strawberries   tomatoes
> trout   tuna   turkey   veal

Underline the stressed syllable in each of the words with more than one syllable.

3 Ask questions to find out which type of food your partner prefers.

4 Work in small groups. Choose one of the following situations and design a suitable meal. The meal should consist of at least three courses.

a) For a friend of yours and her new boyfriend. The boyfriend is vegetarian.
b) For a romantic evening.
c) For a hot summer's day.
d) For a friend who's on a diet.
e) For a child's sixth birthday party.

When you have finished, read out your menu to the rest of the class and ask them to guess which situation you chose.

Incredible edibles

1 Here are some words to describe the taste or texture of things you eat:

> crunchy spicy tasty crisp salty
> bland sweet bitter chewy greasy
> creamy

Use your dictionary if necessary and use the words in the box above to describe the taste or textures of the different kinds of food below.

> raw carrots   salted peanuts
> plain white rice   creme caramel
> plain chocolate   seafood   milk chocolate
> cheap steak   curry   pizza   fresh bread
> apples   your mother's cooking
> English food   tinned anchovies
> strong coffee   fried eggs

2 These are some of the more unusual things people eat around the world. What do you imagine they taste like?

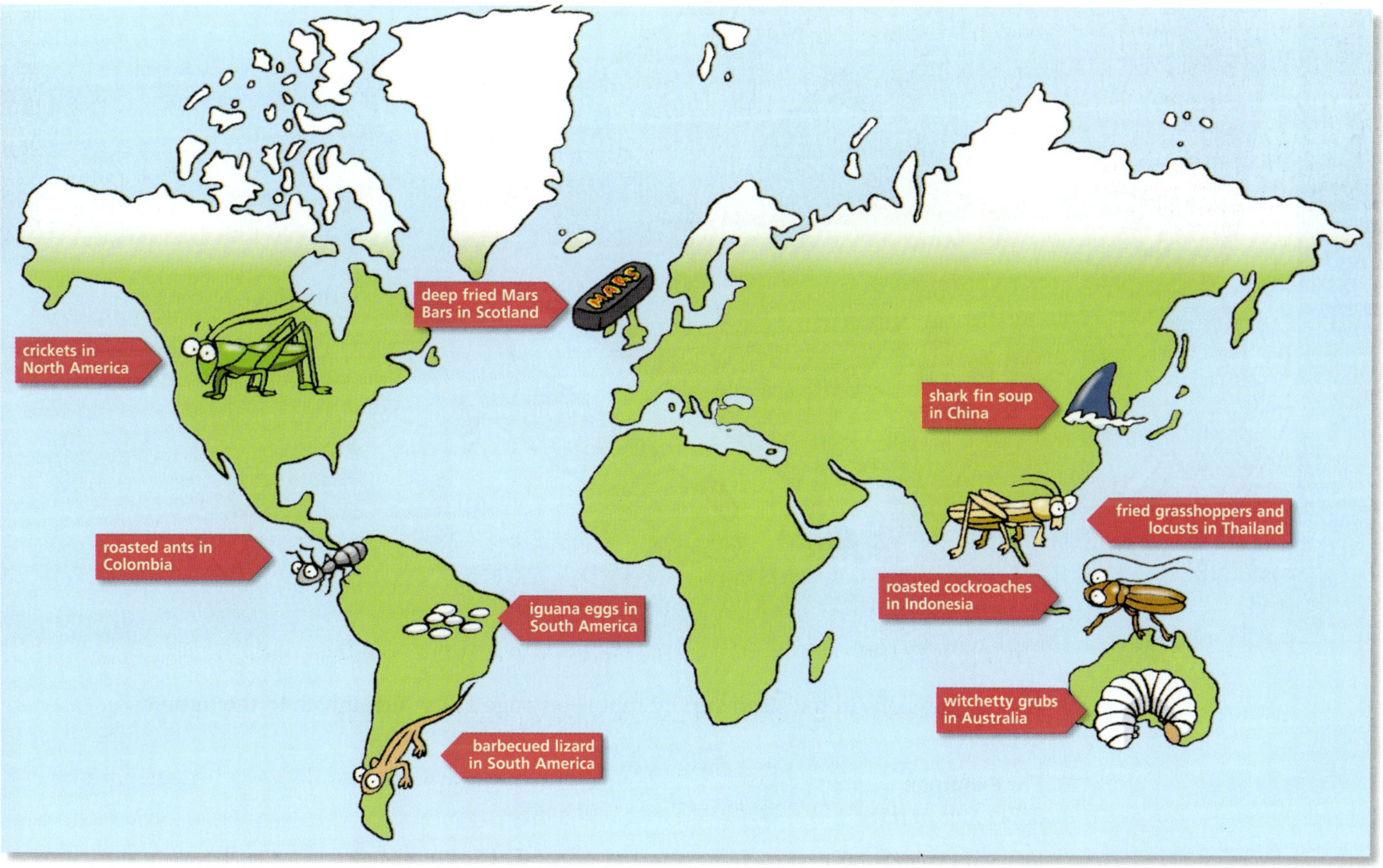

- crickets in North America
- deep fried Mars Bars in Scotland
- shark fin soup in China
- fried grasshoppers and locusts in Thailand
- roasted ants in Colombia
- iguana eggs in South America
- roasted cockroaches in Indonesia
- witchetty grubs in Australia
- barbecued lizard in South America

3 44 Listen to an interview with somebody who has eaten lots of strange things around the world. Write down the words that are used to describe the taste of each dish.

4 Would you consider eating any of the dishes mentioned? What is the strangest thing you have ever eaten? Tell the rest of the class.

Bedtime

1 A survey into people's sleep habits was carried out, based on the questions below. Answer the questions and then compare your answers with a partner.

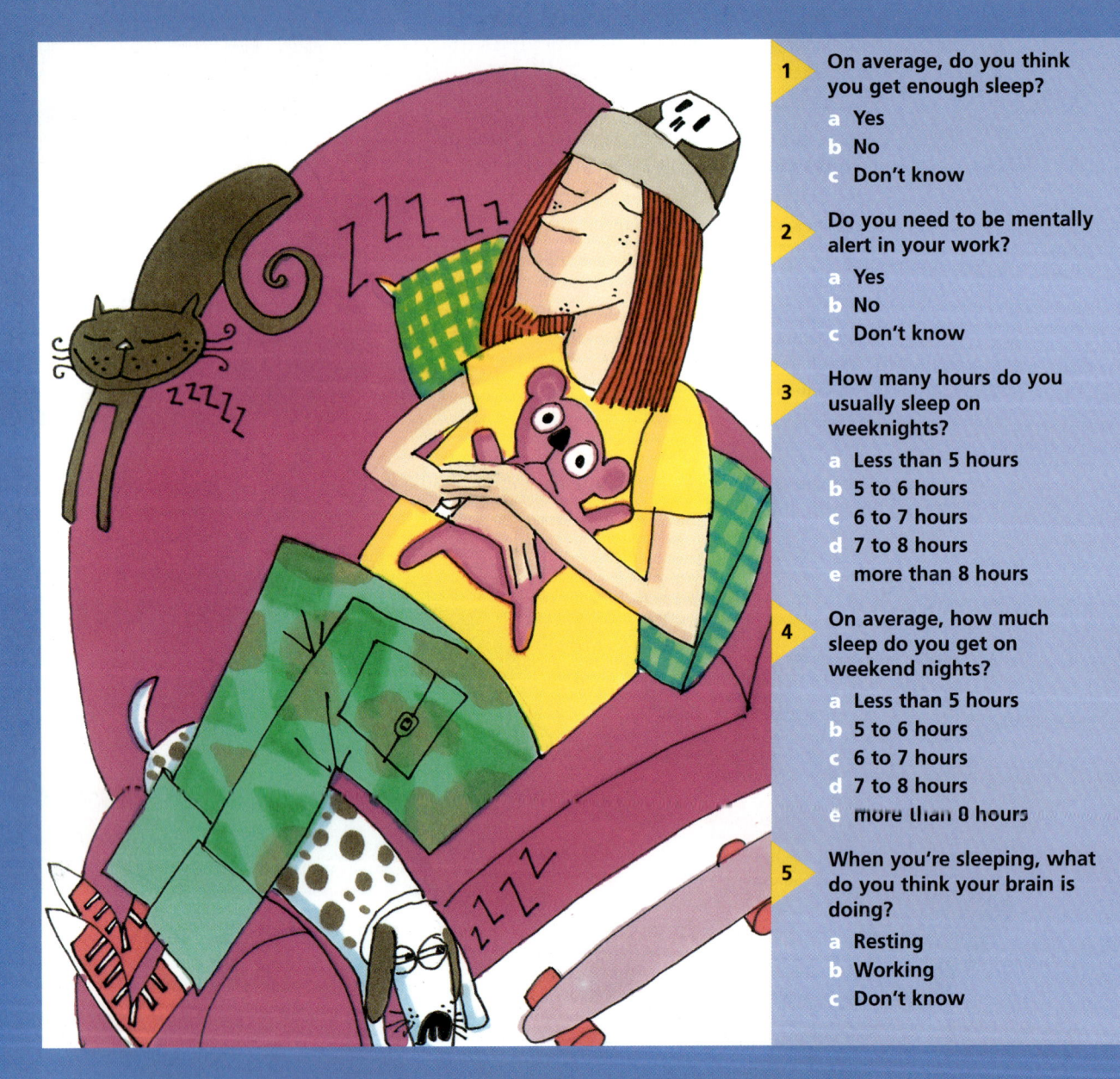

1. On average, do you think you get enough sleep?
   a Yes
   b No
   c Don't know

2. Do you need to be mentally alert in your work?
   a Yes
   b No
   c Don't know

3. How many hours do you usually sleep on weeknights?
   a Less than 5 hours
   b 5 to 6 hours
   c 6 to 7 hours
   d 7 to 8 hours
   e more than 8 hours

4. On average, how much sleep do you get on weekend nights?
   a Less than 5 hours
   b 5 to 6 hours
   c 6 to 7 hours
   d 7 to 8 hours
   e more than 8 hours

5. When you're sleeping, what do you think your brain is doing?
   a Resting
   b Working
   c Don't know

2 Find expressions in the sleep survey report on page 107 which match to the figures below.

For example:
33% – one in three

   a) 5–15% (line 14)
   b) 33% (line 21)
   c) 60–80% (line 27)
   d) 51–60% (line 30)
   e) 80–99% (lines 34 and 52)
   f) 40–49% (line 46)

3 What facts do the figures relate to?

SLEEP SURVEY REPORT

According to recent medical research, sleeping more than nine hours or less than six hours a night can shorten your life expectancy. Those who are likely to live longest are people who regularly get between seven and eight hours a night.

A new survey of 1,000 adults conducted by the Better Sleep Council (BSC) found that few people understand the important role sleep plays in normal daily brain functions and many people actually reduce their brain power by getting too little sleep.

One in three adults admit that they do not get enough sleep, and lack of sleep is leaving millions of people without the energy to work as hard as they should. Although a large number of people say that they need to be mentally alert in their work, over half of the people interviewed say that they sleep just under seven hours a night during the week. On the other hand, most of the people interviewed say that they sleep more than seven hours a night at the weekend. This suggests that a significant number of people try to catch up on their sleep at the weekend instead of getting enough sleep during the week, when they most need it.

According to this survey, nearly half of the population believe that the brain rests when the body sleeps. In fact, the opposite is true. Sleep allows the brain to go to work, filing and storing the day's events. 'Most people incorrectly think the brain is resting or recuperating during sleep. Actually, some parts of the brain are more active when you're asleep,' confirms Dr Mark Mahowald, director of the Minnesota Regional Sleep Disorders Center. 'Your brain is like a cluttered desktop at the end of the day. At night, when you're asleep and no more information can be put on the desk, or in your brain, your brain can then file away the information.' ●

Report writing

1 Work with a partner. Write five questions to ask people about their sleep habits using the words and expressions in the box.

> dream   have nightmares   talk in your sleep   snore   sleepwalk
> sleep on your back, on your side or on your front   have a nap   alarm clock
> feel sleepy   suffer from insomnia   yawn   fall asleep while travelling
> fall asleep in front of the television   early bird   night owl   go without sleep
> in a double bed   have a lie-in at the weekend

2 Now ask other students in the class all five questions and write down their answers.

3 Write sentences reporting the results of your survey. Use expressions from the language toolbox to help you.

LANGUAGE TOOLBOX

According to recent medical research/a recent survey …
A new survey of … conducted by … found that …
On the other hand …
This suggests that a significant number …
In fact …
Actually …

13 Communication

1 🎧 **45** Listen and complete these useful numbers and addresses.

a) BBC website: www. _____ uk
b) CNN website: _____ .cnn _____
c) BBC World Service radio: _____ 20 7557 _____
d) MTV website: www _____
e) Reuters sports results: _____ sports _____ .com
f) Yahoo travel: _____ / recreation _____
g) British Tourist Authority website: www _____
h) Heathrow flight enquiries: _____ 4321

Practise saying the numbers and addresses as fast as you can.

2 How many phone/fax numbers or e-mail/website addresses do you know by heart? Take a few moments to note some of them down. Think of your family, friends, work, etc.

Dictate some of these numbers or addresses to your partner. Then ask each other questions to find out as much as you can about them.

Whose …?   Who …?   What …?   Where …?   How often …?   When … last …?

'Hello… This is the police. If you are being attacked from behind by a mad axe-murderer, press "One"…'

After the beep …

1 Look at this photo of Richard. Imagine what he's like.

- How old is he?
- Is he married?
- girlfriend?
- interests?
- friends?
- job?

2 🎧 **46** Listen and note down the six messages on Richard's answering machine. What clues do you hear about his work, friends and lifestyle?

108   UNIT   13   Communication

Telephone language

1 Richard made two calls after picking up his messages. Read the conversations and complete them with the expressions in the box. One of the expressions in each set of three is wrong. Choose the most appropriate expression from the other two.

> a) Hello./Good morning./Speak!
> b) Is (…) there?/I'd like to speak to (…) please./Is there (…)?
> c) Are you (…)?/Is that (…)?/Who's calling, please?
> d) Hold on, please, I'll try to put you through./Hang on, I'll go and get her./One instant.
> e) I am (…)./It's me./This is (…) here.
> f) What are you up to later?/What do you do later?/Are you available later on today?
> g) I'll look forward to seeing you tomorrow./To tomorrow./See you tomorrow.

Phone conversation 1

Jane:	a) __Hello.__
Richard:	Oh, hi. b) _____
Jane:	c) _____
Richard:	Yes, hello, Jane. How are you?
Jane:	Fine, thanks. d) _____
	…
Maggie:	Hello.
Richard:	Hi! e) _____
Maggie:	You got my message then. I thought you'd forgotten about me.
Richard:	Don't be silly. Of course I haven't forgotten you. I've just been a bit busy, that's all.
Maggie:	Busy playing computer games, I suppose.
Richard:	No, not all the time. Anyway, how are you?
Maggie:	Not too bad. A bit tired. Too much work as usual. Which reminds me, have you heard anything from the travel agent's?
Richard:	Oh, yes. They've got the tickets.
Maggie:	Great! I really need this holiday.
Richard:	Listen, I can't chat now, but f) _____
Maggie:	I've got to work this evening, but I thought we could go to the cinema tomorrow.
Richard:	OK, I'll come round at about seven.
Maggie:	g) _____
Richard:	Bye.

Phone conversation 2

Receptionist:	a) __Good morning.__ South-Western Bank. Can I help you?
Richard:	Yes, b) _____
Receptionist:	c) _____
Richard:	My name's Richard Swainston.
Receptionist:	OK, d) _____
	…
	Oh, Mr Swainston, I'm afraid she's on the other line. Would you like to hold?
Richard:	Yes, thank you.
	…
Alison:	Alison Moore.
Richard:	Oh, hello. e) _____
Alison:	Oh, yes. Mr Swainston. Thank you for getting back to me so promptly. There seems to be a problem with your account.
Richard:	Oh, dear. What sort of problem?
Alison:	Well, you're over your overdraft limit by more than £200. You really need to come to the bank to discuss it. f) _____
Richard:	I'm afraid I'm rather tied up today. Would tomorrow be convenient for you?
Alison:	Yes, that's fine. Ten thirty?
Richard:	Yes, ten thirty's fine for me.
Alison:	Well, thank you for ringing. g) _____
Richard:	Goodbye.

2 ▶ 47 Listen to the telephone conversations and check.

'Just hang on a sec, please.'

Communication UNIT 13

3 Work with a partner. Refer to the answering machine messages on page 108. Write down and practise the following telephone conversations:

- Richard phones his friend Jeff and arranges to meet him this evening.
- Richard phones Smiths Insurance and arranges a meeting with Ian Watson.

4 🔲 48 After his meeting with Alison Moore at the bank, Richard did what any independent young person would do. He phoned his mother. Listen to the conversation once and decide whether the following sentences are true or false:

a) When Richard phones his mother, she tells him that she's feeling lonely because her husband's out playing golf.
b) Richard has had money problems before.
c) Mrs Swainston thinks that Richard is careful with his money.
d) Richard's sister had an expensive wedding.
e) Richard asks his mother to give him some money so that he can get married.
f) Mrs Swainston is unhappy with the way Richard manages his money.
g) Mrs Swainston agrees to lend him £300, but only if he promises to get married.
h) Richard often phones his mother just for a chat.

5 What does this phone call tell us about the relationship between Richard and his mother? Do you ever have similar conversations with your parents?

Close up

Real conditionals

1 Look at tapescript 48. Listen again and complete these sentences.

a) Well, of course it is. What do you expect if _____ .
b) Look, Mum, if you can just help me out this time, _____ .
c) I'll do it this time, but this really is the last time. If you get yourself into trouble again _____ .

2 Think of different ways Mrs Swainston might have completed this sentence:

Oh, Richard, have you got yourself into debt again? Because if you have,

a) don't ...
b) I'm not going to ...
c) you can ...
d) I won't ...
e) ...

3 Here are some sentences said by a parent. Match clauses from Column A with clauses from Column B and add *if* to make realistic sentences.

For example:
Take a front door key if you're going to stay out late.

'Bye, darling – don't forget to write – or phone us on: 01273 516819, or fax us on: 01273 510044, or e-mail on: easycum@fair-ways.co.uk or visit our website on: www.fair-ways.co.uk...'

A

a) take a front door key
b) you're going to listen to that awful music
c) you don't put your toys away
d) you hurt yourself
e) you'll be late for school
f) you've finished your dinner
g) you haven't finished your homework
h) you're going to be silly
i) I might buy you an ice-cream
j) you're going to phone a friend

B

1 I'll give them all away
2 you can leave the table
3 you can't play computer games
4 you're going to stay out late
5 you're good
6 don't come crying to me
7 keep it short
8 shut your bedroom door
9 I'm not playing
10 you don't hurry up

What age (0–18) do you think the child would be for the parent to say these things?

4 Choose five of the sentences from 3 and change *if* to *unless*. What other changes do you have to make?

5 Are you superstitious? Explain any superstitions that exist in your country.

For example:
If you touch wood it protects you against bad luck.

6 Look at the following English sayings. Work in groups and decide what you think they mean. Write sentences explaining the sayings using *if*. Do you have an equivalent saying in your language?

a) Easy come, easy go.
b) You snooze, you lose.
c) No pain, no gain.
d) It's no use crying over spilt milk.
e) When the cat's away, the mice will play.
f) Many hands make light work.
g) An apple a day keeps the doctor away.
h) Strike while the iron is hot.
i) Too many cooks spoil the broth.
j) Absence makes the heart grow fonder.

Language reference: real conditionals

Real conditionals talk about real or possible situations, usually in the present or the future. They generally have two clauses: an *if* clause and a *main clause*.

If you're going to stay out late,	take a front door key.
If you don't put your toys away,	I'll give them all away.

The 'if' clause

In most real conditionals, you use the present in the *if* clause, even when you are talking about the future.

Present simple
If you **arrive** early, wait for me in the station café.

Present continuous
If you**'re going** to Greece for your holidays, I can recommend a great hotel.

Present perfect
If you **haven't finished** by ten, you'll miss the post.

You don't always have to use the present simple, continuous or perfect. Look at the first example in this Language reference section. It uses *going to*.

You can also use *can* and *can't*:
If you **can't finish** the exercise, ask the teacher for help.

Occasionally you can use the past tense, but only when you are talking about something you know or you believe really happened:
If it **rained**, we went to school by bus.
If you **didn't call** me, who did?

There are alternatives to *if*. *Unless* is the most important one. It means *if + not*.
There is no important difference between **Unless** you agree … and **If you don't** agree …

The main clause

In the main clause, the most common structure is the present simple. Some modal auxiliaries (especially *will*, *can*, *must* and *may*) are also common, and so is the imperative.

If he finds out the truth, …
- … it**'s** all over for me and you.
- … we**'ll** be in big trouble.
- … you **can forget** about our holiday in Jamaica.
- … **deny** everything!

The *if* clause and the main clause can often go in either order.
If I feel like going out, I'll give you a call.
I'll give you a call if I feel like going out.
Use a comma after the *if* clause in the first type of sentence.

You will find information about unreal conditionals in units 14 and 15.

If you have studied the 'first conditional' (*if* + present simple + *will*) or the zero conditional (*if* + present simple + present simple), you already know a lot about this type of sentence. The first and zero conditionals are common examples of real conditionals.

Stereotypes

> 1 A **stereotype** is a fixed general image or set of characteristics that a lot of people believe represent a particular type of person or thing. *Accents can reinforce a negative stereotype.*
>
> 2 If someone **is stereotyped** as something, people form a fixed general idea or image of them, so that it is assumed that they will behave in a particular way. *You are likely to find many people who have stereotyped ideas about women.*
>
> (Collins Cobuild English Dictionary)

1 According to an article in the *Daily Mail*, these are some of the things you'll never hear men say:

- Let's ask that woman for directions.
- Hi, Mum, I just rang for a chat.
- Where's the toilet cleaner?

And these are some of the things you'll never hear women say:

- Would you please stop sending me flowers? It's embarrassing.
- Do you think I'd look better if I put on a few kilos?
- I've just killed that enormous spider in the bath.

Do you agree?

2 Which category do you think the *Daily Mail* put the following statements in?

a) Of course I'd love to have dinner with your sister. The only thing on telly tonight is football.
b) Shall I check the tyre pressures when I go to the petrol station?
c) Let's switch off the TV, I want to talk about our relationship.
d) Thanks so much for ironing my shirt.
e) Don't worry, I'll clean that up.
f) Do you think my bottom looks fat in these trousers?
g) I saw this gorgeous suit in that new shop in town. The jacket's a great shape and it wasn't expensive.
h) You drive, darling, you're so much better than me.
i) Look, I'm sick of talking about our relationship, OK?
j) But I just don't need another pair of shoes.

Answers according to the *Daily Mail*:
Things you'll never hear a man say: a, c, e, f, g, h
Things you'll never hear a woman say: b, d, i, j

3 What kinds of stereotypes of men and women could you make from the comments in 1 and 2? If you are a woman, complete the sentences in Column A. If you are a man, complete the sentences in Column B.

A	B
Men are …	Women are …
Men like …	Woman like …
Men never …	Women never …
Men are good at …	Women are good at …
Men aren't very good at …	Women aren't very good at …
The best thing about being a man is …	The best thing about being a woman is …
The worst thing about being a man is …	The worst thing about being a woman is …

Compare your sentences.

4 Complete these expressions using one verb for all the expressions in Column A and one verb for all the expressions in Column B.

A
- … the shopping
- … the cooking
- … the washing-up
- … the odd jobs around the house
- … most of the driving
- … the washing
- … the ironing
- … the family accounts
- … the cleaning
- … the vacuuming

B
- … the beds
- … dinner when there are guests
- … the important decisions
- … an effort to keep in touch with family and friends
- … arrangements for baby-sitters
- … family appointments to see doctors, dentists or teachers
- … the biggest mess in the kitchen
- … the most noise
- … their mind up quickest
- … the longest phone calls

5 Think about your own family. Who makes/does the things in 4?

For example:
My mother does the shopping and cooking, but we take it in turns to do the washing-up.
We make all the important decisions together.

6 Discuss the following questions:

- What things have changed in your lifetime for the family?/ for women?/for men?
- Do you think women should have the same rights as men?
- Do you think women have the same rights as men in your country?
- Do you think women are in a better position now than women of your grandmother's generation were?
- Do you think women are happier now than women of your grandmother's generation were?

ASPIRATION AND REALITY – % of women who think they:

country	should have all the same rights as men	do have the same rights as men	are in a better position than grandmother's generation	are happier than grandmother's generation
Australia	77	25	95	38
Belgium	70	12	90	41
Britain	73	9	93	42
Canada	70	8	93	33
Germany	70	7	94	29
Japan	21	0	96	82
Mexico*	81	18	69	53
Netherlands	80	20	92	25
South Africa*	63	23	77	54
Switzerland	39	14	92	27
United States	62	8	93	28

Source Angus Reid/*The Economist* poll   *Urban sample only

Compare your answers with the results of the poll carried out by *The Economist*, based on interviews with more than 3,000 women.

What do men & women really think?

1 Work with a partner of the opposite sex if possible. Answer the questionnaire for yourself and then guess the answers for your partner.

survey

One thousand men and women between the ages of 18 and 35 were interviewed for a survey to find out the differences between what British men and women really think. This is the survey.

1 After a first date, how soon would you want him or her to telephone you?
 a) The next day.
 b) Within three days.
 c) Within a fortnight.
 d) Any time.

2 When you say 'I'll call you,' do you mean:
 a) I'll phone you tomorrow?
 b) I'll contact you when I feel like seeing you again?
 c) Don't call me?

3 If they didn't arrive on time for a first date, how long would you wait?
 a) Five minutes.
 b) Fifteen minutes.
 c) Half an hour.
 d) No limit.

4 Do you think it's OK for men to:
 a) use beauty products?
 b) still live at home when they are over 30?
 c) stay at home and look after the children while their partner goes out to work?

5 How would you feel if your partner forgot your birthday?
 a) Upset.
 b) Angry.
 c) You don't care – it's only a birthday.

6 Which of the following items would you like to receive as a present?
 a) Flowers.
 b) Computer games.
 c) Clothes.
 d) A mobile phone.

7 Which of the following statements do you agree with?
 a) Men should hold doors open for women.
 b) Men and women are equal, so it's insulting to women if men hold doors open for them.
 c) Men and women are equal, but women still like having doors held open for them.

8 Have you ever done any of the following to attract a member of the opposite sex?
 a) Bought new clothes.
 b) Changed your hair.
 c) Dieted.
 d) Lied about your age.

9 Should the wives/husbands of public figures stand by their partner?
 a) Yes.
 b) No.

10 Do you think marriage is the ideal romantic relationship?
 a) Yes.
 b) No.

Adapted from 'Today's Woman Laid Bare,' *Esquire*, June 1995

2 Here is a summary of some of the more interesting findings to come out of the survey. Complete the gaps with 'men' or 'women' as you think appropriate.

survey HIGHLIGHTS

ON PHONING The majority of both men and women want to be phoned within three days. However, 35% of (1) _____ said they would expect to be phoned the next day, while only 19% of (2) _____ gave this answer.

ON DATES On average, (3) _____ are prepared to wait for their date longer than (4) _____. Eighteen per cent of (5) _____ said that they would only wait for five minutes, whereas 67% of (6) _____ would be prepared to wait half an hour or more.

ON CHILDCARE (7) _____ are far more in favour of men staying at home to look after the children than (8) _____. While 65% of (9) _____ said it was fine, only 30% of (10) _____ agreed. The majority of (11) _____ do not feel that it is appropriate for the man to stay at home with the children.

ON BIRTHDAYS The results of the survey suggest that (12) _____ attach greater importance to birthdays than (13) _____ : 29% said they would be angry and upset if their partner forgot their birthday.

ON ATTRACTION Three out of four (14) _____ have bought new clothes to attract a member of the opposite sex compared with only one in five (15) _____. Similarly, while just under half of the (16) _____ interviewed have changed their hair or dieted, only one in ten (17) _____ admitted to doing the same. However, a significant number of both men and women admitted lying about their age, with the important difference that (18) _____ tended to say they were older while (19) _____ were more likely to knock a few years off their age.

ON MARRIAGE The results of the survey show that (20) _____ are more in favour of marriage than (21) _____. Sixty-one per cent of (22) _____ didn't think much of this institution whereas four out of five (23) _____ interviewed gave a resounding thumbs-up to marriage as the ideal romantic relationship.

ANSWERS ON PAGE 141.

3 Would the results of the survey have been different in your country?

Report writing Work in groups and complete the following tasks:

1 Write a multiple choice questionnaire to find out about people's attitudes to one of the following:
- mobile phones
- computers
- housework
- marriage

2 Do the questionnaire in class and collate the results.

3 Write a report to summarise your findings. Use expressions from the survey highlights above.

14 Style

1. Match the verbs below to the noun phrases from the box to describe the sort of things people do before they leave the house in the morning.

   have   get   make   do   read   put

   | a shower   coffee   my homework   the radio on   the mail   dressed |
   | breakfast   my make-up on   the children ready   the washing-up   the bed |
   | the TV on   the paper   a cup of tea |

2. Think about your own morning routine from the moment you get out of bed to the moment you leave the house.
   - What do you do? What order do you do things in?
   - How long does each activity usually take you?

   Compare routines with a partner. What are the differences?

3. Read through these two morning routines. Choose the most appropriate verb.

PERSON 1

My alarm goes off early and it takes me ten minutes to eat my breakfast, drink two cups of coffee, have a shower, pack my bag and read the post and thirty minutes to (1) **get dressed/wear**. I start thinking about what I'm going to (2) **get dressed/wear** while I have my breakfast. After a shower, I (3) **put on/wear** my underwear and then I look in my wardrobe and choose a pair of trousers. If they still (4) **fit/look** me I put them on. If they feel a bit tight around the waist I (5) **try them on/take them off** and spend a few minutes feeling guilty about all those chocolates I had last night. Then, I choose a looser pair of trousers and think about a top that (6) **goes with/fits** it. I usually (7) **have on/try on** two or three tops before I find one that (8) **looks/wears** right and (9) **feels/fits** comfortable. Finding a pair of socks usually takes about five minutes – I can find two dozen odd pairs, but none that (10) **look/match**. By now, I'm late.

PERSON 2

I get up as late as I possibly can and jump in and out of the shower. I (1) **put on/fit** the trousers I (2) **had on/got dressed** yesterday and take a shirt out of the wardrobe – it doesn't matter which one as long as it's ironed. I find the jacket that (3) **fits/goes with** the trousers, look down and check that my socks (4) **match/feel** and that's it. Nearly all my clothes are either green or brown because I've been told that they are the only colours that (5) **suit/match** me. So I never really have to worry about what I (6) **look like/go with**. The important thing is to make sure I have enough time to enjoy my favourite drink of the day: that first cup of coffee …

Do you think these are descriptions of a man or a woman? Do the descriptions fit anybody you know?

4. On a piece of paper write a short account of how you get ready in the morning. Don't write your name on it. When you've finished, fold the piece of paper and give it to your teacher. Then take another student's piece of paper and guess who it belongs to.

5. Work with a partner. Describe how you would get ready for some of the following:
   - a job interview
   - a first date
   - an evening at the theatre
   - Saturday night out with your friends
   - a wedding
   - a long flight
   - a day on the beach
   - a Sunday afternoon stroll around town

Suits you

1 Which of the sentences below describes your style best? Compare with a partner.

- Comfortable. I like baggy trousers, loose-fitting tops and trainers.
- Up-to-date but original.
- I have to be smart for work, but I wear casual clothes at the weekend.
- I've been wearing the same clothes for ten years. I have no idea what's in fashion and I don't care.
- The only way I could possibly describe my style is scruffy. I wear jeans, sweatshirts and trainers, and I never manage to look neat and tidy.
- My style would be different if I had more money. I'd buy designer labels, especially Gucci and Versace. I love dressing up in glamorous outfits.
- Something else:

2 49 You are going to listen to some people talking about their favourite clothes. Number the pictures below in the order in which you hear about them. Not all of the clothes are mentioned.

3 Which of the items do you think is the ugliest? Which ones do you like?

Close up

Adjective order

1 Put these words in the correct order to describe clothes.

For example:
a polo-neck sweater white – *a white polo-neck sweater*

a) T-shirt an short-sleeved old
b) green a cardigan plain
c) beautiful scarf a cashmere
d) sweater a v-neck striped
e) silk flowery waistcoat a

Make five new combinations of adjectives and nouns.

(Language Reference p119)

2 a) Put the adjectives in the box into these five categories: age; material; pattern; opinion; style.

old	stripy	beautiful	wool	leather	second-hand	horrible	check
short-sleeved	new	full-length	fabulous	plain	Armani	silk	

b) In most languages, when we use two or three adjectives to describe a noun there are rules about the order of the adjectives.

Put the categories in the correct order for English. Is it the same in your language?

3 Write down different combinations of clothing under the following headings:
I've got this in my wardrobe; I wouldn't be seen dead in this.

For example:

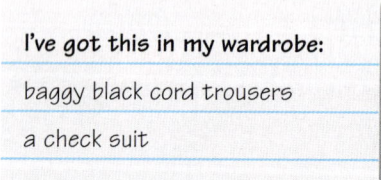

I've got this in my wardrobe:
baggy black cord trousers
a check suit

I wouldn't be seen dead in this!
a second-hand nylon shirt
green leather trousers

Work with a partner. Take turns to read out one of your items, but don't say which heading you wrote it under. Your partner has to guess which heading each item belongs to.

Anecdote

4 Think of a favourite item of clothes or accessory which you have bought. You are going to tell your partner about it. Choose from the list the things you want to talk about. Think about what you will say and the language you will need.

- ☐ What is it?
- ☐ What does it look like?
- ☐ What does it feel like?
- ☐ How long have you had it?
- ☐ Which shop did you buy it in?
- ☐ Who was with you when you bought it?
- ☐ Was it very expensive?
- ☐ Do you think it was worth the money?
- ☐ How often do you wear/use it?
- ☐ Do you have any special memories associated with it?
- ☐ Have you ever lent it to someone?
- ☐ How would you feel if you lost it?
- ☐ What do you like best about it?

5 Tell your partner about the item of clothing or accessory.

Idioms

1. Write down the names of some clothes that have:
   a) zips
   b) buttons
   c) hems
   d) turn-ups
   e) buckles
   f) sleeves
   g) heels

   For example:
   cuffs – shirt, jacket, coat, sweater

2. Test your idioms. Choose the correct word in the expressions below and say what you think the expressions mean.
   a) Don't get shirty **with/into/across** me, I was only trying to help.
   b) I'm sorry, I didn't mean to offend you. It was just an **up/off/around** the cuff remark.
   c) If you want to pass that exam, you'll have to buckle **over/down/round** to work very soon.
   d) It's so obvious when Claire's in love – she wears her heart **under/by/on** her sleeve.
   e) We're saving up to go on holiday so we'll have to **tighten/loosen/forget** our belts for a while.
   f) I haven't seen Bill around for a while – do you think he's been **wearing/given/missing** the boot?
   g) Sorry I'm late. Mike **collared/belted/zipped** me after work and I couldn't get away.
   h) I'm afraid I've run out of ideas – let's ask John. He's usually got something **beside/between/up** his sleeve.

3. Match the expressions in 2 to these definitions:
   1. to behave in a way that makes your feelings obvious
   2. to spend less money
   3. to stop somebody and make them listen to you
   4. to have an idea or a plan
   5. to say something without thinking about it first
   6. to get rid of somebody
   7. to start working seriously
   8. to behave in a bad-tempered and rude way

4. Think of something that happened to you recently. Use one of the expressions in 2 and tell your partner about it.

Language reference: adjective order

In most languages, when you use two or three adjectives to describe a noun, there are rules about the order of the adjectives. In English this is the order:

| | | ADJECTIVES | | | |
Opinion →	Age →	Pattern & colour →	Material →	Style →	NOUN
horrible,	second-hand,	stripy,	cotton,	short-sleeved,	shirt.
fabulous,	old,	leopard-print,	fake fur,	full-length,	coat.
beautiful,	new,	blue,	silk,	Armani,	suit.

Style UNIT 14 119

First impressions

1 Match words from Column A and Column B according to the underlined sounds.

A	B
a) overw<u>ei</u>ght	1 a p<u>ier</u>ced nose
b) br<u>oa</u>d shoulders	2 sm<u>ar</u>t
c) a b<u>ea</u>rd	3 a th<u>i</u>ck neck
d) st<u>u</u>bble	4 eyebr<u>ow</u>s
e) a sc<u>ar</u>	5 a rel<u>a</u>xed style
f) b<u>a</u>ggy trousers	6 ba<u>l</u>d
g) slim b<u>ui</u>ld	7 scr<u>u</u>ffy
h) s<u>ui</u>t	8 a sh<u>a</u>ved head
i) a wide m<u>ou</u>th	9 high-heeled b<u>oo</u>ts

2 Which of these adjectives can you use with *hair*, *eyes* or *skin*?

blue   deep-set   brown   clear   fair   pale   dark   tanned

3 Work with a partner. Use the words in 1 and 2 to describe the people below.

UNIT 14 *Style*

4 If you met the people in the photo in 3 for the first time, what would be the first thing you would notice about each of them?

5 Can you tell anything about a person from a first impression? Are your first impressions usually right?

6 Read the description below and match it to one of the people in 3.

Say you're a girl. Say you're a girl and you're at a party, or in a pub, or in a club. Say you're a girl and you're at a party, or in a pub, or in a club, and I come up to you.

5 Say you've never set eyes on me before.

Some things you'll know immediately. You'll see that I'm just under six feet tall and of average build. If we shake hands, you'll notice that my grip is strong and my fingernails clean. You'll see that I have brown eyes which
10 match my brown hair. And you'll see that I have a scar across the centre of my left eyebrow. You'll guess that I'm somewhere between twenty-five and thirty years old.

You'll ask me what I do for a living and I'll tell you that I'm an artist, which is true, and that I make a living
15 from it, which isn't. I won't tell you that I work in a small art gallery in Mayfair three days a week to make ends meet. You'll look at my clothes, which will probably be my friend's clothes, and wrongly assume that I'm rich. As I won't mention a girlfriend, you'll probably assume
20 correctly that I'm single. I won't ask you if you have a boyfriend, but I will check your finger to see if you're engaged or married.

From *Come Together* by Josie Lloyd and Emlyn Rees

Come Together

Come Together was written by a couple. Each of them wrote alternate chapters of the book. It tells the story of the same relationship from the point of view of the man and the woman.

7 Complete the description below for one of the other people in 3.

Say we meet at a party, and we've never met before, you'll see that I'm _____ tall and of _____ build. You'll see that I've got _____ hair and _____ eyes. You'll guess that I'm somewhere between _____ and _____ years old.
You'll look at my clothes and assume that my style is _____ . If we speak, I'll tell you that I _____ , which is true, and that I _____ , which isn't.

8 Read your description out to a partner and ask them to guess which person you've described.

9 Write a description of yourself or another student in the class.

Ugly

Jon Bon Jovi

Jon Bon Jovi was born John Francis Bongiovi Jr on 2nd March, 1962. His first band was Atlantic City Expressway. He made his breakthrough with the song 'Runaway'.

1 50 Listen to the song.

a) Is it a romantic song?
b) Who is the singer talking to?
c) What does he think of her?
d) What does she think of herself?

2 Look at the lyrics of the first two verses of the song. The lines have been cut in half. In Column A the lines are in the correct order but in Column B they are mixed up. Listen again and match the two halves of each line.

A	B
If you're ugly,	you really are to me
In your eyes	a camera sometimes
If you could see yourself	as beautiful as you
You'd wish you were	for you to see
And I wish I was	I'm ugly too!
So I could take your picture	with my mind
Put it in a frame	like others do
How beautiful	the sky's a different blue

Close up

I wish

1 Look at the lyrics in 2. What tense is used after *I wish*?

2 Make *I wish* sentences for the following situations.

For example:
I'm poor. ➔ *I wish I had more money.*

a) I live in a tiny house in the suburbs.
b) I've got a boring job.
c) My car's 15 years old.
d) My wife doesn't understand me.
e) My children never listen to a word I say.
f) I never have time to do the things I like.
g) I hardly ever see my friends.

3 What wishes do you have about your own life? Write down a few and then tell your partner about them.

I wish I   was/were …
           wasn't/weren't so …
           had …/didn't have …
           lived …
           could …

Interview with Jon Bon Jovi

1. What do you know about Jon Bon Jovi?

2. In the interview below, he answers some of the following questions:

   a) If you could be anywhere in the world right now, where would you like to be?
   b) What do you do in your spare time?
   c) Who would you most like to have lunch with?
   d) What makes you angry?
   e) What would surprise people most about you?
   f) If your best friend was about to marry someone you thought was totally unsuitable, would you give an honest opinion?
   g) What scares you?
   h) If an old flame invited you to dinner, would you go?
   i) If you could change anything, what would it be?
   j) What's the best thing about your work?

   Match a question to each of his answers.

Q&A JON BON JOVI

1 ?

My mother. At the peak of Bon Jovi's early success, the group went through a period of real extravagance. We hired private planes, chartered the biggest yachts in the world, took all our friends on holiday to exotic islands, bought each other Ferraris and gave our parents expensive presents. But Mum would always much rather I went round for Sunday lunch instead of buying her another gift.

2 ?

Being a rock 'n' roll star is not as romantic as people think. It's actually a very strenuous job – especially when you're on the road 240 days a year. Songwriting, creating something that you can have for ever, is what gives me the greatest thrill.

3 ?

People who come to interview me and only want to talk about my hairstyle.

4 ?

I'd spend more time with my wife, Dorothea, and my kids, Stephanie and James. I take them with me whenever possible. They all came to live with me in London for three months while I was filming the thriller *The Leading Man*, but I still don't see enough of them.

5 ?

I used to worry about living up to the success of the last record, especially after *Slippery When Wet* sold 14 million copies. But these days, I'm much more relaxed and personal artistic satisfaction means more than commercial success.

6 ?

That I'm not out on the town every night. When I was in London filming, I would drive to work at 6 am and see people coming out of the clubs and feel thankful that I'd had a good night's sleep. I'm all for going out on a bender now and again, but you can't do it every night.

(Adapted from *Candice*, October 1997)

3. Work in small groups and discuss your own answers to the questions in 2 above.

Close up

Unreal conditionals

1 Look at the interview with Jon Bon Jovi again. Which tense does the interviewer use after the word *if*? Why?

2 51 Listen and read the dialogues below. What is the relationship between the people in each dialogue?

A
Anna: If you're looking for a new skirt, there's a sale on at DKNY.
Dan: Is there? Well, come on. If we don't leave now, the shops'll be closed when we get there.

B
Mark: If I pass the exam, can I have a new pair of Doc Martens? And a CD? And …
Laura: If you spent less time thinking about clothes and music and more time on your schoolwork, I'd be a lot happier.

C
Paul: This is really nice. If I had the money, I'd always wear Hugo Boss suits.
Chris: If you like it, why don't you buy it? You look great in it.

D
Mel: Right. Who's been wearing my Calvin Klein jacket?
Julia: Well, don't look at me.
Mel: Well, if it wasn't you, who was it?
Julia: Well, I don't know. Anyway, what do you expect if you leave your things all around the house?
Mel: That's neither here nor there. If you're going to borrow things, you should ask. Look at this stain.

3 Underline the *conditional* sentences.

Language Reference p125

4 Work with a partner. Discuss these questions with reference to the examples in the conversations.

a) How many clauses are there in each conditional sentence in the conversations?
b) In each case, is the speaker talking about a situation which they see as *real* or *unreal*?
c) What verb tenses are used in the *if* clauses? What happens to the verb tense in the *if* clause in the *unreal* conditionals?
d) How is this similar to *I wish* (page 122)?
e) What happens in the main clause in the unreal conditionals?

5 Write at least five sentences about yourself and talk about them with a partner.

a) If I had more money/time …
b) If I could speak English/Chinese …
c) If I were younger/older …
d) If I could sing/dance/play a musical instrument/drive …
e) If …

'If I was married to you, I'd divorce you!'

Language reference: I wish & unreal conditionals

I wish

I wish is one of the ways of talking about *unreal* situations. After *I wish* the tense backshifts.

FACT	WISH
I'm a teacher	but I **wish** I **wasn't/weren't** a teacher. I **wish** I **was/were** a doctor. *
I **live** in New York	but I **wish** I **didn't live** in New York. I **wish** I **lived** in Paris.
I'm **studying** English	but I **wish** I **wasn't studying** English. I **wish** I **was/were studying** Chinese.

* *were* is often used instead of *was* to make the sentence more formal.

Unreal conditionals

If for unreal conditionals follows the same rule as *I wish*.
If I **was/were** a doctor ...
If I **lived** in Paris ...
If I **was/were studying** Chinese ...

In the second clause of the sentence you generally use *would*. You can also use *might* or *maybe + would* for possible results.
If I was a doctor I**'d** be able to help people more, and I**'d** make more money.
If I lived in Paris, I**'d** visit the Louvre every day and I**'d** have croissants and coffee for breakfast in a pavement café.
If I was studying Chinese I**'d** have fewer problems with grammar. And I **might** be able to study in China for a year.

There is more information about *I wish* and conditionals in units 13 and 15 and about *would* in unit 11.

> If you have studied the 'second conditional' (*if* + past simple + *would* + verb), you already know a lot about this type of sentence.

Style UNIT 14

15 Age

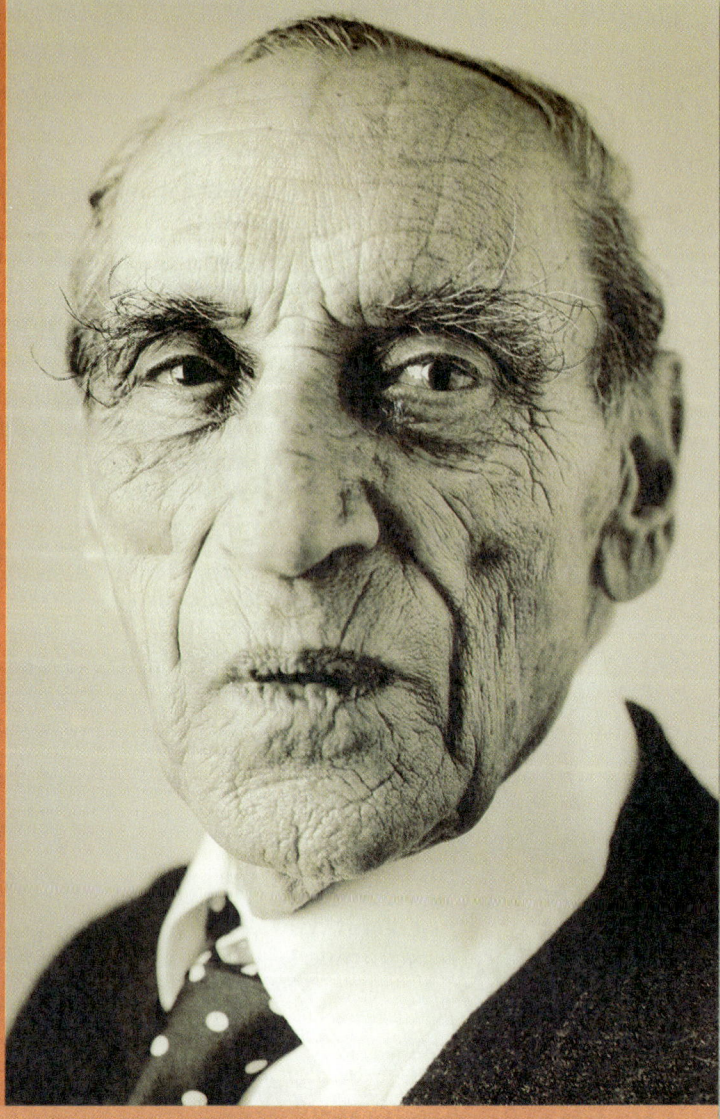

if

If I had my life to live over,
I'd try to make more mistakes next time.

I would relax.

I would be sillier than I have been this trip.

5 I know of very few things I would take
seriously.

I would take more chances.

I would take more trips.

I would climb more mountains, swim more
10 rivers and watch more sunsets.

I would eat more ice cream and less beans.

I would have more actual troubles and
fewer imaginary ones.

You see, I am one of those people who live
15 prophylactically and sanely and sensibly,

hour after hour, day after day.

Oh, I have had my moments and, if I had to
do it over again, I'd have more of them.

In fact, I'd try to have nothing else. Just
20 moments, one after another.

If I had my life to live over,

I would start bare-footed earlier in the
spring and stay that way later in the fall.

I would play hooky more.

25 I would ride on more merry-go-rounds.

I'd pick more daisies.

CALL 0345 883 1340 TODAY. ALTERNATIVELY, YOU COULD WAIT UNTIL TOMORROW.

prophylactically (line 15): very carefully
sanely (line 15): in a normal or reasonable way
bare-footed (line 22): without shoes
fall (US) (line 23): autumn
play hooky (US) (line 24): stay away from school without permission
daisy (line 26): small white wild flower

1 Work in groups. Invent an identity for the man in the advertisement.
- What's his name?
- How old is he?
- Where does he live?
- What's his family background?
- What has he done in his life?
- Is he happy?

Work with students from other groups. Compare descriptions.

2 Read the poem and decide whether it fits the character you have invented. How does the man in the poem feel about his life?

3 Why did Harley Davidson choose this poem to advertise their bikes? What kind of person is the advertisement aimed at?

Wishes

1 The poem you have just read is about an old man looking back over his life. Think about your future. Make a list of five or more things you'd like to do in the future and why you can't do them now.

For example:

What I'd like …	Why it's impossible …
I'd like to *buy a new leather jacket* …	but *I can't find one I like.*
I'd like to *travel round the world* …	but *I've got to finish my studies.*

2 Rewrite your list using conditional sentences.

For example:
If I could find a jacket I liked, I'd buy it.
If I didn't have to finish my studies, I'd travel round the world.

3 Work with a partner. Compare your sentences.

4 Look back at the poem. Complete these sentences for the man. Use the words in the box.

sensible   seriously   adventurous   anxious   fun   risks   enjoy

a) I wish I'd been more …
b) I wish I'd been less …
c) I wish I'd taken more …
d) If only I'd had more …
e) I wish I hadn't been so …
f) I wish I hadn't taken life so …
g) If only I'd done more of the things I …

Close up

I wish & if only

1 Work with a partner. Look at the sentences in 4 above.

a) What verb form follows *I wish …* and *If only …* in these particular sentences?
b) Are the sentences about situations in the past, the present or the future?
c) Are they about things that really happened?
d) Look at the sentences below and find the verbs.

Facts
I studied maths, literature and
business studies at school.
Now I'm studying economics in Oxford.

Sadly, it's all over with Gina.
She went back to Rome last week.

Wishes
I wish I'd studied Italian. If only I'd known
what was going to happen.
I wish I was studying Italian literature.
I wish I lived in Rome.

If only she hadn't finished with me.
I wish I'd gone with her.

What happens to the verbs when you change from a fact to a wish?

Language Reference p128

2 The people in these pictures regret decisions they have made or things they have done. What do you think they regret? Write sentences beginning *I wish ...* or *If only ...* for each picture.

3 Write at least two wishes for the people in these situations.

a) I have to play tennis with Jack on Saturday. The thing is, not only is he dreadful at tennis, he's also a pain in the neck. And now Nico has asked me if I want to play with him. *I wish ...*

b) I went to see *The Texas Chain Saw Massacre* with Carmen last week, and she's had nightmares about it all week. *I wish ...*

c) Ten years ago, when I was 16, I left school and went to work in my dad's business. Now the business has gone bankrupt and I'm out of work. *If only ...*

d) I started smoking when I was a teenager. I'm on two packs a day now and I'm desperate to stop, but I just can't manage it. *If only ...*

e) We got married when we were both 18. We were in love and we thought it would last for ever. But as we've got older we've drifted apart and now we fight all the time. *I wish ...*

4 Have you made any bad decisions in your life so far? Tell your partner about them.

Language reference: I wish & if only

Wish and *if only* are two ways of talking about *unreal* situations. You can use them to express regrets about the present or past.

In *unreal* situations, the tense usually backshifts. For example:

1 Present changes to past

*I **live** in Oxford.*	→	*I wish I **lived** in Rome.*
*I'**m going** to the cinema with Pete on Saturday.*	→	*I wish I **was going** to the cinema with Miguel.*
*I **can't** stop smoking.*	→	*If only I **could** stop smoking.*

2 Past changes to past perfect

*I **studied** economics.*	→	*I wish I'**d studied** Italian literature.*
*I **went** to Scotland for my holidays.*	→	*I wish I'**d gone** to Spain.*
*I **started** smoking when I was a teenager.*	→	*If only I **hadn't started** smoking.*

See also the Language reference section about *I wish* in unit 14.

Act your age

1. Do you think there is an upper or lower age limit for:

   - getting married
   - having children
   - learning a new language
   - travelling around the world
   - worrying about how you look
   - leaving home
   - starting a new career
   - dancing to pop music in public
   - learning to ski
   - riding a motorbike
   - wearing jeans

   Discuss your answers with a partner. Are there any other activities you think have age limits?

2. Read the article and decide which statements are true for the writer.

   a) I wish I'd never met him.
   b) I should have been honest about my age.
   c) If I'd told him my age at the beginning, he might have left me.
   d) I shouldn't have told him about my disastrous existence.
   e) If I was a man, the age difference wouldn't be a problem.
   f) It's all his fault: if I hadn't met him I wouldn't have turned into an ageist and a liar.

> **Ageism**
>
> **Ageism** is prejudice against older people, for example through refusing them employment. It is a new word, following the models of racism and sexism.

Ageism turned her into a liar

For most of my life, age has seemed unimportant. My friends of both sexes have been younger, older or the same age. When I was in my early thirties I had a very enjoyable and fulfilling relationship with a man of 23. One of the most attractive men I know is in his mid fifties.

THE FIRST time I experienced a problem with age was on my fortieth birthday. Much to my surprise, it was a deeply traumatic event. Forty seemed to be so much older than 39. I used to like it when people told me I looked young for my age, but then I realised that they were just telling me how old I was. Anyway, I slowly got over the shock and tried to convince myself that life begins at 40 …

I met him playing badminton. He was impressed with my exciting lifestyle – lots of travelling and some writing. I found him fun, kind, amusing and very attractive. He's 31 and looks about 19. He has no idea how old I am.

All my life I've been totally honest. I return extra change to astonished shopkeepers, I've never travelled without a ticket and in job interviews I always come out with all the reasons why I should not be employed.

Early on in the relationship I told him the truth about my disastrous existence – my divorce, my financial difficulties, the relationship that destroyed my faith in men. I even admitted that I dye my hair. The sky did not fall in and he didn't run screaming from the house. I did tell him I'm older than he is, but something stopped me from coming clean about my actual age.

And now I'm in trouble – serious trouble. Silence has made the problem much greater. If I had told him before, it wouldn't have become such a big issue. If I had been brave enough to admit that I was 11 years older than him, I wouldn't be in this crazy situation now. I lie about jobs, years abroad and education; he wonders how I've managed to fit so much living into my life; I conveniently can't remember the music of my teenage years.

The other day, I even hid my passport under a pile of papers. I'm worried about organising a get-together with my friends in case one of them says something like, 'Doesn't she look good for her age.'

The longer I remain silent, the more likely he is to find out and I'm frightened. For once in a very long time I've found someone who makes me happy and I don't want to lose it.

I know that if I was a man, I would never have got into this mess. Eleven years' difference is nothing for a man. But it's the other way round and the world judges older women harshly, and I'm afraid he would do the same.

I have become an ageist and a liar and I have no one to blame but myself.

3 The following is a summary of the article. Put the lines of the summary in the correct order.

( ) over the shock and tried
(1) She has always had friends
( ) traumatic event. But she got
( ) to convince herself that life begins
( ) but herself for the situation she's in.
(2) of all ages. In fact, one of the most attractive
( ) clean about her age. Silence has made the problem
( ) at 40. She met him playing badminton but didn't come
( ) women so harshly. But she knows that she has no one to blame
( ) much greater and now she thinks that the longer she remains silent
( ) men she knows is in his mid fifties. Her fortieth birthday was a deeply
( ) the more likely he is to find out. She thinks it's unfair that society judges older

4 What would you do if you were the writer?

5 Write the conversation they have when she tells him the truth. Begin like this:

Him: You look worried. What's on your mind?
Her: Actually there *is* something I've been meaning to tell you.

6 52 Listen to the conversation. Did you imagine a similar situation?

7 Work in small groups and discuss these questions:

a) How old are your youngest and oldest friends?
b) Do you know any couples who have a big age difference?
c) What would you do now if you were the writer?
d) Have you ever lied about your age?
e) Can you think of any situations in which you would lie about your age?
f) What ages do you think are turning-points in life?

Close up

Unreal conditionals

1 Here are some comments the woman makes about her difficult situation. Match them to the time sequences in the box.

a) If I had told him before, it wouldn't have become such a big issue.
b) If I had been brave enough to admit that I was 11 years older than him, I wouldn't be in this crazy situation now.
c) I know that if I was a man, I would never have got into this mess.

time sequences		
present situation	→	past result
past situation	→	past result
past situation	→	present result

2 Write conditional sentences according to the prompts. Think carefully about the verb tenses.

For example:
You arrived early. I wasn't ready. → *If you hadn't arrived early, I would have been ready.*

a) I ate too much last night. I'm not feeling very well.
b) He went to university. He got a good job.
c) She's got a fast car. She got here in under two hours.
d) You only had a sandwich at lunch time. You're hungry now.
e) I didn't see you. I didn't say 'hello'.
f) There was a power cut. I lost two vital computer documents.
g) You didn't ask anyone for directions. We're lost.
h) He loves her a lot. He forgave her.

Unreal! The Conditional Game

What would you have done?

1 Read these stories and discuss what you would have done.

A I was in the supermarket yesterday and I saw this elderly woman shuffling up and down the aisles. She didn't have a trolley, and was putting her shopping straight into her basket. Anyway, I thought nothing more about it and carried on doing my shopping and when I went to queue up to pay, there she was in front of me. I watched her put one tin of cat food on the counter and pay for it, then she walked out with her basket full of unpaid shopping.

B Something awful happened to me last week. I'd invited six people round for dinner and you know how I hate cooking. Anyway, I spent all afternoon preparing the meal and actually I was quite pleased with how it turned out. I even managed to get all the vegetables ready at the same time as the meat. So, the vegetables were on the table and I just had to get the chicken out of the oven. I lifted it out and I don't know how it happened, but I dropped it on the kitchen floor and before I could pick it up, the cat had licked it. She regretted it afterwards, because she burnt her tongue.

C My friend put me in a really difficult position the other day. She'd bought this dress for a special 'do' and I don't know why she had to ask me what I thought of it. I mean, she wouldn't have bought it if she didn't like it, would she? And she paid a fortune for it. Anyway, she put it on and I immediately thought, 'No, orange is not your colour.' Not only that, but some people just haven't got the legs for short skirts. To be honest, she looked ridiculous.

D On my last birthday, my husband just gave me an envelope. I was really excited. I thought it was going to be tickets for a holiday to Egypt. He knew that it was my ambition to see the pyramids. Anyway, when I opened the envelope, there was a cheque inside for £5,000 and a little note saying, 'Happy Birthday darling. I've booked you a face-lift.'

E I had a very strange experience the other day. I was up in London for a meeting and it was lunch time. It was a lovely day, so I bought a sandwich and went for a walk. I was just on my way back to the office when I noticed a scruffy, bearded man begging in the street. I recognised him immediately. It was someone I'd been at university with, a brilliant rugby player. He'd always been a bit of a rebel, but a very clever man. We'd been very good friends, but I'd lost touch with him when we left university.

2 🔲 53 Listen and find out what the people did. Do you think they did the right thing?

Language reference: unreal conditionals

The 'if' clause
If the situation is unreal (imaginary or very improbable) we show this by backshifting the verb.

real	unreal
I'm an economist.	If I **wasn't** an economist …
	If I **was** a musician …
	If I **had** a different job …

real past	unreal past
I studied economics at university.	If I **hadn't studied** economics …
	If I'**d studied** music …
	If I **hadn't gone** to university …

The main clause
The main clause generally uses *would* or *might*.

If I **was** a musician, …
… I think I'd **be** happier.
… I'd probably **earn** less money than I do.
… I might **become** world famous.

For the past, use *would have* or *might have*.

If I'**d studied** music, …
I'**d have chosen** the violin as my instrument.
I **might have got** a job with the BBC Symphony Orchestra.

You can usually swap the two clauses round:
I'd probably have chosen the violin as my instrument if I'd studied music.

Notes: Sometimes the *if* clause is in the past and the main clause is in the present, or vice versa.

past + present
If I'**d become** a musician, …
I **would make** less money.

present + past
If I **didn't make** so much money, …
I **wouldn't have been able** to buy my Porsche, or my flat in New York.
See also units 11, 13, 14 and 15.

If you have studied the 'third conditional' (*if* + past perfect + *would* + perfect infinitive), you already know a lot about this type of sentence.

Sweet sixteen

1. Work in small groups and discuss the following questions:
   - Do you think that the age you are is a good age to be?
   - What do you think is the best age to be and why?
   - Have you ever wished you were older or younger?

Freddie (12)   **Jem** (16)   **Yvette** (21)   **Carmel** (mid thirties)

2. 🔊 54 These four people were asked the same questions. Listen to the interviews and note down their answers.

3. Match the person to the question they were asked.
   a) Do you mind if I ask you how old you are?
   b) How old are you now?
   c) You've just had an important birthday, haven't you?
   d) How old are you?

   Which is the most polite form?

Delicate questions

When you want to ask about something delicate, indirect questions are often more polite than direct questions.

For example:
Direct question	Indirect question
How old are you?	Do you mind if I ask (you) how old you are?
Have you got a girlfriend?	Do you mind if I ask (you) whether you've got a girlfriend?

Instead of *Do you mind* + present you can use *Would you mind* + past as a more formal alternative.

1. Make indirect questions from the prompts.

   Do you mind if I ask you ...
   a) where/buy/your/shirt?
   b) why/study/English?
   c) get/here/on/time?
   d) where/go/after/lesson?
   e) enjoy/this/lesson?
   f) what/do/this/evening?

   Now ask your partner the questions.

2. Work with a partner. In your country which of these questions do you not ask somebody you don't know very well?
   a) What perfume are you wearing?
   b) How much do you earn?
   c) Where did you buy your shoes?
   d) How much do you weigh?
   e) Who did you vote for in the last elections?
   f) Are you married?
   g) Is that your natural hair colour?
   h) How much did your house cost?

3. Can you think of any other 'taboo' questions? Add them to the list.

4. Work with a partner. Change the direct questions in 2 into indirect questions using *Do you mind if I ask you ...?*

5. Take it in turns to ask and answer the questions, giving a true answer or politely refusing to answer.

Taboo /təbuː/
taboos. If there is a **taboo** on a subject or activity, it is a social custom to avoid doing that activity or talking about that subject, because people find them embarrassing or offensive. *The topic of addiction remains something of a taboo.* > Also an adjective. *Cancer is a taboo subject and people are frightened or embarrassed to talk openly about it.*

LANGUAGE TOOLBOX

No, I don't mind.
No, not at all.
I'd rather not say.
I'd rather not answer that.
Yes, I do mind, actually.

16 Review 2

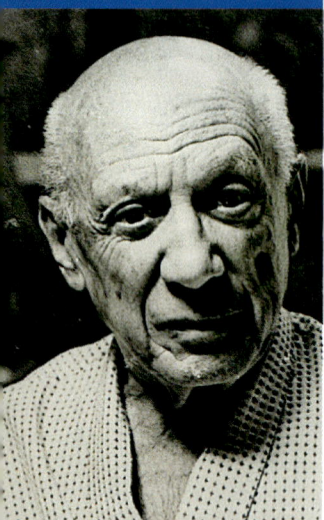
Pablo Picasso

Who said what?

1 Here are some quotes by well-known people. Match the quote to the person.

a) 'The Beatles are more popular than Jesus Christ.'
b) 'In the future, everyone will be famous for fifteen minutes.'
c) 'Rock 'n' roll has no future.'
d) 'Painting a picture is either easy or impossible.'
e) 'England is a nation of shopkeepers.'
f) 'Words are the most powerful drug used by mankind.'
g) 'I love Mickey Mouse more than any woman I've ever known.'
h) 'I've never hated a man enough to give diamonds back.'
i) 'There's no such thing as a bad Picasso.'
j) 'I don't want to belong to any club that will accept me as a member.'
k) 'I never think about the future.'
l) 'There is no sin except stupidity.'

Walt Disney   Salvador Dali   Groucho Marx   Pablo Picasso   Oscar Wilde
Zsa Zsa Gabor   Albert Einstein   Rudyard Kipling   Napoleon Bonaparte
Andy Warhol   Frank Sinatra   John Lennon

Check your answers on page 140.

Groucho Marx

2 Report the quotes in 1.

For example:
John Lennon once said the Beatles were more popular than Jesus Christ.

3 If you could be famous for 15 minutes, as the quote in 1 suggests, what would you like it to be for? Think of three things.

For example:
I'd like to score the winning goal in a World Cup final.

I wish ...

1 Read these three wishes. Then add one of your own.

I wish there were more hours in the day. (Sue)

I wish I'd gone up Mount Fuji when I was in Japan. (Vaughan)

I wish I could play the piano. (Jon)

Wish tree
A tradition in Japan is to write a wish on a piece of paper and then tie it to a tree.

2 Collect your classmates' wishes and write them down.

3 What are the most common wishes in your class? What are the most unusual wishes?

Zsa Zsa Gabor

In your dreams

Conditionals

1 Work in small groups and discuss these questions.

If you …
a) could be anywhere in the world for the next 24 hours, where would you go?
b) were on a five year space mission and could take one of your possessions what would it be?
c) could have the answer to any one question, what would you want to know?
d) could change one thing about your country, what would it be?
e) could relive one week of your life, which week would it be?
f) could have one day with someone from history, who would it be?
g) won £1 million on the lottery next week, what would you do with the money?
h) could change sex for one year, what would you do with the time?
i) could be transported into the future, when and where would you like to go to?
j) could be any animal, what would you be?

2 Report three interesting things from your discussions to the class.

The real you

Conditionals

1 Answer the questionnaire below.

DISCOVER THE REAL YOU!

SECTION 1	SECTION 2	SECTION 3	SECTION 4
1 If you are with a group of people, do you generally … a) like to have the whole group as your audience? b) talk with one person at a time?	1 Would you say you usually get on better with … a) reliable, steady people? b) unpredictable, spontaneous people?	1 Would you be happier if you were known as … a) a person who is always reasonable? b) a person who is always compassionate?	1 If you go somewhere for the day, do you usually … a) plan what you will do and when you'll do it? b) just go?
2 Do you tend to have … a) broad friendships with a lot of people? b) deep friendships with a few people?	2 If you were a teacher, would you rather teach … a) fact-based courses? b) courses involving theory?	2 What is more important, someone's … a) rights? b) feelings?	2 When you have a special job to do, do you … a) organise it carefully before you start? b) find out what is necessary as you go along?
3 If there is some gossip about one of your friends, will you usually be … a) one of the first to hear about it? b) one of the last to find out what's going on?	3 If you could choose, would you prefer to be … a) practical and good at fixing things? b) creative and artistic?	3 Would you say you more often let … a) your head rule your heart? b) your heart rule your head?	3 If you had been asked last Saturday morning what you were going to do that day, would you have … a) known pretty well? b) had no idea?
4 Would you say you … a) can be enthusiastic about most things if necessary? b) can only be enthusiastic about things of particular importance to you?	4 Would you say you are … a) conventional? b) original?	4 Given the choice, would you rather work for someone who is … a) always fair? b) always kind?	4 Do you generally do things at the last minute? a) sometimes b) often
5 If you could choose, would you rather things around you were … a) busy? b) quiet?	5 Which of these words do you prefer? a) certainty b) possibility	5 Which of these words do you prefer? a) determined b) devoted	5 Would you say the routine parts of your day are … a) restful? b) boring?

2 Work with a partner. Exchange questionnaires and turn to page 142 to find out what it all means. Is the description an accurate summary of them?

I predict ...

will 1 Here are some predictions about the future made by some of our students. Put the verb in brackets into an appropriate future form. Then write four predictions of your own.

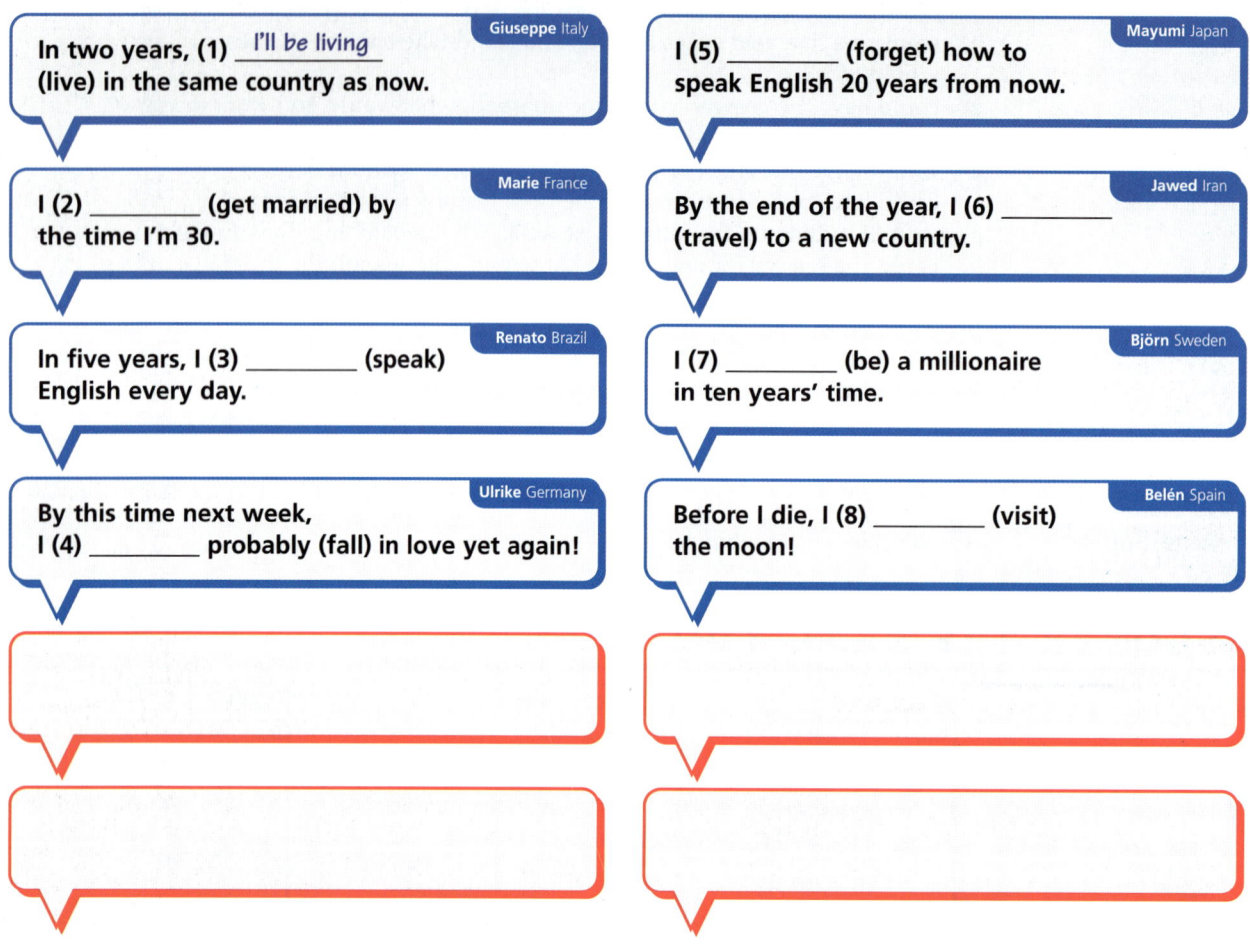

- In two years, (1) _I'll be living_ (live) in the same country as now. — Giuseppe Italy
- I (2) _____ (get married) by the time I'm 30. — Marie France
- In five years, I (3) _____ (speak) English every day. — Renato Brazil
- By this time next week, I (4) _____ probably (fall) in love yet again! — Ulrike Germany
- I (5) _____ (forget) how to speak English 20 years from now. — Mayumi Japan
- By the end of the year, I (6) _____ (travel) to a new country. — Jawed Iran
- I (7) _____ (be) a millionaire in ten years' time. — Björn Sweden
- Before I die, I (8) _____ (visit) the moon! — Belén Spain

2 Interview a classmate to find out whether the statements in 1 are true or false for him or her. Do a class survey.

For example:
Eight people in our class think they'll be living in the same country as now in two years.

The world of languages

Questions 1 Work with a partner and discuss the following questions:

a) When was language first written down?
b) When was the first alphabet developed?
c) How many languages are there in the world?
d) Which are the five most spoken languages in the world?
e) How many words are there in English?
f) Which are the most common words in English?
g) Which languages do the words *ketchup* and *shampoo* originally come from?
h) Which country has got 13 languages on its bank notes?

2 ▶ 55 You are going to hear Kim Thomas, a professor of linguistics, being interviewed. Listen and check your answers to the questions in 1.

3 Listen again. Write five more questions about the interview. Ask some classmates your questions.

For example:
Who were the first people to write down their language?

UNIT 16 *Review 2*

Doing the right thing

Modals   **1**   Work with a partner and do the following quiz.

How would you cope around the world?

Are the following statements TRUE or FALSE?

1. You mustn't give tips in India. ● T ● F
2. In the UK, you don't have to carry ID with you. ● T ● F
3. In Holland, friends are supposed to kiss each other four times when saying hello and goodbye. ● T ● F
4. You should never give a clock as a gift in China. ● T ● F
5. In Japan, you can't vote until you are 19. ● T ● F
6. You can drive as fast as you want in Germany. ● T ● F
7. In Britain, people are expected to take turns to buy drinks in a pub. ● T ● F
8. In Zimbabwe, you can pay fines with flowers. ● T ● F
9. In Spain, children under 16 aren't allowed into bars. ● T ● F
10. You are expected to take some cheese with you when you are invited to dinner in France. ● T ● F
11. In Japan, you shouldn't blow your nose in public. ● T ● F
12. When giving flowers in Germany, you should give an even number. ● T ● F
13. You have to turn out to vote in Australia. ● T ● F
14. In the USA, you can drive a car in most states when you're 15. ● T ● F
15. You must eat with your left hand in Sudan. ● T ● F
16. In Sweden, you aren't allowed to smoke until you are 16. ● T ● F
17. In the UK, you must never turn your back on a picture of the Queen. ● T ● F
18. You don't have to wear a motorcycle helmet in Italy. ● T ● F
19. In Finland you can't buy alcohol in a supermarket. ● T ● F
20. In Saudi Arabia, it's normal for shops to close for about 15 minutes four times a day. ● T ● F

Check your answers on page 142.

2   Can you think of any rules in your country? What would a visitor need to know?

Review 2   UNIT 16

Greetings from Vietnam

General revision Read the letter to Marcella. Choose the correct alternative. In some cases both alternatives are possible.

Dear Marcella,

Well, at last here we are in Vietnam and we (1) **have/'re having** an absolutely (2) **good/wonderful** time. We're now in a (3) **beautiful, small/small, beautiful** market town in the mountains in the very north of the country. The town is at the end of a steep valley and there are the most (4) **amazing/amazed** terraces as far as the eye can see. Miguel (5) **said me/said** he thought they (6) **were/are** the most spectacular views he (7) **had/has** ever seen. I've taken so (8) **much/many** photos since we (9) **are/'ve been** here. I think I (10) **'ve/'d** only taken about a dozen in total before we (11) **arrived/had arrived** here in Sapa. We (12) **go/'ve been** for a long walk every day so far. In the evenings, we're pretty (13) **exhausting/exhausted** and we just have a meal – Vietnamese food is (14) **very/absolutely** great – and a beer or two before bed.

Yesterday, Stefan had his hair cut by the woman (15) **which/who** owns the hotel (16) **which/where** we're staying in. He says he (17) **likes/liked** it, but he (18) **mustn't/can't** have looked in a mirror! It looks awful!

We think we might (19) **to stay/stay** here for a (20) **few/little** more days before heading back south. With a bit of luck, this time next week, we'll (21) **have left/be leaving** the mountains behind us and we'll (22) **lie/be lying** on a deserted, sandy beach! I'm really looking forward to (23) **do/doing** nothing for (24) **a few/few** days! We really wish you (25) **would be/were** here with us. If you (26) **are/were**, you (27) **'d/'ll** really love it! If only you (28) **didn't break/hadn't broken** your arm! Never mind, I suppose things (29) **might/can** have been a lot worse! Anyway, I hope it (30) **gets/is getting** better.

So, how are things back home? Miguel and Stefan want to know how (31) **are you/you are** coping without (32) **them/they**! We're all expecting (33) **lots of/much** juicy gossip when we (34) **'ll get/get** back next month!

It's late, so (35) **I'll finish/am finishing** now. (36) **Say/Tell** Juliette we'll write (37) **her/to her** soon. Take care and have fun!

Lots of love,

Virginia and Lena xxxxxxxx

Additional material

6 News

The passive voice, 6

Student A

Here are your three stories. Don't show them to anyone.

1. (1) A dramatic chase involved police cars (2) after somebody spotted a notice in the back window of a car (3) saying 'Help us, we have been kidnapped.' (4) It had been put there by four unhappy children (5) who didn't want to go on holiday to Bournemouth with their parents.

2. (1) An 85-year-old man was asked to leave the M4 motorway by the police (2) because he was riding in a wheelchair. (3) His 65-year-old son was pushing the wheelchair.

3. (1) After spending many hours practising birdcalls at home, (2) some woods were gone into by French ornithologist Marius Giraud (3) to try them out (4) and was shot dead by a hunter.

3 Dating

Twenty-first century dating, 2

Student A

Read about couple 1.
When you've finished reading, close your book and tell Student B about the couple.

Couple 1

I've finally found the man of my dreams. We have so much in common, we laugh at the same things and talk for hours. There's only one problem. We've never met. Tom lives in the US. I live in Ireland. We met on the Net.

I wasn't looking for Mr Right, I was just hoping to chat to some interesting people. The American singles dating site didn't charge a fee so I filled in a form with my likes and dislikes and a short paragraph about myself. By the end of the week I had about 25 responses. Over the next five months, I went on eight dates with men I met on the Net. One I dated for about two months, others I saw a couple of times before I realised there was no real spark. Then, two months ago, just as I was about to take my details off the Net, I received an e-mail from a guy in America called Tom. His note was amusing and he sounded interesting so I decided to write back.

Soon I found myself rushing back home after work to check my e-mails. Tom made me laugh, he challenged my opinions. We talked about everything. My friends weren't particularly impressed when I told them about him, but I knew this one was different.

We exchanged pictures by e-mail and we liked what we saw, but at this stage looks didn't matter. Then Tom and I had what we consider our first 'date'. We spoke for 11 hours and that phone call changed the course of our relationship. We've decided to meet.

7 Party

Phrasal verbs, 4

Call My Bluff

Call my bluff was a popular TV game in the UK for many years. The aim of the game is for teams to guess the correct meaning of words.

Team A

1. Invent two false definitions for each of the phrasal verbs below:

   get on. If you *get on* with someone, you like them and have a friendly relationship with them.
   go round with. You regularly meet or go to different places with the same group of people.

   run out of. If you *run out of* something you no longer have any of it left. *We've run out of milk. Can you buy some at the supermarket?*
   take in. If you *take someone in* you allow someone to stay in your house or country, especially when they are homeless or in trouble.

2. Read out your three definitions (one true, two false) for the first phrasal verb. Team B guess which definition is correct. If they guess correctly, they get a point. If they guess incorrectly, you get a point.

3. Now listen to Team B's definitions and guess the correct one. Take turns. The winning team is the team with the most points.

4. If you want to continue the game, here is an extra set of phrasal verbs:

   get away. To leave a place or a person's company. *I'm sorry I'm late. I couldn't get away from the office until now.*
   put up with (something or someone). To tolerate or accept something or someone. *I can't put up with this noise anymore.*

   run into. If you *run into* (someone), you meet someone unexpectedly. *I ran into Jim at the station.*
   turn up. To arrive, often unexpectedly or after you have been waiting a long time. *After waiting for 50 minutes the bus finally turned up.*

8 Review 1
Sound & vision, 2

16 Review 2
Who said what?, 1

Answers

a) John Lennon   b) Andy Warhol   c) Frank Sinatra
d) Salvador Dali   e) Napoleon Bonaparte
f) Rudyard Kipling   g) Walt Disney   h) Zsa Zsa Gabor
i) Pablo Picasso   j) Groucho Marx   k) Albert Einstein
l) Oscar Wilde

11 Journey
Conrad's round-the-world trip, 3

Answers

Photo 1 Patagonia, Argentina
Photo 2 The Basque country, Spain
Photo 3 Lake Como, Italy
Photo 4 New Delhi, India
Photo 5 Fiji
Photo 6 Petra, Jordan

3 Dating
Twenty-first century dating, 2

Student B

Read about couple 2.
When you've finished reading, close your book and tell Student A about the couple.

Couple 2

It was <u>love</u> at first <u>sight</u> for Joel Emerson and Lisa Bunyan, which was lucky because they met for the first time on their wedding day!
As a publicity stunt, a local Australian radio station ran a seven-week competition which they called 'Two Strangers and a Wedding'. The radio station voted Joel Emerson, 24 and a marketing consultant, the 'most eligible bachelor'. Lisa Bunyan, 22, who works at a management training centre, was one of 300 <u>single</u> women who rushed to the phone to offer herself as his bride.
The only direct contact they had before their wedding day was when Joel <u>proposed</u> over the telephone on the radio. An estimated 50,000 listeners witnessed the romantic (but not particularly intimate) moment when Lisa said 'yes'.
The <u>groom</u>'s mother was not amused and told a local newspaper that she was shocked and appalled. As the couple left for their <u>honeymoon</u> in Paris, they told the same newspaper, 'We know that we're doing the right thing.'

1 Friends
Noughts & Crosses, 1

Team A

FACTS FOR QUIZ QUESTIONS

Choose ten facts and write questions for them.

1. A spider has got eight legs.
2. Greenland is the largest island in the world.
3. The Atlas mountains are in north Africa.
4. There are 11 players in a cricket team.
5. The Russian alphabet uses the Cyrillic script.
6. The capital of Colombia is Bogota.
7. Tutankhamen was a king of Egypt.
8. Ringo was the smallest Beatle.
9. Margaret Thatcher was the first woman prime minister of England.
10. Neil Armstrong was the first man on the moon.
11. The Black Forest is in Germany.
12. Hollywood is in Los Angeles, California.
13. Alaska is the largest state in the USA.
14. Leonardo da Vinci painted the *Mona Lisa (La Giaconda)*.
15. St Valentine's Day is on 14th February.
16. The capital of Algeria is Algiers.
17. Schipol Airport is in Amsterdam.

3 Dating

Dream date. Lexis, 3

Calculating your *Ki* Astrology sign.

Think of your year of birth. The Chinese year runs from February to February, so anyone born between 1st January and 3rd February needs to count the previous year as their year of birth.

Add up the last two numbers of your year of birth. For example, if you were born in 1970, add seven to zero (7 + 0) to get seven. If you were born in 1985, add eight to five (8 + 5) to get thirteen.

If the number you have is 9 or less, subtract it from 10 to find your Ki sign. For example, for a person born in 1970, 10 − 7 = 3.

If the number you have is 10 or more, add up the two digits. For example, with thirteen add one and three to get four (1 + 3 = 4). Then subtract the new number from 10 to find your Ki sign. For example, for a person born in 1985, 10 − 4 = 6.

13 Communication

What do men and women really think?, 2

Answers

(1) women (2) men (3) men (4) women
(5) women (6) men (7) women (8) men
(9) women (10) men (11) men (12) women
(13) men (14) women (15) men (16) women
(17) men (18) men (19) women (20) men
(21) women (22) women (23) men

1 Friends

You've got a friend. Lexis, 3

Answers

a) The Beatles, *I Wanna Hold Your Hand*
b) Lighthouse Family, *Ocean Drive*
c) Bob Dylan, *It Ain't Me Babe*
d) All Saints, *Never Ever*
e) The Rolling Stones, *Satisfaction*
f) Oasis, *Roll With It*

6 News

The passive voice, 6

Student B

Here are your three stories. Don't show them to anyone.

1. (1) Police cars were involved in a dramatic chase (2) after a notice was spotted in the back window of a car (3) saying 'Help us, somebody has kidnapped us.' (4) Four unhappy children had put it there (5) who didn't want to be taken on holiday to Bournemouth by their parents.

2. (1) The police asked an 85-year-old man in a wheelchair to leave the M4 motorway (2) because a wheelchair was being ridden in by him. (3) The wheelchair was being pushed by his 65-year-old son.

3. (1) After many hours had been spent by him practising birdcalls at home, (2) French ornithologist Marius Giraud went into some woods (3) for them to be tried out (4) and a hunter shot him dead.

10 Time

To whom it may concern, 6

```
                          1566b 49th East Street
                          Santa Barbara, CA

Worldwide Airlines Inc
PO Box 2983
Chicago

5th February 2000

Dear Sir or Madam,

Application for the post of flight
attendant

I am writing in response to your
advertisement in the Morning Post and
would like to apply for the position of
flight attendant.

I am 21 years old, and I have just
graduated from university. I enclose my
curriculum vitae for your attention and I
would be pleased to attend an interview at
any time convenient to you.

I would be grateful if you could send me
an application form and some additional
information about the job.

I look forward to hearing from you.

Yours faithfully,

Anthony Clifford

Anthony Clifford
```

16 Review 2

The real you

1 Find out about your classmate.

SECTION 1	SECTION 2	SECTION 3	SECTION 4
If you have scored mostly As, you are an extrovert.	If you have scored mostly As, you are sensitive.	If you have scored mostly As, you are intellectual.	If you have scored mostly As, you evaluate.
If you have scored mostly Bs, you are an introvert.	If you have scored mostly Bs, you are instinctive.	If you have scored mostly Bs, you are emotional.	If you have scored mostly Bs, you observe.

2 Find your classmate in the table.

BAAA	Likes to take responsibility and organise things. Orderly, duty-bound, systematic, thorough.
BABA	Hardworking, meticulous, patient, responsible. Gives stability to people and projects.
BAAB	Onlooker. Quietly observing and analysing life. Independent, logical, realistic.
BABB	Retiring, sensitive, caring, gentle. Dislikes disagreement and does not force opinions on others.
BBBA	Individualistic, intense. Determined and committed to their ideals, principles and work.
BBAA	Has great drive for their own ideas and interests. Sceptical and critical of others. Stubborn.
BBBB	Reserved, curious and reticent until they know someone well. Warm, loyal, enthusiastic.
BBAB	Logical, analytical, precise, likes solving problems. Scientific interests. Doesn't like small talk.
AAAB	Practical, mechanically-minded, versatile, tolerant. Good at on-the-spot problem solving.
AABB	Outgoing, sociable, friendly, enjoys everything. Sporty and active. Has a lot of common sense.
AAAA	Likes to organise and control. Direct, impersonal, matter-of-fact, business-minded, systematic.
AABA	Warm-hearted, helpful, co-operative, hard-working, talkative. Needs harmony around them.
ABBB	Able to do almost anything if interested. High-spirited, imaginative, spontaneous, quick-thinking.
ABAB	Quick, outspoken, resourceful, clever. Likes to play 'devil's advocate'. Doesn't like routine.
ADDA	Concerned about what others think. Considerate, sympathetic, diplomatic, supportive.
ABAA	Frank, fair, tough, decisive. Intelligent, knowledgeable, confident. Good at reasoning

7 Party

Parties, 5

Are you a party animal or a party pooper?

KEY
1 a = 1 b = 2 c = 3
2 a = 2 b = 3 c = 1
3 a = 1 b = 3 c = 2
4 a = 3 b = 1 c = 1
5 a = 2 b = 1 c = 3
6 a = 3 b = 2 c = 1

What it means
- If you scored between 6 and 10: You are definitely the life and soul of any party.
- If you scored between 11 and 14: You could afford to let your hair down occasionally.
- If you scored between 15 and 18: You obviously like the quiet life – but you don't have to take everything so seriously!

11 Journey

Coast to coast, 3

He removed the seat. On the underside was the inscription:

'To Elvis, love James Dean.'

16 Review 2

Doing the right thing

Answers	What it means
(1) F (2) T (3) F – it's three times (4) T (5) F (6) T (7) T (8) F – but you can with animals (9) F (10) F (11) T (12) F – except on someone's 20th birthday when you give them 20 (13) T (14) F – in most states it's sixteen (15) F (16) F (17) F (18) F (19) F (20) T	If you scored between 15 and 20: you're either extremely well-travelled or extremely intuitive. You'll have no problems wherever you go. If you scored between 10 and 15: you should be OK in most situations, but be careful! If you scored between 5 and 10: you might make life difficult for yourself from time to time, but you'll survive. If you scored between 0 and 5: don't go anywhere without a good friend!

1 Friends

Noughts & Crosses, 1

Team B

FACTS FOR QUIZ QUESTIONS:

Choose ten facts and write questions for them.

1. JF Kennedy was assassinated in Dallas.
2. An insect has got six legs.
3. The longest river in Europe is the Volga.
4. Picasso was from Spain.
5. Madonna's first name is 'Madonna'.
6. The last president of the USSR was Mikhail Gorbachev.
7. Yuri Gagarin was the first man in space.
8. The first modern Olympic Games were in Athens.
9. Patagonia is in Argentina.
10. Roger Moore was the third James Bond.
11. Mount Etna is in Sicily.
12. Quito is the capital of Ecuador.
13. Mickey Mouse has got four fingers.
14. The longest river in the world is the Nile.
15. The ancient city of Petra is in Jordan.
16. Riyadh is the capital of Saudi Arabia.
17. Uruguay were the first country to win the World Cup.

6 News

The passive voice, 6

Student C

You are the editor for your group. You will need a pen and a piece of paper.

Explain the task to your partners.

1. Ask your partners to read their stories aloud.
2. Discuss the two versions and decide together which are the best parts from each one. Sometimes the passive is better, sometimes the active is better, and sometimes it doesn't matter.
3. Ask your partners to dictate the best parts to you and write the final versions of the three stories.
4. When you have finished, think of a headline for each story.

3 Dating

A boyfriend's worst nightmare, 3

'Pleased to meet you,' I lied.
'Hi, I'm Eddie,' he said, 'and this is my fiancée, Sarah. We got engaged last week.'
I mumbled something and shook both their hands. At that moment, an enormous weight was lifted from my mind. Eddie is in fact a great guy and we get on really well together. But best of all, he's completely devoted to his girlfriend.

7 Party

Phrasal verbs, 4

Call My Bluff

Call My Bluff was a popular TV game in the UK for many years. The aim of the game is for teams to guess the correct meaning of words.

Team B

1. Invent two false definitions for each of the phrasal verbs below:

cut down on. If you *cut down on* something you consume or do less of it.
get down. If something or someone *gets you down* it makes you unhappy.

let down. If you *let* someone *down* you disappoint them.
take after. If you *take after* a member of your family, you resemble them in your appearance, your behaviour, or your character.

2. Read out your three definitions (one true, two false) for the first phrasal verb. Team A guess which definition is correct. If they guess correctly, they get a point. If they guess incorrectly, you get a point.

3. Now listen to Team A's definitions and guess the correct one. Take turns. The winning team is the team with the most points.

4. If you want to continue the game, here is an extra set of phrasal verbs:

get over. To recover from an unpleasant experience or an illness.
put off. If you *put* something *off* you delay doing it. *The match was put off for a week because of the heavy rain.*

take up. To start a hobby or an activity. *I've taken up scuba-diving.*
turn down. If you *turn down* a person or their request or offer, you refuse their request or offer.

Verb structures

Basic structures

ASPECT	VOICE	TENSES		MODALS
		Present	Past	*will (would, must ...)*
simple	active	He **writes** letters.	He **wrote** letters.	He **will write** letters.
	passive	Letters **are written**.	Letters **were written**.	Letters **will be written**.
continuous	active	He **is writing** letters.	He **was writing** letters.	He **will be writing** letters.
	passive	Letters **are being written**.	Letters **were being written**.	Letters **will be being written**.*
perfect	active	He **has written** letters.	He **had written** letters.	He **will have written** letters.
	passive	Letters **have been written**.	Letters **had been written**.	Letters **will have been written**.

* rarer structure

Present simple
See units 1 and 2.

Affirmative	Negative	Question
I/You/We/They **write**.	I/You/We/They **don't (do not) write**.	**Do** I/you/we/they **write**?
He/She/It **writes**.	He/She/It **doesn't (does not) write**.	**Does** he/she/it **write**?

Present continuous
See units 1, 2 and 7.

Affirmative	Negative	Question
I**'m (am) writing**.	I**'m not (am not) writing**.	**Am** I **writing**?
You/We/They**'re (are) writing**.	You/We/They**'re not/aren't (are not) writing**.	**Are** you/we/they **writing**?
He/She/It**'s (is) writing**.	He/She/It **isn't (is not) writing**.	**Is** he/she/it **writing**?

Present perfect
See units 1, 2, 3 and 4.

Affirmative	Negative	Question
I/You/We/They**'ve (have) written**.	I/You/We/They **haven't (have not) written**.	**Have** I/you/we/they **written**?
He/She/It**'s (has) written**.	He/She/It **hasn't (has not) written**.	**Has** he/she/it **written**?

Note: see list of irregular verbs on page 147.

Past simple
See units 1, 3 and 4.

Affirmative	Negative	Question
I/You/He/She/It/We/They **wrote**.	I/You/He/She/It/We/They **didn't (did not) write**.	**Did** I/you/he/she/it/we/they **write**?

Note: see list of irregular verbs on page 147.

Past continuous
See units 1 and 4.

Affirmative	Negative	Question
I/He/She/It **was writing**.	I/He/She/It **wasn't (was not) writing**.	**Was** I/he/she/it **writing**?
You/We/They **were writing**.	You/We/They **weren't (were not) writing**.	**Were** you/we/they **writing**?

Past perfect
See units 1 and 11.

Affirmative	Negative	Question
I/You/He/She/It/We/They**'d (had) written**.	I/You/He/She/It/We/They **hadn't (had not) written**.	**Had** I/you/he/she/it/we/they **written**?

Note: see list of irregular verbs on page 147.

Future forms
Will
See units 7 and 10.

Affirmative	Negative	Question
Simple		
I/You/He/She/It/We/They **will write**.	I/You/He/She/It/We/They **won't write**.	**Will** I/you/he/she/it/we/they **write**?
Continuous		
I/You/He/She/It/We/They **will be writing**.	I/You/He/She/It/We/They **won't be writing**.	**Will** I/you/he/she/it/we/they **be writing**?
Perfect		
I/You/He/She/It/We/They **will have written**.	I/You/He/She/It/We/They **won't have written**.	**Will** I/you/he/she/it/we/they **have written**?

Future (be) going to
See unit 7.

Affirmative	Negative	Question
I'm (am) going to write.	I'm not (am not) going to write.	Am I going to write?
You/We/They're (are) going to write.	You/We/They 're not/aren't (are not) going to write.	Are you/we/they going to write?
He/She/It's (is) going to write.	He/She/It isn't (is not) going to write.	Is he/she/it going to write?

Present continuous for future
See unit 7.

Modals

A modal verb has the same forms in all persons.
For example:
I/You/He/She/It/We/They **can come**.

Affirmative	Negative	Question
Can: see units 1, 10 and 11.		
I **can** come.	I **can't (cannot)** come.	**Can** I come?
Could: see units 1 and 11.		
I **could** come.	I **couldn't (could not)** come.	**Could** I come?
Must: see units 1, 10 and 11.		
I **must** come.	I **mustn't (must not)** come.	**Must** I come?
May: see units 1 and 11.		
I **may** come.	I **may not** come.	**May** I come?
Might: see unit 1		
I **might** come.	I **mightn't (might not)** come.	**Might** I come?
Shall: see unit 1.		
I'**ll (shall)** come.	I **shan't (shall not)** come.	**Shall** I come?
Shall is usually only used with questions in the first person (I and we).		
Should: see units 1 and 10.		
I **should** come.	I **shouldn't (should not)** come.	**Should** I come?
Will: see units 1, 7, 9, 10 and 13.		
I'**ll (will)** come.	I **won't (will not)** come.	**Will** I come?
Would: see units 1, 5, 11, 14 and 15.		
I'**d (would)** come.	I **wouldn't (would not)** come.	**Would** I come?

Reported speech with backshift
See unit 9.

Present		
'I **write**.'		he **wrote**.
'I'm **writing**.'	He said/told me …	he **was writing**.
'I've **written**.'		he **had written**.

Past		
'I **have written**.'		he **had written**.
'I **was writing**.'	He said/told me …	he **had been writing**.

Modals		
'I **will/would**.'		he **would**.
'I **can/could**.'	He said/told me …	he **could**.
'I **must**.'		he **had to**. *

Must has no past form. The practical solution is often to use *had to*.

Questions		
'**Do** you **work** here?'		if I **worked** there.
'When **are** you **leaving**?'	He asked me …	when I **was leaving**.
'**Have** you **been** to Istanbul?'		if I **had been** to Istanbul.

Imperative		
'**Come** to my office.'	He told me …	**to come** to his office.

Real conditionals
See unit 13.

If clause	Main clause
If you **have** any problems,	**call** me. I'**ll help** you.
If you **aren't going to** the theatre,	**can** I have your ticket? **do** you **want** to come out for a meal?
If you'**ve finished** your work,	you **can go** home. **go** and help Annie.

Unreal conditionals
See units 14 and 15.

If clause	Main clause
If you **were** better organised,	you **wouldn't have** so many problems. you **wouldn't have had** that problem yesterday.
If I'**d known** earlier,	I **wouldn't be** in this situation now. I **could have done** something about it.

I wish …
See units 14 and 15.

Fact	Wish
I'**m not** rich.	I **wish** I **was/were** rich.
I **didn't study** hard at school.	I **wish** I'**d (had) studied** harder at school.

VERB STRUCTURES

Grammar glossary

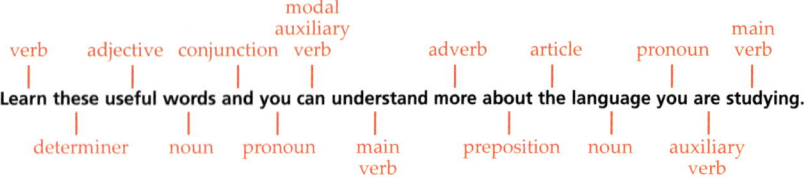

Learn these useful words and you can understand more about the language you are studying.

Agents are people or things that perform an action in a passive sentence.
For example: *He was brought up by his grandparents.*

Backshift is when a verb moves 'one tense back' in a conditional clause or reported statement.
For example: *'I can't come.'* → *He said he couldn't come.*

Clauses are groups of words containing a verb.
For example: *He said* (main clause) *that he'll be late.* (subordinate clause)
NB: subordinate clauses are introduced by conjunctions.

Collocations refer to words that frequently occur together.
For example: *Common sense … Get on well … Merry Christmas.*

Complements refer to adjective or noun phrases which give more information about the subject of a clause.
For example: *She was very happy … It's my fault … I feel a complete idiot.*
NB: usually after verbs like *be, seem, feel*.

Expressions are groups of words that belong together where the words and word order never or rarely change.
For example: *black and white … That reminds me, I must buy some toothpaste … How do you do?*

Objects usually come after the verb and show who or what is affected by the verb.
For example: *She closed the window … My neighbour hates me … I've made a cup of tea.*
NB: some verbs take a direct object (DO) and indirect object (IO).
For example: *She gave him (IO) a kiss (DO) … He sent her (IO) some flowers (DO) … I teach students (IO) English (DO).*

Partitives used with *of* can make uncountable nouns countable.
For example: *a litre of petrol … a piece of advice … an item of news.*

Relative clauses can be either defining or non-defining. A defining relative clause is necessary to identify the person or thing being talked about in the main clause.
For example: *The people who live next door have got three kids.*
A non-defining relative clause is not necessary for identification and just gives extra information.
For example: *The Smiths, who have got three children, live next door.*
NB: relative clauses are usually introduced by relative pronouns *who, that* or *which* or by relative adverbs *whose, when, where, why.*

Subjects usually come before the verb and refer to the main person or thing you are talking about.
For example: *Money doesn't grow on trees … My tailor is rich … The biggest rock and roll group in the world have started their world tour.*

Phonetic symbols

VOWELS AND DIPHTHONGS

/ɪ/	big fish	/bɪg fɪʃ/
/iː/	green beans	/griːn biːnz/
/ʊ/	should look	/ʃʊd lʊk/
/uː/	blue moon	/bluː muːn/
/e/	ten eggs	/ten egz/
/ə/	about mother	/əbaʊt mʌðə/
/ɜː/	learn words	/lɜːn wɜːdz/
/ɔː/	short talk	/ʃɔːt tɔːk/
/æ/	fat cat	/fæt kæt/
/ʌ/	must come	/mʌst kʌm/
/ɑː/	calm start	/kɑːm stɑːt/
/ɒ/	hot spot	/hɒt spɒt/
/ɪə/	ear	/ɪə/
/eɪ/	face	/feɪs/
/ʊə/	pure	/pjʊər/
/ɔɪ/	boy	/bɔɪ/
/əʊ/	nose	/nəʊz/
/eə/	hair	/heə/
/aɪ/	eye	/aɪ/
/aʊ/	mouth	/maʊθ/

CONSONANTS

/p/	pen	/pen/
/b/	bad	/bæd/
/t/	tea	/tiː/
/d/	dog	/dɒg/
/tʃ/	church	/tʃɜːtʃ/
/dʒ/	jazz	/dʒæz/
/k/	cost	/kɒst/
/g/	girl	/gɜːl/
/f/	far	/fɑːr/
/v/	voice	/vɔɪs/
/θ/	thin	/θɪn/
/ð/	then	/ðen/
/s/	snake	/sneɪk/
/z/	noise	/nɔɪz/
/ʃ/	shop	/ʃɒp/
/ʒ/	measure	/meʒər/
/m/	make	/meɪk/
/n/	nine	/naɪn/
/ŋ/	sing	/sɪŋ/
/h/	house	/haʊs/
/l/	leg	/leg/
/r/	red	/red/
/w/	wet	/wet/
/j/	yes	/jes/

STRESS

In this book, word stress is shown by underlining the stressed syllable.
For example: water /wɔːtər/; result /rɪsʌlt/; disappointing /dɪsəpɔɪntɪŋ/

LETTERS OF THE ALPHABET

/eɪ/	/iː/	/e/	/aɪ/	/əʊ/	/uː/	/ɑː/
Aa	Bb	Ff	Ii	Oo	Qq	Rr
Hh	Cc	Ll	Yy		Uu	
Jj	Dd	Mm			Ww	
Kk	Ee	Nn				
	Gg	Ss				
	Pp	Xx				
	Tt	Zz				
	Vv					

Irregular verbs

Infinitive	Past simple	Past participle
be	was/were	been
beat	beat	beaten
become	became	become
begin	began	begun
bend	bent	bent
bet	bet	bet
bite	bit	bitten
blow	blew	blown
break	broke	broken
bring	brought	brought
build	built	built
burn	burnt/burned	burnt/burned
burst	burst	burst
buy	bought	bought
can	could	(been able)
catch	caught	caught
choose	chose	chosen
come	came	come
cost	cost	cost
cut	cut	cut
deal	dealt	dealt
do	did	done
draw	drew	drawn
dream	dreamt/dreamed	dreamt/dreamed
drink	drank	drunk
drive	drove	driven
eat	ate	eaten
fall	fell	fallen
feed	fed	fed
feel	felt	felt
fight	fought	fought
find	found	found
fly	flew	flown
forget	forgot	forgotten
forgive	forgave	forgiven
freeze	froze	frozen
get	got	got
give	gave	given
go	went	gone/been
grow	grew	grown
hang	hung/hanged	hung/hanged
have	had	had
hear	heard	heard
hide	hid	hidden
hit	hit	hit
hold	held	held
hurt	hurt	hurt
keep	kept	kept
kneel	knelt/kneeled	knelt/kneeled
know	knew	known
lay	laid	laid
lead	led	led
learn	learnt/learned	learnt/learned
leave	left	left
lend	lent	lent
let	let	let
lie	lay/lied	lied/lain
light	lit/lighted	lit/lighted
lose	lost	lost
make	made	made
mean	meant	meant
meet	met	met
must	had to	(had to)
pay	paid	paid
put	put	put
read	read /red/	read /red/
ride	rode	ridden
ring	rang	rung
rise	rose	risen
run	ran	run
say	said	said
see	saw	seen
sell	sold	sold
send	sent	sent
set	set	set
shake	shook	shaken
shine	shone	shone
shoot	shot	shot
show	showed	shown
shrink	shrank	shrunk
shut	shut	shut
sing	sang	sung
sink	sank	sunk
sit	sat	sat
sleep	slept	slept
slide	slid	slid
smell	smelt/smelled	smelt/smelled
speak	spoke	spoken
spell	spelt/spelled	spelt/spelled
spend	spent	spent
spill	spilt/spilled	spilt/spilled
split	split	split
spoil	spoilt/spoiled	spoilt/spoiled
spread	spread	spread
stand	stood	stood
steal	stole	stolen
stick	stuck	stuck
swear	swore	sworn
swell	swelled	swollen/swelled
swim	swam	swum
take	took	taken
teach	taught	taught
tear	tore	torn
tell	told	told
think	thought	thought
throw	threw	thrown
understand	understood	understood
wake	woke	woken
wear	wore	worn
win	won	won
write	wrote	written

Tapescripts

1 Friends

01

(I = Interviewer; C = Celebrity)
I: Could you tell us a little bit about yourself?
C: Sure.
I: First of all, where were you born?
C: I was born in London, but I've got dual nationality because my mother's from Nicaragua.
I: Do you still live in London?
C: No, I'm living in Ibiza now.
I: Oh, really? How long have you been there?
C: Not long. I moved from London with my two daughters, Assisi and Amba, about six months ago.
I: Are you happy there?
C: Yeah, very happy. We love the outdoor life. Also, my mother's a Spanish speaker and I feel more comfortable in a Latin country.
I: Have you made any new friends?
C: Yeah, I've made lots of new friends here. A few English, but my two best friends are Argentinian and Spanish.
I: What do you do for a living?
C: I'm a painter, but I've recently started a jewellery business with a friend, and that takes up most of my time. I also do some modelling when I need the cash!
I: And what do you do in your free time?
C: Well, with a business and two young children I don't have much free time, but I love reading and listening to music.
I: What sort of music do you like?
C: All sorts: pop music and classical.
I: Do you ever listen to the Rolling Stones?
C: No, never, but don't tell my father.
I: How often do you see your parents?
C: Not very often. My mother's in New York and my father's often on tour. But we all love big family get-togethers.
I: You've obviously travelled a lot. What's your favourite place in the world?
C: That's a difficult question because I've been to so many amazing places, but I think Brazil is my favourite. The children love it there too.
I: Finally, can I ask one last question – who chose your name?
C: I think my father chose it. My mother wanted me to have a Spanish name.

02

a) Where were you born?
b) Do you still live in London?
c) How long have you been there?
d) Are you happy there?
e) Have you made any new friends?
f) What do you do for a living?
g) What do you do in your free time?
h) What sort of music do you like?
i) Do you ever listen to the Rolling Stones?
j) How often do you see your parents?
k) What's your favourite place in the world?
l) Who chose your name?

03

(B = Balvir; T = Tim)
B: … No, I went out with my friend last night. Well, actually, she's my best friend. Have you ever met her?
T: Er, I don't know.
B: Lisa?
T: You told me about her.
B: I did. She's the Greek girl.
T: Er, yeah.
B: Really pretty … and she's got long, dark hair and she's um, she's very petite. Um, yeah, we had a great time. We met … gosh … we've known each other now … about 15 years. Can you believe that?
T: Oh, wow.
B: Yeah, we met … I was working for her dad. He had a casino. Oh, I tell you, those were wild days but, er, we met working there together and um, she's a sister, a younger sister, and she doesn't get along with her very well, so I always like to say that I'm like her sister. I'm like the sister she never had.
T: Hah, hah, hah …
B: We don't have a lot in common, but, er … cause she doesn't work, she's a full-time mum. She's got a little boy.
T: Oh, yeah.
B: He's about … he's about 11 now … difficult age. Hum. Uhm, um, but we still get together about once or twice a month, and it's always good to see her.
T: Nice.
B: Yeah.

04

(See page 11.)

05

You've Got a Friend by the Brand New Heavies

When you're down and troubled
And you need some loving care
And nothing, no, is going right
Close your eyes and think of me
Oh, and soon I will be there
To brighten up even your darkest night

You just call out my name
And you know wherever I am
I'll come running, yeah, to see you again
Don't you know that winter, spring, summer or fall
All you've got to do is call
And I'll be there, yes I will
You've got a friend
(You've got a friend in me)

Ain't it good to know that you've got a friend
People can be so cold
They'll hurt you and desert you
Take your very soul if you let them
So don't let them

You just call out my name
And you know wherever I am
I'll come running, yeah, to see you again
Don't you know that winter, spring, summer or fall
All you've got to do is call
And I'll be there, yes I will
You've got a friend
(You've got a friend)
You've got a friend
(You've got a friend in me …)

2 Relax

06 ADVERBIOS DE TIEMPO

Barbara
(I = Interviewer; B = Barbara)
I: Do you think you're a relaxed person?
B: Yes, I think so.
I: What do you think of *The Little Book of Calm*?
B: Well, I think it's interesting, but I work from eight thirty in the morning until about seven in the evening, so I don't have much time to relax. I never have time for a nap during the day. I have a massage from time to time, but I hardly ever have a leisurely bath.
I: Do you ever do any physical exercise?
B: Yes, I go to the gym two or three times a week and I sometimes walk to work.
I: And how do you relax in the evenings?
B: I have a glass of wine and watch television.

Robert
(I = Interviewer; R = Robert)
I: Do you think you're a relaxed person?
R: I don't know – I thought I was until I read *The Little Book of Calm*.
I: What do think of it?
R: Hah … I think it's rubbish. I mean, I like warm water, but only if it's got tea or coffee in it. And I've never had a massage or a nap during the day, but I don't get stressed out very often.
I: How do you relax when you're not working?
R: Well, I go for a walk in the park now and again. I often read in the evening. I like reading, but I'm so tired after work that I frequently fall asleep with a book in my hands and the light on.

Peter
(I = Interviewer; P = Peter)
I: Do you think you're a relaxed person?
P: Oh, yes, definitely.
I: What do you think of *The Little Book of Calm*?
P: I think it's brilliant. It's changed my life.
I: Really? Which advice do you follow?
P: I never drink tea or coffee. I drink two glasses of milk every morning and a cup of hot water in the evening. Um, I go running every morning before work and I spend at least 10 minutes alone in a quiet room when I get home in the evening. Then I float in the bath for about 20 minutes.
I: What does your wife think about that?
P: Oh, she thinks I'm mad.

Sally
(I = Interviewer; S = Sally)
I: Do you think you're a relaxed person?
S: Not really.
I: Why not?
S: I don't think I'm very good at relaxing. I don't like sitting around doing nothing.
I: So what do you do in your free time?
S: Well, I've got three children, so I don't have much free time. But <u>once a month</u>, I get a babysitter and go dancing with my friends. We laugh a lot, and that's what I find relaxing.
I: What do you think of *The Little Book of Calm*?
S: I don't think it was written for people with three children.

📼 07

1
A: Which is your favourite track on the album?
B: The last one – it's amazing. I can't wait to see them live.

2
C: What did you think of it?
D: I thought the acting was brilliant and the photography's superb. Apart from that, it was dead boring.

3
E: Have you finished it yet?
F: Nearly.
E: What's it like?
F: Really good. I reckon it's going to be a best-seller.

4
G: I enjoyed that. What did you think of it?
H: I thought it was rubbish – a sentimental tearjerker – and the ending was so predictable.
G: Well, it made you cry anyway.
H: No, it didn't – I've got a cold.

5
I: Are you enjoying it?
J: Yeah, I found it a bit difficult to get into, but now that I'm past the first few chapters, I can't put it down.

6
K: What did you think of the special effects?
L: What special effects?
K: It was all done with computers.
L: Oh, no ... I thought it was real. You've spoilt it now.

7
M: Did you have a good time?
N: Not really ... I can't stand all that techno stuff. I like it when you can actually hear the lyrics.
M: Old hippy.
N: What did you say?
M: Nothing.

📼 08

[Film music]

3 Dating
📼 09

Tom and Kathy
(J = Journalist; K = Kathy)
J: Kathy, we last heard from you when you were about to meet Tom for the first time.
K: That's right. It was easier for me to take time off work, so I booked a flight to Denver.
J: Wow! That's a long way to go for a date! And rather expensive too.
K: Oh, we shared the cost of the flight. Tom's a very generous man. Anyway, he arranged to meet me at the airport.
J: And when was that?
K: It was almost a year ago. I felt really nervous, but I couldn't wait to meet Tom.
J: And was he there?
K: Oh, yes. I spotted him immediately. He looked just like his photograph.
J: Hah. Was it love at first sight?
K: I'm afraid not. I couldn't have predicted what happened but something put me off him straightaway. I didn't even leave the airport. I just turned round and came straight back to Ireland. We haven't been in touch since that day.
J: Wow, what was it that put you off?
K: Well, it's going to sound really stupid, but I hated his shoes.

Lisa and Joel
(J = Journalist; L = Lisa; Jo = Joel)
J: Lisa and Joel, are you still married?
L: Oh, yes, very much so. We've been married for a year now. In fact we've just celebrated our first wedding anniversary.
J: Oh, congratulations! How have your lives changed since your unusual marriage?
Jo: Well, my mother hasn't spoken to me since the day we got married! Hah. That's the good news.
J: Hah, hah, hah.
Jo: But, no, I'm joking. We're really upset about it. But we've moved away from our home town.
J: Really? Why did you decide to do that?
Jo: Well, everybody knew about the competition and the wedding and we turned into tourist attractions. We couldn't walk down the street without strangers coming up to us and asking us all these personal questions.
J: So, where do you live now?
Jo: In Adelaide. Er, we've been there for about six months now, and we love it.

📼 10

a) What's a nice girl like you doing in a place like this?
b) You know, I'm not just an interesting person, I have a body too.
c) I'm in advertising. Would you like to be in our next photo shoot?
d) Do you believe in love at first sight or do I have to walk past you again?
e) A: Do you have a boyfriend?
   B: Yes.
   A: Want another one?
f) Your father must be a thief, because he's stolen the stars from the sky and put them in your eyes.
g) I've just moved next door and I was wondering if you could recommend a good restaurant nearby. Would you like to join me?

📼 11

(R = Rose; M = Meg)
R: What do you think of Jake?
M: He's all right.
R: You don't like him, do you?
M: Well, he wasn't exactly friendly.
R: Oh, he's just a bit shy, that's all.
M: Shy? You must be joking. Five minutes after meeting me he asked me to buy him a drink! That's not what I call shy!
R: OK, that was a bit cheeky, but he's broke.
M: Huh, I'm not particularly well-off myself and I'm trying to save up for my holiday.
R: All right, all right, I'll pay you back. He's not bad-looking, though, is he?
M: No, I suppose not – but he knows it. I think he's really big-headed.
R: You're just jealous.
M: No, I'm not. I don't want him. He's mean, big-headed and stupid.
R: What do you mean stupid? You're not exactly Miss Einstein yourself.
M: Shut up!
R: No, you shut up!
M: Mum!

4 Adrenalin
📼 12

a
A: Have you ever been skydiving?
B: Yes, I have.
A: Was it good?
B: Good? It was absolutely incredible!

b
C: Have you ever been surfing?
D: Yes, I have.
C: Were you scared?
D: Scared? I was absolutely terrified!

📼 13

Interview with Jane Couch
(I = Interviewer; JC = Jane Couch)
I: Now this is a question that everyone asks you, I know, but, h ... when ... how did you get interested in boxing?
JC: I saw a documentary about women boxing in America about six years ago, it was there, just a li ... a little television programme, it was about an hour long, and I ... I watched the programme and it just changed my life, I was just fascinated from there on in, from like a half an hour programme, I just went ... 'I'm going to do that'.
I: And were you interested in sport at school?
JC: No, nothing. I wasn't even fit or anything. I used to smoke. I used to drink. Um, just didn't look after meself at all. Didn't eat very well, and this just changed my life. Hah ...
I: How long did it take you to get fit?
JC: It took me, I'd say, to get to the level that I'm at, it took me ... about two years to reach ... to reach the level I needed to be at.
I: And do you know how many female boxers there are in ... the ... in Britain?
JC: In the UK, um, there's ... there's about three hundred women boxing as

amateurs, and there's about eight women boxing professionally in the UK at the moment, but throughout the world there's about thirty thousand women, throughout the world.

I: And what do your critics say?
JC: Um, at … at the … at the outset it was difficult. It was, like, women shouldn't box, you know, … they shouldn't be doing this, and they shouldn't be doing that, and should be at home looking after the kids, and everything. But, um … and she's never be as good as a man, but my last three fights have been live on TV. I've just signed a five fo … fight deal with Bravo Television.
I: What do you think are the prime, um, skills to have as a boxer?
JC: Um, believe it or not, you've got to be … you've got to have a pretty good brain to be a good boxer. Anyone can fight, but to make it to the top you've to know your skills, and you've to have a pretty cute brain, and … and the fitness … the fitness side of it is very, very important.
I: And how do you relax?
JC: I don't. I never do … I … I nev … I don't sleep much. I just … and when I do, I dream about boxing, and when I'm trying to get to sleep it's about my fights. I'm just, I can't … I work really hard. I'm just constantly working, working …
I: How do you prepare for a match?
JC: Um, for a … for a ten-round, um, world title fight, obviously I go to training camp just outside Bristol, for eight weeks before each fight, and, um, once I go to training camp that's it. I don't do anything. I've got a … a very good trainer, I've got a very good team round me, so …
I: Have you ever been seriously hurt in a match?
JC: Er, not really seriously, Not lasting damage. Things that take a couple of weeks to mend, like broken cheek bone, broken nose, lost a few teeth, but just, er …
I: Your teeth look great to me from where I'm sitting, I can tell you …
JC: Hah … no, I only lost the back ones. Hah, hah …
I: Now, just finally, do you think you've changed since your success.
JC: Um, changed as a person? I … I … I think … I think I've changed as in … in the life-style that I live now, is um, it's just constantly I'm travelling. I live out of a suitcase. But I think, um, as a person, definitely not, no, I've j … my feet are just so firmly on the ground, you wouldn't believe it. Um, …
I: I would believe it, having met you. I can assure you.
JC: Hah.
I: And, just lastly, when's your next big fight?
JC: Er, the next one's going to be the end of February, beginning of March. I'm going to be defending my world … my three world titles.
I: And where will it be?
JC: In London! Hah, hah.
I: Well, that's great. Thank you very, very much.

14

a
(I = Interviewer; B = Ben)
I: Have you ever had a sports injury?
B: Yes, I have. I was playing rugby for the local team and it was just after kick-off. I was jumping up to catch the ball when a player from the other team knocked me over and I fell heavily on my left leg.
I: Oh, dear. Were you badly hurt?
B: Ah, yes, I twisted my ankle and couldn't play rugby for more than three months.

b
(I = Interviewer; D = Dina)
I: Have you ever been in a dangerous situation?
D: Yes, I … I have. I was walking my dog one day with my sister and we were crossing this field. There was a horse in it and it suddenly started running towards us, looking really mad.
I: What did you do?
D: Well, I know you're not supposed to run away from animals because they can sense your fear. But we ran away as fast as we could.

c
(I = Interviewer; F = Frank)
I: Have you ever broken a bone?
F: Yes, I've broken my nose twice. The first time I was playing football and one of the other players hit me in the face. The second time, I was playing tennis. I missed the ball and it hit me right on my nose.

d
(I = Interviewer; P = Paula)
I: Have you ever been really frightened?
P: Yes, I have. Last summer I was driving on the motorway in Spain and we were getting close to Barcelona. So I got into the right-hand lane ready to turn off the motorway when this car screeched up next to me, pulled in front of me and slammed on his brakes. I don't know how I managed to slow down fast enough to avoid him. I've never been so frightened in my life.

e)
(I = Interviewer; G = Glenn)
I: Have you ever thought you were going to die?
G: Yeah. It was when I was eight or nine and I was at the beach with my parents. I was playing in the sea, but on the edge because I couldn't swim. Suddenly, I realised that I couldn't feel the bottom and the sea was pulling me further away from the beach. For a few seconds, I panicked and I started swallowing a lot of water. Then I felt really calm, as if I was floating away. I was drowning. Fortunately, someone saw me and pulled me out in time.

15

George
(I = Interviewer; G = George)
I: George, is it similar to skiing?
G: Actually, it's slightly easier and I think it's a lot more exhilarating.
I: Is it cheaper?
G: No, not really. The equipment is just as expensive.
I: What do you need?
G: A board, of course, and that can cost about £400. Then you have to have bindings to attach your feet to the board, and you also need special clothes and boots which are quite expensive.
I: Is it as popular as skiing?
G: With young people, yes.

Katrina
(I = Interviewer; K = Katrina)
I: Katrina, where did you learn?
K: I did my preliminary certificate in Malta when I was on holiday.
I: I suppose you have to learn in the sea, don't you? I mean, you don't live near the sea, do you?
K: Er, no, but I could have had lessons at home in a lake, although it's much more pleasant to learn in the Mediterranean because it's nice and warm.
I: Did you have to buy all the equipment?
K: No, you can hire it but it's far better to have your own wetsuit because it's important for it to be exactly the right size.
I: Are lessons very expensive?
K: Quite expensive, but it's worth having lessons with professionals because it's much safer.
I: Were you nervous on your first dive?
K: Yes, but it was one of the most amazing experiences I've ever had.

Paul
(I = Interviewer; P = Paul)
I: Paul, who do you support?
P: I used to support Notts Forest, but then I changed to Man U.
I: Why?
P: Because they're by far the most exciting team in England.
I: Did you watch their last match?
P: Yes. They didn't play as well as usual and one of their best players was sent off in the first half.
I: Why?
P: Er, the referee said that he kicked a player from the other team.
I: So, did they lose?
P: No, it was a draw.

Eva
(I = Interviewer; E = Eva)
I: Eva, was it your first time?
E: Yes, and it was amazing.
I: What did you have to do?
E: Well, the first time you do it they attach the elastic around your waist and you just jump. At first, you free fall, and then the elastic pulls you back and you bounce up and down a few times.
I: How did it feel?
E: Incredible. … I can't explain the feeling … it's … it's much better than anything else I've ever done. It's exciting, but it isn't nearly as frightening as you imagine.
I: What made you do it?
E: It was a birthday present and it's definitely the best birthday present I've ever had.

16

River Deep Mountain High by Ike and Tina Turner

When I was a little girl
I had a rag doll
Only doll I've ever owned
Now I love you just the way I loved that rag doll
But only now my love has grown
And it gets stronger, in every way
And it gets deeper, let me say
And it gets higher, day by day
And do I love you my oh my
Yeah, river deep mountain high
Yeah, yeah, yeah
If I lost you would I cry
Oh how I love you baby, baby, baby, baby

When you were a young boy
Did you have a puppy
That always followed you around
Well I'm gonna be as faithful as that puppy
No I'll never let you down
Cause it goes on and on, like a river flows
And it gets bigger baby, and heaven knows
And it gets sweeter baby, as it grows
And do I love you my oh my
Yeah, river deep mountain high
Yeah, yeah, yeah
If I lost you would I cry
Oh how I love you baby, baby, baby, baby

I love you baby like a flower loves the spring
And I love you baby like a robin loves to sing
And I love you baby like a schoolboy loves his pet
And I love you baby, river deep mountain high
baby, baby, baby … oh baby … oh … oh …
Do I love you my oh my
Yeah, river deep mountain high
Yeah, yeah, yeah
If I lost you would I cry
Oh how I love you baby, baby, baby, baby

5 Kids

17

1
A: Um, it's something that lived a l… a very long time ago. It looks very scary.
B: A thing that lived long time ago.
C: Um … It's a big monster.

2
D: It's a man and, and um … he lives in … he lives up in space.
E: It's someone who um … made the world and um … he made the animals.
F: He's someone who lives … who's died and he … he, um … looks down on people.
G: He's a man up in heaven.
H: A person that helps people, in heaven.

3
I: It's something that's er … er, very cold and it's in … it's a … it's a … it's a, um … it's a stone.
J: It's something that crashes down on people and it's got ice.
K: It's a sort of big piece of, um … ice that cracks off a bigger piece.
L: It's a big ice cube.

4
M: A place where … where animals … have been put up to show.
N: Somewhere where um … they show you things that are very old.
O: It's somewhere where er, people will show things like dinosaurs and olden days things.
P: A place … a place that um … you see loads and loads of … you see bones or things and pictures.
Q: It's in the country and you see dinosaur bones there.

5
R: It's a person who takes toys away.
S: It's someone that in the middle of the night … and it's got um … it's got a … it's got um, a ba … something around his face with, with, um … round holes and he's … he's got um … a T-shirt that's got black and white and he robs things.
T: It's someone who steals things when you're asleep.
U: A person that steals things at night.

18

(See page 46.)

19

Doctor Foster went to Gloucester
In a shower of rain
He stepped in a puddle right up to his middle
And never went there again

20

(See page 48.)

21

Her name was Mrs Pratchett. She was a small skinny old hag with a moustache on her upper lip and a mouth as sour as a green gooseberry. She never smiled.

Her apron was grey and greasy. Her blouse had bits of breakfast all over it, toast-crumbs and tea stains and splotches of dried egg-yolk. It was her hands, however, that disturbed us most. They were disgusting. They were black with dirt and grime.

And do not forget that it was these hands and fingers that she would plunge into the sweet-jars when we asked for a pennyworth of Treacle Toffee or Wine Gums or Nut Clusters or whatever. There were precious few health laws in those days, and nobody, least of all Mrs Pratchett, ever thought of using a little shovel for getting sweets out as they do today.

The other thing we hated Mrs Pratchett for was her meanness. Unless you spent a whole sixpence all in one go, she wouldn't give you a bag. Instead you got your sweets twisted up in a small piece of newspaper which she tore off a pile of old Daily Mirrors lying on the counter.

So you can well understand that we had it in for Mrs Pratchett in a big way, but we didn't quite know what to do about it. Many schemes were put forward, but none of them was any good. None of them, that is, until suddenly, one memorable afternoon, we found the dead mouse.

My four friends and I had come across a loose floor-board at the back of the classroom, and when we prised it up with the blade of a pocket-knife, we discovered a big hollow space underneath. This, we decided, would be our secret hiding place for sweets and other small treasures such as conkers and monkey-nuts and birds' eggs.

Every afternoon, when the last lesson was over, the five of us would wait until the classroom had emptied, then we would lift up the floor-board and examine our secret hoard, perhaps adding to it or taking something away.

One day, when we lifted it up, we found a dead mouse lying among our treasures. It was an exciting discovery.

Thwaites took it out by its tail and waved it in front of our faces. 'What shall we do with it?' he cried.

'It stinks!' someone shouted. 'Throw it out of the window!'

'Hold on a tick,' I said. 'Don't throw it away.'

Thwaites hesitated. They all looked at me.

When writing about oneself, one must strive to be truthful. Truth is more important than modesty. I must tell you, therefore, that it was I and I alone who had the idea for the great and daring Mouse Plot. We all have our moments of brilliance and glory, and this was mine.

'Why don't we', I said, 'slip it into one of Mrs Pratchett's jars of sweets? Then when she puts her dirty hand in to grab a handful, she'll grab a stinky dead mouse instead '.

The other four stared at me in wonder.

Then, as the sheer genius of the plot began to sink in, they all started grinning. They slapped me on the back. They cheered me and danced around the classroom. 'We'll do it today!' they cried. 'We'll do it on the way home! You had the idea,' they said to me, 'so you can be the one to put the mouse in the jar.'

Thwaites handed me the mouse. I put it into my trouser pocket. Then the five of us left the school, crossed the village green and headed for the sweet-shop. We were tremendously jazzed up. We felt like a gang of desperados setting out to rob a train or blow up the sheriff's office.

We were the victors now and Mrs Pratchett was the victim. She stood behind the counter, and her small malignant pig-eyes watched us suspiciously as we came forward.

'One Sherbet Sucker, please,' Thwaites said to her, holding out his penny.

I kept to the rear of the group, and when I saw Mrs Pratchett turn her head away for a couple of seconds to fish a Sherbet Sucker out of the box, I lifted the heavy glass lid of the Gobstopper jar and dropped the mouse in. Then I replaced the lid as silently as possible. My heart was thumping like mad and my hands had gone all sweaty.

As soon as we were outside, we broke into a run. 'Did you do it?' they shouted at me.

'Of course I did!' I said.

'Well done you!' they cried. What a super show!'

I felt like a hero. I was a hero. It was marvellous to be so popular.

The flush of triumph over the dead mouse was carried forward to the next morning as we met again to walk to school.

'Let's go in and see if it's still in the jar,' somebody said as we approached the sweet-shop.

'Don't,' Thwaites said firmly. 'It's too dangerous. Walk past as though nothing has happened.'

As we came level with the shop we saw a cardboard notice hanging on the door.
CLOSED.

We stopped and stared. We had never known the sweet-shop to be closed at this time in the morning, even on Sundays.

'What's happened?' we asked each other. 'What's going on?'

We pressed our faces against the window and looked inside. Mrs Pratchett was nowhere to be seen.

'Look!' I cried. 'The Gobstopper jar's gone! It's not on the shelf! There's a gap where it used to be!'

'It's on the floor!' someone said. 'It's smashed to bits and there's Gobstoppers everywhere!'

'There's the mouse!' someone else shouted.

We could see it all, the huge glass jar smashed to smithereens with the dead mouse lying in the wreckage and hundreds of many-coloured Gobstoppers littering the floor.

'She got such a shock when she grabbed hold of the mouse that she dropped everything,' somebody was saying.

'But why didn't she sweep it all up and open the shop?' I asked.

Nobody answered me.

After a while, Thwaites broke the silence. 'She must have got one heck of a shock,' he said. He paused. We all looked at him, wondering what wisdom the great medical authority was going to come out with next.

'Well now,' Thwaites went on, 'when an old person like Mrs Pratchett suddenly gets a very big shock, I suppose you know what happens next?'

'What?' we said. 'What happens?'

'You ask my father,' Thwaites said. 'He'll tell you.'

'You tell us,' we said.

'It gives her a heart attack,' Thwaites announced. 'Her heart stops beating and she's dead in five seconds.'

For a moment or two my own heart stopped beating. Thwaites pointed a finger at me and said darkly, 'I'm afraid you've killed her.'

'Me?' I cried. 'Why just me?'

'It was your idea,' he said. 'And what's more, you put the mouse in.'

All of a sudden, I was a murderer.

At exactly that point, we heard the school bell ringing in the distance and we had to gallop the rest of the way so as not to be late for prayers.

The Headmaster is the only teacher at Llandaff Cathedral School that I can remember, and for a reason you will soon discover, I can remember him very clearly indeed. His name was Mr Coombes.

Mr Coombes now proceeded to mumble through the same old prayers we had every day, but this morning, when the last amen had been spoken, he did not turn and lead his group rapidly out of the Hall as usual. He remained standing before us, and it was clear he had an announcement to make.

'The whole school is to go out and line up around the playground immediately,' he said. 'Leave your books behind. And no talking.'

Mr Coombes was looking grim. His hammy pink face had taken on that dangerous scowl which only appeared when he was extremely cross and somebody was for the high-jump. I sat there small and frightened among the rows and rows of other boys, and to me at that moment the Headmaster, with his black gown draped over his shoulders, was like a judge at a murder trial.

'He's after the killer,' Thwaites whispered to me.

I began to shiver.

As we made our way out into the playground my whole stomach began to feel as though it was filling up with swirling water. I am only eight years old, I told myself. No little boy of eight has ever murdered anyone. It's not possible.

I half-expected to see two policemen come bounding out of the school to grab me by the arms and put handcuffs on my wrists.

A single door led out from the school on to the playground. Suddenly it swung open and through it, like the angel of death, strode Mr Coombes, huge and bulky in his tweed suit and black gown, and beside him, believe it or not, right beside him trotted the tiny figure of Mrs Pratchett herself!

Mrs Pratchett was alive!

The relief was tremendous.

Suddenly she let out a high-pitched yell and pointed a dirty finger straight at Thwaites. 'That's 'im!' she yelled. 'That's one of 'em! I'd know 'im a mile away, the scummy little bounder!'

The entire school turned to look at Thwaites. 'W-what have I done?' he stuttered, appealing to Mr Coombes.

'Shut up,' Mr Coombes said.

Mrs Pratchett's eyes flicked over and settled on my own face. I looked down and studied the black asphalt surface of the playground.

''Ere's another of 'em!' I heard her yelling. 'That one there!' She pointed at me now. 'You're quite sure?' Mr Coombes said.

'Of course I'm sure!' she cried. 'I never forget a face, least of all when it's as sly as that! 'Ee's one of 'em all right! There was five altogether. Now where's them other three?'

The other three, I knew very well, were coming up next.

'There they are!' she cried out, stabbing the air with her finger. ''Im … and 'im … and 'im! That's the five of 'em all right! We don't need to look no farther than this, 'Eadmaster! They're all 'ere, the nasty little pigs! You've got their names 'ave you?'

'I've got their names, Mrs Pratchett,' Mr Coombes told her. 'I'm very much obliged to you.'

6 News

📼 22

(A1 = Announcer 1; A2 = Announcer 2)
A1: And here are the news headlines. Following severe droughts in Africa, the President of the USA has announced that he is going to send food and provisions to the people of Somalia, who have lost their homes and livelihood.
A2: Robert Holmes, Minister for the Environment, has resigned. The Prime Minister has ordered an investigation into the mysterious disappearance of a large sum of money. A spokesman for the minister told us that he was out of the country and not available for comment.
A1: Schoolgirl Pauline Gates has not been allowed back into school after the summer holidays, because she has had her nose pierced. According to headmistress Jean Bradley, Pauline knew that piercing was against the school rules. The girl will be allowed back into school when she removes the offending ring.
A2: And finally, to end on a happier note, wedding bells are ringing for 81-year-old Max Williams, who won £16 million in the lottery last month. He's going to marry 22-year-old dancer Sally Lister. The happy couple posed for photographers outside the millionaire's luxury home in Essex and Sally held out her hand to show off her £10,000 engagement ring for the cameras.

📼 23

(K = Ken; S = Steve)
K: Hi, Steve. How are you?
S: Oh, not too bad. Actually, it's my wedding anniversary today.
K: Oh, congratulations!
S: But um, I forgot and my wife was really upset.
K: Oh, no. That's terrible.
S: But I just rang Le Petit Blanc and they actually had a table free, so we're going out for dinner.
K: Excellent.
S: Anyway, I must go.
K: Er, yeah, me too. See you!

📼 24

a
A: Have you heard about Chris and Shirley?
B: No … what about them?
A: They've split up.
B: That's terrible!

b
C: Hello. You're looking very pleased with yourself.
D: I am! I've just passed my driving test!
C: Well done! Can I have a lift?

E: Guess what. I've won a holiday to Florida.
F: Lucky you! Is it a holiday for two?
E: Yes, I'm taking my mum.
F: Oh.

G: I've just had some bad news.
H: What's happened?
G: I've failed my final exams.
H: Oh, I'm sorry to hear that. Are you going to resit them?

I: Oh, no!
J: What's the matter?
I: I've left my bag on the bus.
J: You idiot! What are you going to do?
I: I suppose I'd better ring the bus company.

K: Have a glass of champagne!
L: Thank you. What are you celebrating?
K: My wife's just had a baby.
L: Congratulations! Boy or a girl?

g
M: You don't usually take the bus!
N: No – my car's broken down again.
M: Oh, no!

h
O: I didn't know you had a car.
P: My parents have bought a new car and they've given me their old one.
O: Excellent!

25

That's terrible!
Well done!
Lucky you!
Oh, I'm sorry to hear that.
You idiot!
Congratulations!
Oh, no!
Excellent!

26

1 We got engaged last week.
2 My bicycle's been stolen again.
3 I've decided to move to Australia.
4 My husband's been taken into hospital.
5 My daughter has just had a baby.
6 I got off the bus, slipped and fell flat on my face.
7 I've won £1,000 on the National Lottery!
8 My car wouldn't start this morning.
9 When I got to the party, there was someone there wearing exactly the same dress as me.
10 I've just got my exam results and I've passed.

7 Party

27

1 /ɪ/ – busy   city
2 /e/ – festival   guest
3 /ɒ/ – holiday   modern
4 /æ/ – band   candle
5 /ə/ – around   different
6 /ʊ/ – full   good
7 /ʌ/ – fund   public

28

(Z = Zoë; S = Sandy)
Z: Hi!
S: Oh, hello.
Z: You don't look very happy. What's the matter?
S: David hasn't rung.
Z: You only saw him yesterday.
S: Yes, and the last thing he said was, 'I'll ring you tomorrow.'
Z: Well, tomorrow isn't finished yet.
S: No, but it's eight o'clock. What are you doing tonight? Do you fancy going for a drink?
Z: Um, I'd love to, but John's coming round and we're going for a meal.
S: Well, I'm not going to sit here waiting for the phone to ring. I know – I'll phone Becky.

29

(B = Becky; S = Sandy; Z =Zoë; D = David)
B: Hello.
S: Hi, Becky, it's Sandy.
B: Hiya.
S: Becky, are you doing anything tonight?
B: Yes. I'm meeting Alex and Suzy in about half an hour.
S: Where are you going?
B: To the cinema. Would you like to come with us?
S: Yes, I'd love to. Where are you meeting?
B: At their house, but we could meet you in front of the cinema in George Street at half past eight.
S: OK, thanks. See you later.
…
I'm going to the cinema with Becky.
Z: Good idea.
S: And next time I see David, I'm going to tell him to get lost.
Z: Hmm. I'll believe that when I see it.

…
Z: Hello.
D: Is Sandy there, please?
Z: Yeah, hold on a moment – I'll get her for you.
… It's David.
S: Oh, hello, David.
D: Look, I'm really sorry I didn't call earlier, but I had to work late.
S: Oh, that's all right. I … I forgot you were going to ring anyway.
D: Listen, I'm afraid I can't see you tonight, I'm having dinner with my parents.
S: It doesn't matter – I'm going to the cinema anyway.
D: Oh, right. OK, well I'll call you.
S: When? I mean, all right. Bye.
D: Bye.

…
Z: You didn't tell him to get lost.
S: Well, he apologised – and he's having dinner with his parents. Anyway, I … I must go. See you later.

…
S: Hi, Alex. Hi, Becky. Where's Suzy?
B: Oh, she changed her mind at the last minute. David phoned her and asked her to go for a meal at that new Japanese restaurant.
S: What?! Now I'm definitely going to tell him to get lost!

30

(R = Rachel; A = Alyson; G = Geoff)
R: What do you think makes a good party then?
A: Um … I think the place is really important. It should be big enough but not too big.
G: Yes, it needs to be quite crowded to make an atmosphere … and dark.
R: Oh, I don't like it when you can't see who you're talking to.
G: No… no, I mean soft lighting. I like it when there are some decorations too. You know, a few balloons and things, just to make it special.
A: What, like a children's party?
G: Yeah, I suppose so – or candles and things on the wall.
R: Candles make a nice atmosphere, but you have to be careful the house doesn't catch fire.
G: W … well, you can get those candle-holders. But the most important thing is the food and drink.
A: Oh, yes. There must be lots of drink and enough food. It's terrible when there isn't enough food.
R: What sort of food do you think is good for parties?
A: Um, the sort of thing you can eat with your fingers. I mean, you don't want to have loads of washing-up at the end of the party.
R: Actually, I think the music is the most important thing. Loud, but not too loud, and the sort of music you can dance to.
G: I think the best thing is to prepare party tapes with all the best dance tracks, then you don't have to worry about it.
A: But what about people? That's quite important, isn't it?
G: Um, yes, you do need people for a party!
A: No, I … I mean the right people. You need some party animals who get up and start the dancing.
R: And you need a mix of men and women. I went to a party recently where there were five women for every man.
G: Sounds all right to me.
A: Oh, shut up. So what do we think are the three most important things?
R: Food and drink, music and the right mix of people.
G: Right.

31

It's My Party by Lesley Gore

It's my party and I'll cry if I want to,
Cry if I want to, cry if I want to.
You would cry too if it happened to you.

Nobody knows where my Johnny has gone,
But Judy left the same time.
Why was he holding her hand,
When he's supposed to be mine?

It's my party …

Play all my records, keep dancing all night,
But leave me alone for a while,
'Til Johnny's dancing with me,
I've got no reason to smile.

It's my party …

Judy and Johnny just walked thru' the door,
Like a queen with her king.
Oh, what a birthday surprise,
Judy's wearing his ring.

It's my party …

8 Review 1

32

Sue
We met at university – we both studied music actually and I suppose we hit it off straightaway. Afterwards, I went away travelling for a year or so and we lost touch for a while, but really we've been friends since we were students. We see each other, say, three or four times a week I guess. We're both very outgoing and energetic, which I suppose is why we get on so well in the band …

Juan
It was an amazing coincidence really. Not only to meet like that, but to get on so well and have so much in common. We helped each other with our studying as well. And there was no time at all to feel homesick or anything. From the moment we got on the plane we had lots to talk about. And when

we finished, we had a brilliant time seeing the place and, well, it was just one big party 'till it was time to come back home. I wish we could see each other more often these days.

Elisa

It was in India, just after university. I'd been there for a few months at the time. At first, we didn't get on too well, but we kept bumping into each other, as you do when you're travelling, so we, um, well, we ended up travelling together. We found we had similar interests ... you know, we like the same music and like going to gigs, and we had similar outlooks and so on. I suppose we've been friends for about, well, three or four years now.

Enrico

We've got similar interests, particularly music. We like to see as many bands as we can. We like going out a lot. We, er, don't get to travel as much as we used to, but we're planning to go back to Asia together for a few weeks next year. That's where we met in the first place actually, about four years ago.

Sindy

We've known each other for a few years now and we still get on well, most of the time anyway! We see each other a lot. Of course we're together twice a week when the band rehearses and we often go to pubs or to friends' houses and just, sort of, hang out and chat really. Yeah, we both love a good party!

Hans

We first met in the, er, airport actually. We just bumped into each other at the check-in. It turned out we were both going to the same place to study and we ended up living in rooms on the same corridor in the hall. It was pretty amazing really! We got on from the word go. It just happened naturally, you know, two people away from home and all that. We did almost everything together and then when the course was over we travelled around the country for a month or so, before coming home. Now, I guess we only see each other three or four times a year or so.

📼 33

(See page 69.)

9 Soap

📼 34

(See page 74.)

📼 35

Pacific Heights. Scene 2

(P = Penny; E = Ella; Ph = Phil; M = Mara)
P: So, what have you been up to today?
E: We've been to the travel agent's to get some brochures.
Ph: I thought we'd talked about that.
M: But Dad ...
Ph: Look, I've told you once and I'll tell you again – you're not going travelling on your own. You're too young.
E: But Becky's parents let *her* go travelling last year.
Ph: Yes, but she went with her brother.
M: Well, let's ask Charlie. Where is he, by the way?
P: Oh, he's taking part in a big surfing competition out of town.
Ph: But his surfboard's here.
P: Oh, that's strange. I must have made a mistake.
M: Come on, Ella ... let's go round to Becky's.
P: Er, don't be late for dinner.

Pacific Heights. Scene 3

(M = Mara; E = Ella)
M: I think I know where Charlie is.
E: Where?
M: He's gone to see Clare. I'm sure there's something going on.
E: Oh, between Charlie and Clare?
M: Yes.
E: But Clare's married to Uncle Dave.
M: So? Lots of married people have affairs.
E: Well, I don't think it's right. Anyway, how do you know?
M: Well, I heard him talking to her on the phone yesterday. He asked her if Dave had left for America and then he said he couldn't wait to be in her arms again!
E: Oh, what a creep. Poor Becky.
M: Oh, don't worry, she'll get over it. But listen, I've got an idea.
E: If it's about Charlie coming travelling with us, forget it. He's already said he doesn't want to.
M: Yes, but if we catch him with Clare, we can blackmail him to come travelling with us.
E: Oh, yes. I see what you mean. But don't you think we should tell Becky about him and Clare?
M: No, stupid. If we tell her, we won't be able to blackmail him. Come on, let's make a plan.

Pacific Heights. Scene 4

(A = Amy; M = Mark)
A: I don't know what to do. If I don't take part in the demonstration I'll have to leave the group.
M: Just think about those poor little animals. Have you any idea what they do to them?
A: I know, but it's my step-father's company.
M: Well, it serves him right for experimenting on animals.
A: Are they going to do any damage?
M: No, it's a peaceful demonstration, that's all. Anyway, it's up to you.
A: Um, OK, I'll come, but my mom will kill me if she finds out.

10 Time

📼 36

(PR = Paul Roesch; RW = Roberta Wilson)
PR: ... That was Sonny Best with *Midnight in Vermont*. Now, do you make the best of your time? In the studio today we've got Roberta Wilson, who's a time management consultant. Good morning, Roberta.
RW: Good morning, Paul.
PR: Roberta, what exactly do time management consultants do?
RW: Well, Paul, it's all about helping people to organise their work in an effective way: maximum efficiency; minimum stress.
PR: Hah, sounds like something I need. Er, who are your clients?
RW: Um, mainly business people, but I've also worked with politicians, civil servants and university lecturers.
PR: Um, quite a range, then. And what sort of things help people to organise their time? I suppose punctuality is important?
RW: Um, yes and no. It's easier to finish a meeting on time if it starts on time. But in international contexts, you do have to be aware of cultural differences.
PR: For example?
RW: Well, in Britain big, formal meetings usually start on time, but less formal meetings often begin a few minutes late. In Germany, on the other hand, people expect all meetings to begin on time. In some countries, er, for example in Latin America, there's a more ... relaxed attitude. So, you do have to adapt to circumstances.
PR: When in Rome ...
RW: Er, to some extent, yes.
PR: Um, it sounds like even if you manage your own time very well, you still can't control what other people do.
RW: Well, you can set limits. If you're meeting a friend who always arrives late, you can say, 'Well, I'm going to wait for 15 minutes. If they aren't there by then, I'll leave.'
PR: Hmm. I've got one friend who's always late. I don't think I'd ever see her if I did that.
RW: Hah, but people who are always late are the ones you need to set limits with. If they know that you won't wait, then, perhaps they'll make an effort.
PR: Isn't that rather harsh?
RW: No, not really. Someone who constantly turns up late is putting a low value on your time. Let them know you've got other things to do. And I'm not suggesting you do that with everyone – just the persistent latecomers. Though, again, different cultures do have different viewpoints on what constitutes serious lateness.
PR: What about interruptions? I often come in to the studio with something important I need to do. Then the phone rings or someone comes to see me ... Before I know it, the day's over and I haven't done what I planned.
RW: Um, you need to defend your time. If you're working on something important and someone drops in to see you, get your diary out. Politely tell them you're busy and make an appointment for another time. If it isn't important anyway, they'll just go away. If it is, they'll make an appointment and you can deal with it properly.
PR: That sounds practical.
RW: Um, again, you do have to be careful. In some cultures, particularly Latin ones, this technique can upset people. But here in the United States, almost no-one will be offended.
PR: Hmm. So, does everything depend on culture?
RW: No. Attitudes to time are one of the big differences between cultures. But how you organise your own work is up to you. And there are lots of techniques here. For example, imagine you've got two important things to do. One of them is pleasant, and the other isn't. Always try to do the unpleasant task first. That way, the pleasant task is a reward for finishing. If you do it the

other way round, you'll tend to slow down the pleasant task because you don't want to do the unpleasant one.
PR: Hah, hah. I'll remember that. Finally, what, for you, is a hard-working person?
RW: Oh, I'm not very interested in hard-working people. You can spend twelve hours a day at the office without doing very much. I'm interested in productive – and happy – people.
PR: And on that note, I have to say we've run out of time. Thank you Roberta and over to Jasmine Dahar with the news …

📼 37

1 /s/ – Sunday
second
Saturday
weeks
first

2 /z/ – days
Tuesday
weekends
Wednesday
hours

3 /θ/ – three
thirty
month
Thursday
third

4 /ð/ – then
there
weather
that
these

📼 38

(J = Julie; M = Martin)
M: OK, so what dates did you get?
J: I've got 20th February 1997.
M: OK, I'll write that down … '97.
J: Um, 24th May 1972.
M: OK.
J: Then I've got 5th November, 1999.
M: OK.
J: Then there's 31st July, 1991.
M: … '91. OK, and the last one?
J: The last one … I've got 15th July next year.
M: Right. OK, well, let's go for the oldest one. 24th May '72. What's that?
J: That's my birthday.
M: Hah, hah, hah.
J: Hah … and I'm a Gemini.
M: Oh, right. OK. Er, 20th February '97?
J: That is my cat's birthday.
M: … I don't even know my cat's …
J: She's called 'Sparkle'.
M: Hah, hah, hah. 31st July '91?
J: Ah. This is the date that I left college and I got my first job in Habitat Superstore.
M: Hah, hah. Right, OK. Er, 5th November … 5th November '99.
J: Well, that's bonfire night, of course.
M: Oh, right.
J: Yeah. A huge party takes place.
M: And finally, what's this 15th July next year?
J: Well, I'm going on a world trip.
M: Oh, where are you going?
J: I'm going to Australia, Sri Lanka, to India, the Far East, then to America … . All over the place.
M: Oh, lucky you. It sounds great.

📼 39

1
We're supposed to start work at nine, but I often come in later because I have to take my children to school first, but then I stay a bit later. Of course, if I've got an early meeting or if I've got to be in court first thing in the morning, my wife has to take the kids to school. We're supposed to work a 40-hour week, but I think most people actually work more than that. We're supposed to dress smartly, particularly if we have contact with clients, so I always wear a suit and tie to work. Female lawyers aren't allowed to wear trousers or even dark tights. They have to wear knee-length skirts – no minis. The secretaries can wear tailored trousers, but no jeans. A weekly dress-down day has been introduced recently – it's an idea from America, where everybody comes into work in casual dress on a Friday. Personally, I have no desire to come into work wearing jeans and a T-shirt. I like to make a difference between work and home, and I can wear casual clothes at home. I think people should dress smartly for work – it gives a good impression.
Smoking, eating and drinking are strictly forbidden in the office. There's a non-smoking cafeteria downstairs, and smokers have to go outside. Personally, I think smoking ought to be banned in all public places.

2
As you can see, it's a really busy office and we have to work long hours. Everybody works different hours because people are coming in and out all the time. We can have a drink at our desks but we're not allowed to bring food into the offices. There's a canteen downstairs. We're supposed to have a break every two hours, but when you're working to a deadline, you can't afford to take time for a break. Sometimes I work right through my lunch hour – it's mad really. In fact, you have to be mad to work here. Hah. We're not supposed to smoke in the office but some of the reporters and journalists do when they're working late. You know they've been smoking because the place smells horrible in the morning. As far as dress is concerned, it depends. The editors and senior staff dress smartly. I think our senior editor has two suits and about twenty identical striped shirts because I've never seen him wearing anything else. The younger men are a bit more fashion-conscious and they don't have to wear suits. The women can wear trousers or skirts, but we can't wear jeans. Smart-casual clothes are OK.

3
As you can imagine, people who work here are pretty fashion-conscious. They can wear whatever they like, but people usually choose to dress smartly for work. They're the sort of people who enjoy dressing up and they're quite competitive. Most people wear black – it's a bit like wearing a uniform really! Um, black polo-neck pullovers, black bootleg trousers, black leather jackets and boots – and that's just the girls. Hah. The men tend to be more imaginative with their colours. They wear nice brightly coloured shirts … and then colour their hair to match! Personally, I go for a more elegant look – suits and high heels.
Unfortunately, most of the young models who come to the agency are smokers – but they're not allowed to smoke in the building. In fact, they can't smoke anywhere near the building. It gives such a bad impression when you see people smoking in the entrance.
The agency is open from ten o'clock in the morning, but the staff arrive any time after eight. They have to work a nine-hour day, but the starting and finishing times are flexible.
Coffee is available whenever you want it, but food isn't allowed in the office. Nobody here eats anyway!

11 Journey

📼 40

(F = Friend; C = Conrad)
F: It must be very strange to be back home after such a long time.
C: Yes, it is. I … I mean, it's lovely to see everybody and I really appreciate my bed.
F: Let's have a look at these photos then.
C: Well, they're all mixed up at the moment. I've got to sort them out.
F: Um, this looks nice. Where is it?
C: Where do you think it is?
F: Ah, well … it must be somewhere really hot. It looks like paradise. I suppose it could be Thailand or Bali, or it could even be India.
C: No. I'll give you a clue. It's an island in the Pacific Ocean.
F: Hawaii.
C: No, I didn't go to Hawaii.
F: Oh, right … I thought you'd been everywhere! It's probably Fiji then.
C: That's right. Oh, it was lovely. This man wanted me to marry his daughter. She was beautiful.
F: Oh, a Fijian wedding … that would've been fun.
C: Yeah, that's what I thought. But I don't think my mum would've been very pleased. Hah. Anyway, what about this one?
F: Ah, this is a bit different. Well, must be Switzerland or somewhere in the French Alps?
C: Nope.
F: Who's the girl by the way?
C: Oh, yes … that's er, what's-her-name, er? She's Argentinian.
F: Oh, was she travelling around Europe then?
C: No. In this picture, she wasn't far from home.
F: Well, it can't be Argentina, can it? Maybe it's Chile?
C: No, it's the southern part of Argentina … Patagonia.
F: Oh …
C: They call it the Switzerland of the southern hemisphere.
F: Really? That's amazing. It really does look like Switzerland. So anyway, did you meet a girl in every country you visited?

📼 41

Liz
(I = Interviewer; L = Liz)
I: So, who would your ideal companion be?
L: My friend, Anna, who's doing a course in Oriental studies.
I: Ahah, and how would you get around?

come on, this is silly. How much do you need?
R: £300.
MS: Oh, honestly, Richard, you really must learn to budget.
R: Look, Mum, if you can just help me out this time, I promise I'll try to be more careful in future.
MS: Well, we'll see about that. Listen, I … I'll do it this time, but this really is the last time. If you get yourself into trouble again you'll just have to sort it out yourself.
R: Oh, thanks, Mum.
MS: But I'm doing this on one condition …
R: Yes?
MS: You never say you're not going to get married again.
R: OK, I promise. Thanks Mum. Bye.
MS: Bye … and next time, you could phone up just for a chat!

14 Style

📼 49

1
I think my favourite thing at the moment is my white polo-neck sweater. It goes with everything and it's really easy to wear.

2
I love my flowery silk waistcoat. I only wear it on very special occasions and I usually wear it with a suit. It cheers me up.

3
My favourite thing is my black leather jacket which I bought in America and is really old. It gets better as it gets older.

4
My baseball cap is my favourite thing. I've got very short hair and I feel really cold without it. The colour's great, bright orange and pink.

5
I spend quite a lot of money on clothes, but my favourite things aren't usually the most expensive. For example, I love my old short-sleeved T-shirt with a big banana on the front. I got that from the market for less than five pounds.

6
My favourite thing is definitely my leopard-print fake fur coat. I got it from a second-hand shop and it looks fabulous with my high-heeled boots.

7
I tend to like comfortable clothes best … my favourite outfit is my baggy trousers and check shirt.

8
My gran sent me a beautiful tartan cashmere scarf for Christmas and I love it.

📼 50

Ugly by Jon Bon Jovi
If you're ugly, I'm ugly too!
In your eyes the sky's a different blue
If you could see yourself like others do
You'd wish you were as beautiful as you

And I wish I was a camera sometimes
So I could take your picture with my mind
Put it in a frame for you to see
How beautiful you really are to me

Ugly, ugly
All of us just feel like that some day
Ain't no rainbow in the sky
When you feel U.G.L.Y.
And that's ugly
Yeah yeah yeah
Yeah yeah yeah

Ugly, ugly
All of us just feel like that some day
Ain't no rainbow in the sky
When you feel U.G.L.Y.
And that's ugly, ugly
All of us just feel like that some day
Ain't no cure that you can buy
When you feel U.G.L.Y.
And that's ugly

So, if you're ugly, I'm ugly too
If you're a nut, then I must be a screw
If you could see yourself the way I do
You'd wish you were as beautiful as you
I wish I was as beautiful as you

📼 51

(See page 124.)

15 Age

📼 52

(M = Man; W = Woman)
M: You look worried. What's on your mind?
W: Actually, there is something I've been meaning to tell you …
M: Look, if it's about last night, it really doesn't matter. I shouldn't have said anything.
W: No, no, it's nothing to do with that. Or rather I suppose it is, in a way.
M: I knew it. If only I'd kept my mouth shut.
W: Look, I agree with you. The Rolling Stones are old-fashioned and I wish I'd never put that record on.
M: It's not a bad record. It's my fault. I shouldn't have called them boring old dinosaurs.
W: No, it's my fault. I shouldn't have reacted like I did. It's just that that record brings back special memories for me.
M: Look, I understand. My parents used to play The Rolling Stones too.
W: No, you don't understand. I was in my teens when that record first came out.
M: Ah, right. I see what you mean. Well, you look very good for your age.
W: Oh, shut up.
M: No, no, no. What I mean is that I don't care how old you are … and anyway, I've got something to tell you. I'm not 31, I'm 26.
W: What!

📼 53

a
Of course I didn't say anything … I mean, the cashier should have asked to look in her bag, shouldn't she? If it had been a small shop, I probably would have said something, but a big supermarket like that can afford it.

b
Well, I picked it up, brushed the cat hairs off and served it. Well, what you don't see you don't worry about, do you?

c
So I said, 'It looks lovely,' and then spent the rest of the day wishing I'd told her the truth.

d
I was so shocked. It took me a few days to decide what to do, but once I'd made up my mind, I was sure it was the right thing. I cashed the cheque and went straight to the travel agent's where I bought tickets to Egypt for myself and a couple of friends. At least they love me as I am. The divorce will be through next month.

e
I don't know if he saw me, but I didn't want to embarrass him so I just carried on walking. I often think about him and wonder how he ended up on the streets.

📼 54

Freddie
(I = Interviewer; F = Freddie)
I: How old are you now, Freddie?
F: Twelve.
I: Is that a good age to be?
F: Yeah … you're grown up enough to be semi-independent but still young. At school I've just gone from being one of the oldest in my old school to being one of the youngest in secondary school.
I: Oh, and which do you prefer?
F: Well, it was good being the oldest because I could boss people around but it's quite good being the youngest too because we're let out early for lunch and we get to go home at two o'clock on Wednesday afternoons. Also having an older brother in the same school helps.
I: What are the advantages of being 12?
F: You're not a teenager yet so you're not annoyed and uptight about everything.
I: How old's your brother?
F: Sixteen.
I: What differences are there between being 12 and being 16?
F: He smells and I don't. Hah. Also, he's got exams and I haven't.
I: Have you ever wished you were older or younger than you are?
F: Yeah … I'd like to be old enough not to tidy my room.
I: Hah. But you have to tidy your room whatever age you are.
F: Yeah, but if I was old enough to leave home and have my own place, I wouldn't have to tidy my room.

Jem
(I = Interviewer; J = Jem)
I: How old are you, Jem?
J: Sixteen.
I: What's it like being 16? Is that a good age to be?
J: Er, well, I'd prefer to be 18.
I: Why?

J: Because of the things I could do legally, like go to bars and clubs ... oh yeah, and vote.
I: Are you looking forward to voting?
J: Yeah.
I: Do you mind if I ask you who you might vote for?
J: Well, I don't really know. Um, it might all have changed in two years.
I: What do you think is the best age to be?
J: Er, probably when you're really young, before you go to school. You don't have a care in the world.
I: You've got a brother who's 12, haven't you?
J: Yes, unfortunately.
I: Hah. In what way are your lives different?
J: I've got a lot more responsibilities. I've got a part-time job at the weekend and I've got more of a workload from school. But I've also got a lot more freedom. He's not allowed out after six o'clock.
I: Ah. Do you mind if I ask you whether you've got a girlfriend?
J: Er, not really.

Yvette
(I = Interviewer; Y = Yvette)
I: You've just had an important birthday, haven't you?
Y: Oh, well, not really. These days 18 is the important one.
I: So, how does it feel to be 21?
Y: Oh, exactly the same as 20.
I: Is there anything you can do now that you couldn't do before you were 21?
Y: Um, no, not really. But I suppose when you're 21, you have more responsibilities. You're supposed to be more independent and er, you can't depend on your parents so much. Er, like I have to pay for my holidays myself now, so these are the disadvantages. And er, people expect grown-up behaviour from you.
I: Ah. What do you reckon is the best age to be?
Y: Um, maybe five years old. You go to play school and you play all day. Everybody spoils you and life is just fun.
I: Have you ever wished you were older or younger?
Y: Oh, yes. When I was about 15, my brother was allowed out and I wasn't. He's three years older than me and I wanted to be the same age as him.

Carmel
(I = Interviewer; C = Carmel)
I: Do you mind if I ask you how old you are?
C: Actually, I'd rather not say. But put it this way, I'm the wrong side of 30.
I: Is that a good age to be?
C: Um, yes, pretty good. But it's a lot older than 25, which is how old I feel.
I: What's life like when you're in your thirties?
C: Well, not very different from my twenties except that I'm seriously thinking of buying more expensive face creams, and wondering if they really work.
I: What do you think is the best age to be?
C: I think between 25 and 30 is a good age, because you've kind of sorted out what you want and you know how to get it and you've got some experience of trying to get it. At that age you don't think about the consequences of what you do whereas when you're a bit older you do tend to worry about the consequences.
I: So do you wish you were still 25?
C: No, I'm happy at the age I am now. I mean, I had a good time in my twenties, but I wouldn't necessarily want to relive them.
I: Hah.

16 Review 2

 55

(I = Interviewer; KT = Kim Thomas)
I: ... so, if we could turn to the origin of language? Um, do we know when, where and how language originated?
KT: Ah, that's a difficult question to answer, or rather the answer is no one really knows. What we do know is when language was first written down.
I: Ah hah, and that was ...
KT: That was about five and a half thousand years ago, in about 3500 BC. The Sumerians, who lived in Mesopotamia, were the first people to write down their language. They used symbols called pictographs to represent everyday objects – a bit like Egyptian hieroglyphics – and the first actual alphabet was developed around 3,500 years ago by the Phoenicians, who lived on the eastern coast of what is now Syria. Today there are around 65 alphabets in the world. Interestingly, the shortest of them, the one used in the Solomon Islands, has only 11 letters.
I: Hah, hah. And the longest?
KT: Er, the Cambodian, I think. I believe it's got 74 letters.
I: So, how many languages are there in the world today?
KT: Somewhere in the region of 4,000. I don't think we'll ever find out the exact figure.
I: Um, and which of these are the most spoken?
KT: Well, Mandarin Chinese has about a billion speakers. English is next with about half a billion speakers and Hindi, Spanish and Russian are not too far behind. These five languages account for half of all the conversations in the world!
I: Hah, hah, hah. And is it true that Mandarin is the biggest language? I mean the one with the most number of words.
KT: Again, it's difficult to say, but the latest thinking is that English is actually the biggest, largely due to the number of technical and scientific words it contains. There are at least a million words in English. Most native speakers only use about 10,000 words, that's one per cent of them.
I: Hah. Only 10,000?
KT: Yeah, and can you guess which are the most common of these? The most used words in English.
I: Huh. Let me think. Um, maybe 'be'?
KT: Well, according to recent research, where tens of thousands of hours of conversation have been fed into computers and analysed, the most common word is 'the'.
I: Oh, and 'be'?
KT: Well, 'be', we think, is the most used verb in English. But of course there are different forms. Er, what do you think the most common noun in spoken English is?
I: Mm, The most common noun? Erm, maybe something like ... er, oh, I've no idea. You're going to have to tell us.
KT: Hah, hah, hah. Well, you just said it, actually. Apparently it's 'thing'.
I: Mm. Hah ... OK ... hah. What about the origins of words? Where does English come from?
KT: Well, modern English, which is about 500 years old, is a mixture of mainly Romance and Germanic languages. Greek and Arabic have also provided English with many words. Er, did you know 'sugar' comes from Arabic? And, surprisingly, so does 'alcohol'. In fact many, many words have been 'borrowed' from other languages. For example, did you know that 'coffee' comes from Turkish and that 'chess', the game, is a Persian word?
I: Oh, no.
KT: Where do you think 'ketchup', as in tomato ketchup, comes from?
I: Er, I've never really thought about it. I've no idea. Hah, hah, hah. America?
KT: Hah, hah, hah. It's from the Malay language. A traditional Malaysian sauce I believe.
I: Ah.
KT: How about 'shampoo'?
I: Mmm, it sounds a bit oriental to me. Maybe Japanese?
KT: It's actually a Hindi word, from India. The list is endless.
I: Er, you mentioned India just then. Isn't that a country with hundreds of languages?
KT: Well, I don't know about hundreds. I think Papua New Guinea has got the most with over eight hundred and fifty separate languages, but India has got dozens of languages. The bank notes there have got thirteen languages written on them. I suppose they're the main languages. Um, most people there speak at least two or three languages.
I: Um, talking of which ... and one final question. To speak two languages fluently is difficult enough, but have you any idea what the highest number of languages spoken by one person is?
KT: There is, or was, a Frenchman, I, er, can't remember his name, but he spoke 31 different languages. All of them fluently!
I: Oh. On that note, Professor Thomas, we'll say thank you very much and, er, au revoir, auf Wiedersehen, arrivaderci, or, sayonara, adios ...

Carmen Cadierno & Mabel Soracco

Inside Out

Student's Book

Intermediate

**MACMILLAN
HEINEMANN**
English Language Teaching

Special Edition

Units & topics	Speaking & writing	Reading & listening texts	**G**rammar, **L**exis & **P**ronunciation
S1 Fame (Friends) Life as an Oscar winner Qualities of a good host page 164	Talking about the qualities of a good host	Interview with Tom Hanks Interview questions	**G** Asking questions **L** Classrooms language False friends **P** Intonation of questions
S2 Movies (Relax) Books, films & music Cultural events page 166	Writing dialogues Planning a presentation Giving a presentation	Preview of what's on: entertainment guide	**L** Giving & asking for opinions **P** Long & short vowel sounds
S3 Compatibility (Dating) Relationships page 168	Giving criticisms tactfully Writing an advertisement for the lonely hearts section of a magazine	*The Importance of Being Earnest* by Oscar Wilde 'Lonely hearts' advertisements People talking about themselves	**G** Question tags **L** Criticisms & generalisations: *can be; tends to be* **P** Verbs ending with *-ed*
S4 Risk (Adrenalin) Taking risks Story telling page 170	Talking about attitudes to risk taking Telling stories Evaluating stories	Questionnaire: *Are you a risk taker?* – measuring your capacity for risk A story with sound effects	**G** Past experiences: past simple; present perfect & present perfect continuous **P** Adjectives ending with *-ed*
S5 Development (Kids) Changing habits Genetics Dangerous games page 172	Talking about how society has changed Talking about dangerous games children play & how to warn them about the dangers	Article: *What do we learn from twins?* – researching identical twins People talking about children & dangerous games	**G** Past habits & states: *used to* & *would* Defining & non-defining relative clauses
S6 Headlines (News) News Addiction page 174	Talking about news	Newspaper headlines and articles A woman talking about her addiction to shopping	**G** Repeated past events Present perfect for recent events Expressing contrast: *although, despite, however, nevertheless* **L** Newspaper language
S7 Fiesta (Party) Festivals & parties page 176	Writing a recipe	Article: preview of a music festival Phone calls: inviting people out & making arrangements	**G** Future tenses & uses of the future **L** The language of parties
S8 Exam practice 1 page 178			

Units & topics	Speaking & writing	Reading & listening texts	Grammar, Lexis & Pronunciation
S9 Lies (Soap) Telling stories Robbery page 184	Telling lies	📖 An employee progress report 📼 A job interview 📼 A hold-up in a bank	**G** Reporting commands & requests *say* & *tell* Reporting verbs
S10 Connected (Time) Working from home New technology page 186	Talking about new technology	📼 A journalist talking about the pros and cons of working from home	**G** Modals of obligation, prohibition & permission: *must(n't); can('t); could*, plus *(don't) have to; need to* Reporting modal verbs **L** Agreeing, disagreeing, interrupting and asking for clarification **P** Strong & weak forms
S11 Expedition (Journey) Sherpas Entertainment page 188	Talking about Sherpas Discussing events in an entertainment guide	📼 A climber talking about Sherpas & their role in mountaineering expeditions 📖 A hotel & entertainment guide 📼 Dialogues to do with air travel	**L** Vocabulary of air travel **P** Contractions
S12 Food (Basics) Diets Eating styles page 190	Talking about diets Writing a menu	📼 Two flatmates talking about dieting 📖 Article describing different types of eaters & giving advice on good eating habits	**G** Countable & uncountable nouns Definite article **L** Food vocabulary; ways of cooking Comparing English & Spanish food vocabulary **P** Linking words
S13 Habit (Communication) Stereotypes Computers page 192	Talking about national stereotypes Talking about computers Writing tips on buying a car or hi-fi system	📼 *How to be an Alien* by George Mikes 📖 Tips on buying a computer	**L** False friends **P** Rising & falling intonation
S14 Fashion (Style) Being fashionable Body piercing page 194	Talking about body piercing Talking about fashion & pressure to be fashionable	📖 Article: *But it's cool!* – film stars & fashion 📼 Conversation about body piercing	**G** Purpose clauses **L** Vocabulary of clothes Word formation: adjectives & adverbs
S15 Memory (Age) Ambitions & regrets Growing old page 196	Talking about living to an old age	📼 People talking about their job situation, ambitions & regrets 📖 Article: *Can I live to be 125* – living to an old age	**G** Real & unreal conditionals; *I wish* + past simple & past perfect
S16 Exam practice 2 page 198			
Tapescripts page 204			

S1 Fame

Friends

Classroom language

Here are some useful phrases for you to use in class. Match the phrases to the uses below.

a) What does ' … ' mean?
How do you say ' … ' in English?
I don't understand.

b) You're right, but …
That's not what it says here.
What *I* understand is that …

c) Who starts?
Why don't you do the first part?

d) Excuse me, what do we have to do?
Could you explain that again, please?

e) That's all. We've finished.
What did you think of the activity?

> starting an activity   asking for clarification   asking about meaning
> ending an activity   disagreeing

Interview with Tom Hanks

1 You are going to listen to a radio interview in which Tom Hanks was asked the following questions. Write the questions from the prompts then match the questions to each of his answers.

a) What / the disadvantages / being / two-time Oscar winner?
b) What kind / films / you like / be in?
c) you / feel like / veteran?
d) How far / you go in playing / character?
e) What effect / winning the Oscars had / you?
f) What / Tom Hanks do when he finally gets some privacy?
g) it true you first worked as / hotel bellboy?
h) you ever turned down / comedy?

Tom Hanks in *Saving Private Ryan*

He's won two Academy awards, and has had a straight run of several commercially successful films. Despite all his success, Tom Hanks has a reputation for being one of the most humble and level-headed guys in the business.

1 *Tom, the younger actors in 'Saving Private Ryan' refer to you as 'the Veteran'.*
_____ ?

I sure feel that way. I've made about 20 movies. And five of them are pretty good!

2 _____ ?

Well, I seem to be doing more serious dramas now, which is an interesting change.

3 _____ ?

The disadvantages are probably very obvious. My family is under constant scrutiny, which they don't deserve to be under, and privacy is quite complicated to get.

4 _____ ?

He takes a nap! I can sleep any time, anywhere. I wake up refreshed and ready to go.

5 _____ ?

Yes, it's true, and being a hotel boy was a perfect job for someone like me. Not much is expected of you except for lugging bags, and you can peep through keyholes!

6 _____ ?

Ones with stories that I think I understand and that move me emotionally.

7 _____ ?

Of course not. I never sat around and said, 'No more comedies!'

8 _____ ?

I'll do anything on camera if that's what it takes. I'm not really afraid of anything. If you want me to swing from a tree, I'll swing from a tree. It doesn't matter.

Intonation

2 🔊 01 Listen to the questions. How many did you get right?

Listen to the questions again. Does the speaker's voice go up ↗ or down ↘ on the underlined syllables?

For example:
1 *Do you feel like a veteran?* ↗

2 What effect has winning the Oscars had on you? _____
3 What are the disadvantages of being a two-time Oscar winner? _____
4 What does Tom Hanks do when he finally gets some privacy? _____
5 Is it true you first worked as a hotel bellboy? _____
6 What kind of films do you like to be in? _____
7 Have you ever turned down a comedy? _____
8 How far will you go in playing a character? _____

False friends

1 A false friend is a word that deceives you about its meaning. Here are some examples of *false friends*. Work with a partner and discuss the differences in meanings between these words. Use a dictionary if you need to.

   a) season and station   c) diary and agenda   e) sensible and sensitive
   b) library and bookshop   d) educated and polite   f) destiny and destination

2 Translate the following sentences:

   a) No encontré el libro que necesito en la librería, así que tendré que sacarlo de la biblioteca.
   b) En mi país hay una estación de tren que se llama *Spring* como la estación del año.
   c) Éste es el orden del día de la próxima reunión – no olvides apuntar la fecha en tu agenda.
   d) Una persona educada no dice tacos. Una persona educada puede hablar de muchos temas diferentes.
   e) Mi padre solía darme consejos muy sensatos. Yo era un niño muy sensible y todo me hacía llorar.
   f) Tu destino puede estar escrito en las estrellas, pero tu lugar de destino está escrito en tu billete.

3 Manuela, a Spanish student of English, wrote a description of her neighbour, Mr Hernández. Read her description on the right. Find the false friends and correct them.

> What an unpleasant man Mr Hernández is! He's not sympathetic at all, and he hasn't got educated manners, either. He's got lots of money. But you know what? He's bought the most economic car on the market, and he refuses to take particular lessons because he says they're too expensive. I can't support him!

Home & away

Speaking

'Some folks make you feel at home. Others make you wish you were.' (Arnold Glasgow)

1 Which adjectives would you associate with the idea of making you feel at home and which ones with making you wish you were?

   uneasy   warm   cosy   embarrassing   noisy   worried   comfortable   aggressive
   relaxing   frightening   unpleasant   friendly   calm

2 Work in groups. What are the qualities of a good host? What should you do to make someone feel at home?

S2 Movies

Relax

Do you remember ...?

Humphrey Bogart in the film classic *Casablanca*

1. Work with a partner or in groups. Decide whether each of the titles below is a book, song, film or play and put a cross (✗) in the correct column. Then match the titles to the quotations.

				Title	Quote
				1 The Godfather	a) That is the question.
				2 When I'm 64	b) We made him an offer he couldn't refuse.
				3 Animal Farm	c) Play it again, Sam.
				4 Gone with the Wind	d) Home! Home!
				5 Hamlet	e) You know how to whistle, don't you?
				6 To Have and Have Not	f) Big Brother is watching you.
				7 What a Wonderful World	g) Will you still need me, will you still feed me?
				8 Casablanca	h) Frankly, my dear, I don't give a damn.
				9 E.T.	i) Napoleon is always right.
				10 1984	j) Don't know much about geography.

2. Choose at least three quotes and write a dialogue of no more than ten lines using them.

3. Read or act out the dialogue in front of the class. Which ones do you like best?

Odd one out

Long & short vowel sounds

1. 02 Three of the words in each of the lines below have the same vowel sound, but one is different. Identify the odd one out. Is the vowel sound in this word long or short?

a) thriller films feel drink
b) sing leave eat tree
c) dawn problem story boring
d) plot horror comedy horse
e) book woman movie put
f) rude foot soup blue

Listen and check.

2. How many spellings can you find for each of the sounds in 1?

/ɪ/ /iː/ /ɔː/ /ɒ/ /uː/ /ʊ/

How to organise a one-minute presentation

You have to give a one-minute presentation of a film you've seen recently. Here's some advice on how to do it.

Divide the presentation in two parts: Introduction and Evaluation.

Introduction
Include the following information:
- type of film   • director   • main actor/actress   • supporting actor/actress
- place   • time   • plot summary

For example:
It is a _____ (type) film. It takes place in _____ (place) in _____ (time). It is directed by _____ .

The main actor / actress and the supporting actors / actresses are _____ . The film is about _____ .

Evaluation
Give your opinion. Look at the adjectives below and decide which of them are positive and which are negative. Use some of them in your evaluation.

> superb   brilliant   disappointing   interesting   gripping   incredible   exciting
> boring   fascinating   annoying   depressing   terrible   amazing   excellent   OK
> awful   rubbish   dull   appalling   great   sensational   pretentious

Now give your presentation to the class.

Language awareness

1 Think of other ways of giving your opinions. Write down examples of the language you use in the appropriate column.

giving your opinion	asking someone for their opinion
I think/believe that ...	*What do you think of ...?*

2 Go round the class and ask other students for their opinions about films you've seen.

What's on?

Read the following extracts from a magazine advertising cultural events. Choose the events you find most interesting and translate them into English.

agenda

música

Tears of Stone
The Chieftains, el grupo de música tradicional irlandesa más popular del mundo, acaba de lanzar su último trabajo: *Tears of Stone*, un CD en el que exploran las muchas facetas del amor desde la perspectiva femenina. Por eso han contado con la participación de The Corrs, Bonnie Rait, Loreena McKenitt y Sinead O'Connor.

exposiciones

Chillida
La muestra presenta la trayectoria creadora de este artista vasco a lo largo de más de 50 años. Chillida es uno de los artistas españoles vivos más importantes y de mayor proyección internacional y esta retrospectiva se presenta coincidiendo con su 75 cumpleaños.

teatro

La Casa de Bernarda Alba
Considerada un clásico del teatro español, esta obra muestra la España de una época de un erotismo reprimido, de religión fanática y de un profundo sentimiento de muerte. Se trata de un documento vivo de una sociedad rural en la que el amor se subordina al interés económico, el honor a la opinión de los demás, y la mujer a un machismo desenfrenado.

libros

Amanecer con Hormigas en la Boca
Esta novela, con todos los ingredientes de la mejor tradición americana del género negro, pero con carácter esencialmente latino, se desarrolla en la Cuba de Batista, un lugar en manos de la mafia, repleto de casinos y juego ilegal, de chicas, de los últimos modelos de Chevrolet, y que pronto se convertiría en la Cuba de Fidel Castro.

cine

Todo sobre mi Madre
Tras la muerte de su hijo en un accidente, Manuela descubre que la mayor ilusión de éste era conocer a su padre. Decide buscarle, pero lo único que sabe es que es un travesti que vive en Barcelona. La búsqueda no va a resultar sencilla.

(Adapted from *Ronda Iberia*, May 1999)

S3 Compatibility

Dating

Criticisms & generalisations

1   Here are some comments which avoid saying things directly. Match them to their true meanings below:

1. He wasn't exactly helpful.
2. My parents appear to be modern, but they can be quite old-fashioned.
3. What he said wasn't particularly inspiring.
4. She tends to drink a little too much at parties.
5. They're not particularly punctual.
6. He's a bit overweight, isn't he?
7. He gets rather angry when we break the rules.
8. You tend to worry too much.
9. She can be very talkative at times.
10. He tends to mumble when he gets nervous.

a) They often arrive late.
b) She always gets drunk.
c) I don't understand a word he says.
d) You should try to take things easy.
e) He didn't help me at all.
f) She never stops talking.
g) What a boring speech!
h) They never let me do what I want.
i) Wow, he's fat!
j) He gets mad at us.

2   Think about the last time you had problems dealing with someone: an assistant, a friend, your parents, a government official, the plumber, your boss, etc. Choose a comment from 1, or think of a new one. Then describe the situation including that comment.

For example:
I asked the receptionist at the hotel to recommend a good restaurant, but he wasn't exactly helpful. He just said he didn't know. So I walked into the nearest restaurant, which of course wasn't very good.

These questions may help you: Where were you? Who with? What were you doing there? What made you feel uncomfortable? What did you do? What happened in the end?

The importance of being Earnest

Listening

1   03 You are going to listen to an extract from Oscar Wilde's comedy, *The Importance of Being Earnest*. Complete the following sentences with question tags from the box:

a) And you'll always call me Gwendolen, _____ ?
b) Then that's all settled, _____ ?
c) You've never heard of papa, _____ .
d) And certainly once a man begins to neglect his domestic duties he becomes painfully effeminate, _____ ?

> isn't it?   doesn't he?   won't you?   have you?

Listen to the extract and check your answers. Is the intonation of the questions rising or falling?

The Importance of Being Earnest

The Importance of Being Earnest is one of Oscar Wilde's most witty and light hearted plays. It was published in 1895.

168 UNIT S3 *Compatibility*

2 Listen to the extract again and decide whether the following sentences are True (T), False (F) or Not stated (NS).

a) Gwendolen thinks she has the gift of telling what a person is like right from the beginning. ☐

b) Gwendolen and Cecily have known each other for some time. ☐

c) Cecily hasn't heard of Gwendolen's father. ☐

d) Gwendolen blames the fact that she can't see very well on her mother. ☐

e) Gwendolen has an unusual opinion about the way men should behave. ☐

f) Cecily is very shy and she doesn't like people to look at her. ☐

g) Gwendolen pretends she doesn't know anything about Cecily's background. ☐

Pronunciation of -ed

1 04 Listen and identify the pronunciation of *-ed* in each of the following groups of regular verbs. Is it /d/, /t/ or /ɪd/?

a) laughed looked hoped kissed mixed washed reached
b) dated persuaded voted added succeeded celebrated chatted reported
c) feared played married stored glued robbed mugged circled filmed happened answered loved borrowed closed exchanged

2 Work with a partner. What are the rules for the pronunciation of *-ed*?

Lonely hearts

Listening

1 05 Read these advertisements from the Lonely Hearts section of a popular magazine and listen to some people talking about themselves. Match the speaker to the advertisement. There are more advertisements than speakers.

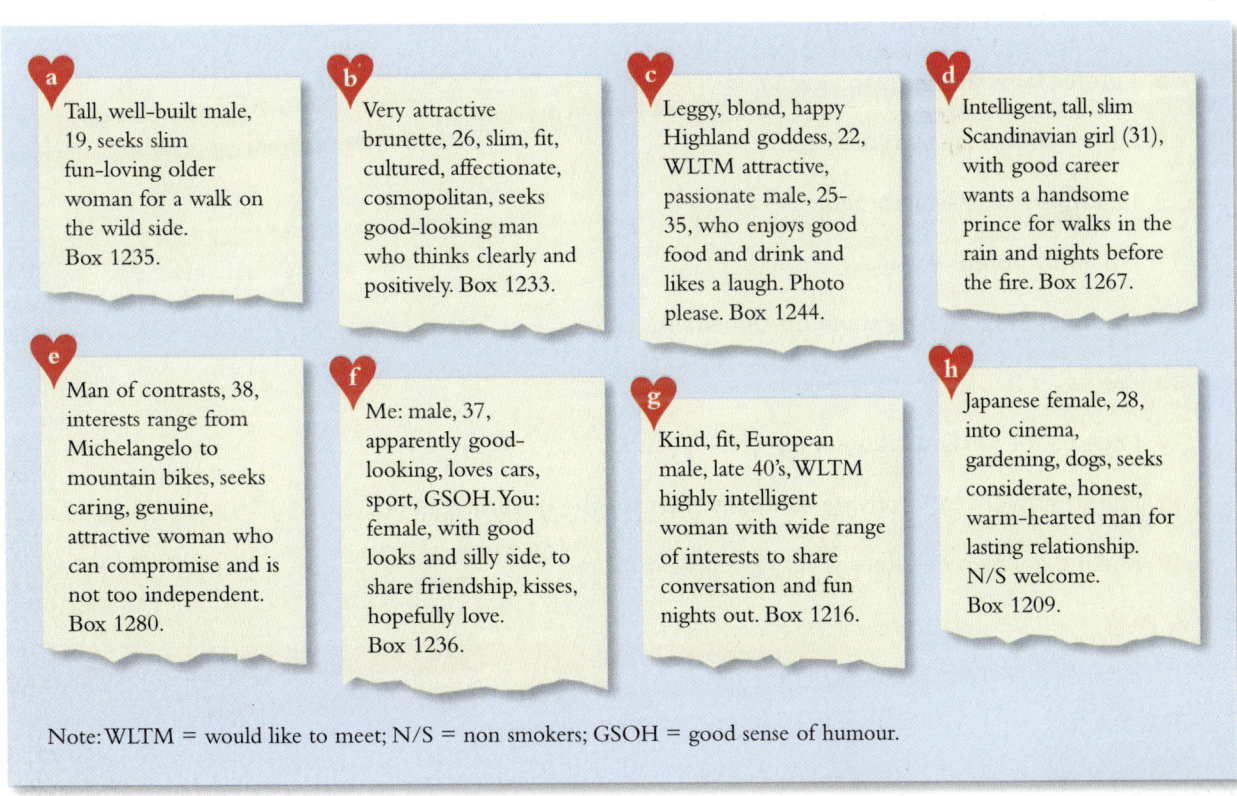

a Tall, well-built male, 19, seeks slim fun-loving older woman for a walk on the wild side. Box 1235.

b Very attractive brunette, 26, slim, fit, cultured, affectionate, cosmopolitan, seeks good-looking man who thinks clearly and positively. Box 1233.

c Leggy, blond, happy Highland goddess, 22, WLTM attractive, passionate male, 25-35, who enjoys good food and drink and likes a laugh. Photo please. Box 1244.

d Intelligent, tall, slim Scandinavian girl (31), with good career wants a handsome prince for walks in the rain and nights before the fire. Box 1267.

e Man of contrasts, 38, interests range from Michelangelo to mountain bikes, seeks caring, genuine, attractive woman who can compromise and is not too independent. Box 1280.

f Me: male, 37, apparently good-looking, loves cars, sport, GSOH. You: female, with good looks and silly side, to share friendship, kisses, hopefully love. Box 1236.

g Kind, fit, European male, late 40's, WLTM highly intelligent woman with wide range of interests to share conversation and fun nights out. Box 1216.

h Japanese female, 28, into cinema, gardening, dogs, seeks considerate, honest, warm-hearted man for lasting relationship. N/S welcome. Box 1209.

Note: WLTM = would like to meet; N/S = non smokers; GSOH = good sense of humour.

2 What kind of people are the writers? Are they sexist; authoritarian; immature; feminine; conceited; fun to be with; self-confident; sensitive; shy …?

3 Write a similar advertisement of up to 20 words, either about yourself, (tell as many lies as you want to), or about a celebrity.

S4 Risk

Adrenalin

Reading

1 Answer the questionnaire below to find out how comfortable you are about taking risks.

ARE YOU A risk taker?

	True	False
1 I don't like my opinions being challenged.	☐	☐
2 I'd rather be an accountant than a TV presenter.	☐	☐
3 I believe that I control my destiny.	☐	☐
4 I'm a highly creative person.	☐	☐
5 I don't like trying exotic foods.	☐	☐
6 I'd rather have a savings account than play the Stock Exchange.	☐	☐
7 I like to challenge authority.	☐	☐
8 I prefer familiar things to new things.	☐	☐
9 I'd like to run my own business.	☐	☐
10 I'd rather not travel abroad.	☐	☐
11 I'm easily bored.	☐	☐
12 I wouldn't like to be a stand-up comedian.	☐	☐
13 I've never had a speeding ticket.	☐	☐
14 I need a lot of stimulation in my life.	☐	☐
15 I'd rather work for a private company than for the government.	☐	☐
16 Making my own decisions is very important for me.	☐	☐

key

1 F	5 F	9 T	13 F
2 F	6 F	10 F	14 T
3 T	7 T	11 T	15 T
4 T	8 F	12 F	16 T

Give yourself one point each time your answer agrees with the key.
If you score:
12–16, you're probably just back from a hang-gliding trip in the Andes.
8–11: You'd go to the Andes, but you'd give hang-gliding a miss.
4–7: Don't forget the umbrella. It might rain.
0–3: So, how long have you been in life insurance?

(Adapted from *Time*, September 6, 1999 Quiz (c) 1999 by Frank Farley, PhD)

2 Work in groups. Discuss your answers to the quiz and your attitudes to risk taking.

Time for a story

Listening

1 What sounds do the words in the box describe? Look up the words you don't know in a dictionary.

> screaming   squealing   slamming   squeaking   clattering   creaking   croaking
> snoring   panting

2 06 You are going to listen to a story. First, listen to all the sound affects from the story. Try to imagine what is happening. Work in groups and invent a story to go with the sounds.

3 Tell your story to the class. Which story do you like best? Consider the following:
- Was the content interesting?
- How clear was the presentation?
- Was the language and vocabulary used varied and appropriate to the story?

Vote for the best story.

4 07 Listen to the original story and compare it with the one your group wrote.

Language awareness

Present perfect simple & continuous

Look at this sentence from the story:

Someone's been eating out of my bowl and has eaten all my porridge up, and someone's broken my chair.

a) Two tenses are used: the present perfect simple and the present perfect continuous. Find them in the sentence.
b) Which tense focuses on the activity and which tense focuses on the result?
c) Can you say *has been breaking* instead of *has broken*?

Pronunciation

1 08 How do you pronounce the *-ed* endings of these adjectives? Practise saying them with a partner and then listen to the recording and check.

> amused   shocked   bored   tired   surprised   annoyed   interested   two-faced
> thick-skinned   broad-minded   big-headed   old-fashioned   self-centred

2 Complete these sentences with adjectives from 1.

a) He was _____ that we weren't _____ in his proposal.
b) What _____ clothes she wears!
c) I was so _____ I fell asleep.
d) A: What do you call someone who is _____ , _____ and often _____ ?
   B: A politician.

S6 Headlines

News

Meet the press

1 Match the headlines to the first paragraphs of the newspaper stories.

a LITERACY HOUR TO BE EXTENDED TO SECONDARY SCHOOL PUPILS

b CANCER FUND HEAD QUITS OVER DONATIONS

c JUST GREAT, KATE

d BOY IN GUN KILL SPREE

e CANOEIST IN SPIDER BITE ERROR

f SICK OR TREAT

g KING WAS WRITE-OFF

h BIG CUT IN CLASS SIZES

1 Two teenage trick-or-treaters killed a girl's kitten on Halloween after being turned away from a house.

2 A teenage sniper shot at hospital visitors and inmates yesterday killing two and injuring seven.

3 A British Olympic canoeist needed emergency treatment after being bitten by a deadly spider.

4 Horror writer Stephen King feared he would never finish another novel after being critically injured in an accident.

5 The Government will extend its national 'literacy hour' to secondary schools after research showed it had a startling effect on learning.

6 In the self-obsessed, narcissistic world of showbusiness Kate Winslet reveals herself, not for the first time, to be a breath of fresh air.

7 The number of children in infant classes of more than thirty has almost halved this year, according to government figures published yesterday.

8 The head of the Roy Castle Lung Cancer Foundation has resigned after a reported dispute over fund-raising.

2 There are some language differences between headlines and other written forms. Look at the headlines in 1.

a) What kinds of words are omitted?
b) Three of the headlines include verb tenses. What verb tenses are used? Do they refer to the past, present or future?
c) Give examples of nouns functioning as adjectives.
d) Which short words are used instead of resigns and reduction?
e) Find an example of a rhyme.

Born to shop

Listening

🔊 10 You are going to listen to Janet's account of how she got into debt. First read the beginning of an article about her on the right. Then listen to the recording and mark the following statements True (T), False (F) or Not stated (NS).

> **My friends used to say I was a born shopper ... now I'm a bankrupt at just 25.**
> Janet Wayne was one of the estimated 700,000 shopping addicts who get a kick from spending money. Aged 25, with no income, she now owes thousands of pounds. Here is her story.

a) She lived on her own in Liverpool. ☐
b) She had no real friends there. ☐
c) Her parents came to visit her regularly. ☐
d) She passed the shops on her way to work. ☐
e) After a while, she stopped buying make-up. ☐
f) She used to go shopping as soon as she left the office. ☐
g) Occasionally she went into a shop but didn't buy anything. ☐
h) After each shopping binge, she used to promise herself she wouldn't do it again. ☐
i) She stopped shopping when she lost her job. ☐

Language awareness

Past actions & events

Look at the tapescript of Janet's story on page 205 and underline all examples of the statements expressing things that happened repeatedly in the past.

a) How many did you find?   b) What two structures are used?
c) What is the difference in meaning between them?

Expressing contrast

1 The examples below show different ways of expressing the idea of contrast in English.

Janet knew it was wrong, but she couldn't help it.
Although Janet knew it was wrong, she couldn't help it.
Despite / In spite of knowing it was wrong, Janet couldn't help it.
Janet knew it was wrong. However, / Nevertheless, she couldn't help it.

Read Janet's tapescript again and ⓒircle connectors expressing contrast: *but, although, despite, in spite of, however, nevertheless.*

2 Match the phrases in Spanish to their closest English translations.

a pesar de   however, nevertheless
sin embargo,   despite, in spite of
aunque   although

3 Discuss with a partner:

a) What grammatical structure do you use after *although*?
b) What grammatical structure do you use after *despite* and *in spite of*?
c) Which punctuation mark should we use after *however/nevertheless*?

4 Rewrite the sentences beginning with the word shown without changing the meaning.

a) She promised to pay back her debts, but she never did.

(1) Although _____ .   (2) Despite _____ .

b) She felt guilty, but never left a shop without buying something.

In spite of _____ .

c) Despite having other alternatives, Janet decided to declare herself bankrupt.

Although _____ .

d) She ran into debt, but she continued to go shopping.

1) Although _____ .   (2) In spite of _____ .

S7 Fiesta

Party

The article on the right comes from the *Irish Times* selective guide to entertainment. Read the article and then answer the questions below.

a) What does *south of the border* refer to?
b) How many times has the festival taken place in Ireland?
c) How long does the festival last?
d) What do *conga line* and *Cuban heels* mean?

Latin night

You don't have to go south of the border to find a salsa party – just take a quick drive to Kilkenny, and you'll arrive at Ireland's first Latin music festival, the Kilkenny Beer Karnivale. Better get there before sundown, though, because tonight is the final night of this two-day extravaganza of exotic Latin sounds. Last night's festivities were led by the Night in Havana Orchestra, but there's still time to catch Pucho & His Latin Soul Brothers at Langton's tonight (10 pm) or form a conga line and follow the Ruta Loca, which takes in a number of free gigs in various pubs around the town. So get your Cuban heels on and get ready to rumba.

Listening

1. 🎧 11 Danny, Asumpta and Liam are having a mid-morning coffee. Danny has just read the newspaper article about the Latin music festival and is now going to tell his friends about it. Listen and <u>underline</u> the information he mentions in the article above.

2. What do they agree to do?

3. 🎧 12 Asumpta has phoned her friend, Kevin. Complete the conversation with the sentences below and then listen and check.

   a) We'll have a laugh, I'm sure.
   b) When does it start?
   c) 're going to a salsa party tonight
   d) how are we going?
   e) But we're meeting at my place at half past seven.
   f) I think we'll come.
   g) There are loads of bands playing

   > A: Hello, Kevin, we (1) _____ and we thought you and Josie would like to come. The twins may be coming too.
   >
   > K: A salsa party? I can't dance the salsa. Nor can Josie.
   >
   > A: Oh, don't worry about that. (2) _____ including a Cuban one, and it's all free. And we could try some cocktails, and you know, by the end of the night we'll be doing the conga. (3) _____ .
   >
   > K: Sounds grand. OK. (4) _____ . We've nothing on tonight. (5) _____ .
   >
   > A: Eight. (6) _____ .
   >
   > K: Seven thirty. Right. By the way, (7) _____ . Do you want me to drive?
   >
   > A: Why, yes, great.
   >
   > K: OK. See you later.
   >
   > A: Bye.

4. 🎧 13 Danny invites the twins. Listen and find out who can go to the festival and who can't. What reasons do they give? Then complete the summary.

   a) _____ can't go because she's got the flu.
   b) _____ 're going in _____ car.
   c) _____ doesn't want to go because she's revising and she can't stand _____ .
   d) _____ won't have another chance to see the festival until next year.

Uses of the future

Look at the sentences in 3 on page 176.

a) <u>Underline</u> the structures used for the future.
b) Which form is used for promises? Which form is used for fixed plans? Which form is used for making decisions at the moment of speaking?

A recipe

1 Asumpta was given a copy of several typical Cuban and Mexican cocktail recipes. Unfortunately, Liam spilt some drink on it and some of the words were blotted out. Complete the recipes with the words and phrases below.

> lime juice   add a twist of lime   plenty of   Stir together in
> and fill with   dash of   not stir   and strain. Serve

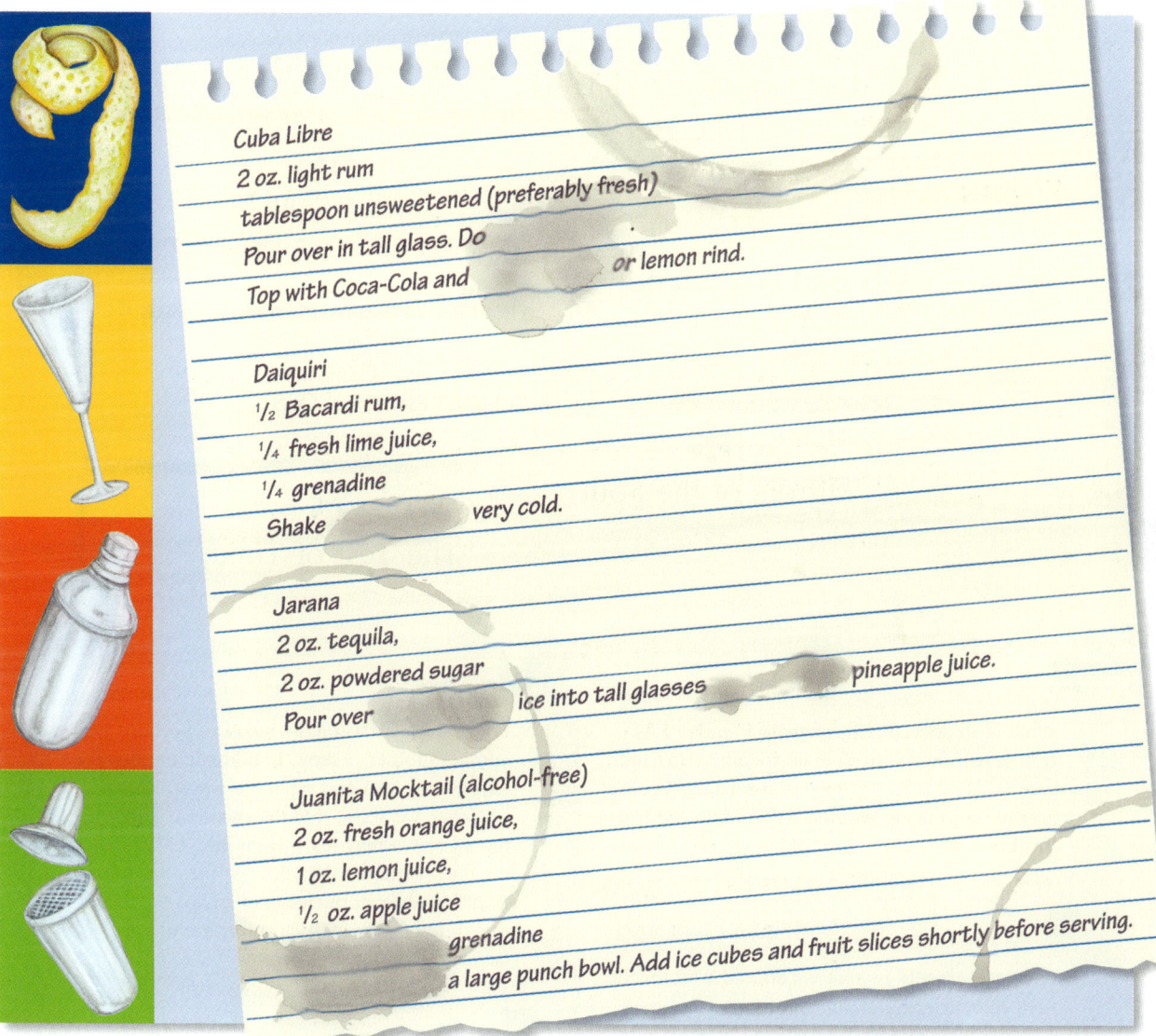

Cuba Libre
2 oz. light rum
tablespoon unsweetened (preferably fresh)
Pour over in tall glass. Do
Top with Coca-Cola and   or lemon rind.

Daiquiri
½ Bacardi rum,
¼ fresh lime juice,
¼ grenadine
Shake   very cold.

Jarana
2 oz. tequila,
2 oz. powdered sugar
Pour over   ice into tall glasses   pineapple juice.

Juanita Mocktail (alcohol-free)
2 oz. fresh orange juice,
1 oz. lemon juice,
½ oz. apple juice
          grenadine
          a large punch bowl. Add ice cubes and fruit slices shortly before serving.

The language of parties

2 Do you have a recipe for Sangría or a favourite cocktail? Write it for a partner.

When would you say the following?
a) Thank you very much. They're lovely. But you shouldn't have bothered.
b) Many happy returns!
c) Here's to the best of friends! Good luck in your new job!
d) Cheers!
e) Yes, I'd love to come.
f) Sorry, I'm busy on Saturday. Some other time, perhaps.

Exam practice 1

Reading comprehension

Part I

Read the following extracts from a book about friendships between women. Match the headings to the extracts. There are two more headings than extracts.

a. I Always Wanted To Be Like Her
b. Losing Touch
c. A Friend is a Friend, Who Cares About the Gender?
d. Surviving Loss
e. Mirrors of the Soul
f. The Test of Time

1
What is so special about female friends? Why distinguish female from male friends? Can't men give what women can give in a relationship? Not according to many women we interviewed for this book.

2
Our mothers told us that we should wait for the right man to come along. But few told us that we may have to wait for the right women friends as well. How do we recognise these women? What is the common characteristic that distinguishes our closest and best friends from our acquaintances? The answer seems to be, in part, that they are like us.

3
Friendships occasionally blossom because we admire another person. In admiration, aren't we expressing who and what we would like to become? We sense that the more we know her, the more we may learn from her. As we mature, we find ourselves drawn to women we perceive as different from ourselves. Perhaps we are ripe for some new growth, and our friend will facilitate that development.

4
At moments of our deepest grief, women who have shared our experience can give uniquely satisfying comfort. When a crisis hits us, we are often knocked off balance and bruised by the fall. Having a girlfriend there to give us a private place to heal can make all the difference.

(Adapted from *Girlfriends*, by C. Renee Berry and Tamara Traeder)

1 _____ 2 _____ 3 _____ 4 _____

Reading comprehension

Part II

Put the paragraphs below in the correct order.

THE NUN WHO REBELLED

a) I realised that the only way to test what I was feeling was to join a convent or something similar, and find out for myself what it was all about. I didn't see this as the end of my legal career because it was still possible for me to work as a lawyer with the order.

b) Since leaving, I've missed the companionship that comes from living in a community. Being a nun is seen as a marriage, but it didn't feel like a divorce when I left, more like breaking off an engagement.

c) Moreover, I found I missed the pressure and the intellectual dimension I was used to. Orders are hierarchical systems, too; your age and the time you've been there are important.

d) I now live on my own in Brighton. I still have my faith in God, but I know leaving the convent was the right thing to do. I'm thinking of returning to law again, although I haven't practised for six years. I became so used to referring to my superiors that it's good to be able to make decisions for myself again.

e) So I joined the Society of the Sacred Heart where I spent five years. I was due to renew my vows when I decided that I no longer liked the direction of the order and therefore, I left. Besides, I felt too secure there. My brother was unemployed at the time, and my cousin was a single mother. They were both struggling, and there I was in a protected environment.

f) Despite being brought up an atheist, I became a Catholic at Cambridge University. I worked as a criminal defence law barrister in London for a year, then I felt a desire to serve God in a more radical way.

(Adapted from *She*, December 1997)

1 _____ 2 _____ 3 _____ 4 _____ 5 _____ 6 _____

Listening comprehension

Part I

14 You are going to listen to a recording about an English girl who lived in Malaya, (now called Malaysia). Listen and mark the four TRUE statements with a cross (✗).

a) Jean didn't have a house of her own.
b) She shared a room with another English girl.
c) She had to work long hours.
d) She led a pleasant life there.
e) She couldn't imagine her future life.
f) She wanted to stay in Malaya.
g) She wouldn't have help with the housework there.
h) Things would be different from what she had thought.

Listening comprehension

Part II

15 You are going to listen to an interview with a sociologist who gives reasons for the rising popularity of risk sports. Read these sentences and choose the best alternative. Mark it with a cross (✗).

1. a) Rugby is not a dangerous sport now.
   b) Football and rugby don't have things in common.
   c) The new sports offer more challenge.

2. Risk sports are becoming more popular because …
   a) millions of people participate in them.
   b) they require skill.
   c) they mix danger, ability and fear.

3. a) Only men want to find out how strong they are.
   b) Dangerous sports help people know themselves.
   c) If you don't take risks, you enjoy life more.

4. Thousands of years ago, man needed …
   a) basically a strong body.
   b) a strong body and an alert mind.
   c) to be strong to attract a mate.

5. In the old times …
   a) there was risk in ordinary life.
   b) the main diseases were flu and polio.
   c) science and governments didn't reduce risks.

Listening comprehension

Part III

16 You are going to listen to three news items. Listen to the recording and mark the seven TRUE statements with a cross (✗).

News item 1: *Natural disasters*

A In Mexico …
   a) the earthquake has only killed 20 people.
   b) it has killed people and damaged buildings.
   c) it has caused floods.

B In Nicaragua …
   a) it has been raining for weeks.
   b) 14 people have died.
   c) the floods have covered the whole country.

News item 2: *Günter Grass*

a) Günter Grass wrote about the Second World War.
b) He is the first German author to get the Nobel prize.
c) He is popular outside Germany.
d) He refuses to have his books made into films.

News item 3: *The Eurochocolate festival*

a) The Eurochocolate Festival lasts from 15–24 October.
b) To take a course in chocolate-making go to the Etruscan Chocohotel.
c) There will be a chocolate fashion parade at the 'Sweet Tooth' theatre.
d) Visitors will be able to try different kinds of chocolate in the streets.

Grammatical competence

Part I

Read the following article and choose the best answer.

Happy birthday

The Internet is the 20th century's most dynamic legacy to the 21st. The first recorded transmission of data took place in 1969, (1) _____ a computer at the University of California in Los Angeles to (2) _____ one at a research centre at Stanford near San Francisco.

(3) _____ those distant days hardly (4) _____ took any notice. It was (5) _____ the 1990s when the explosion in activity happened as the World Wide Web (6) _____ transplanted to the Internet. Actually, it was not until May 1995 that Bill Gates of Microsoft (7) _____ its significance and assigned it 'the highest priority'.

In less than a decade the Web (8) _____ that it will completely transform the way commerce is conducted, and (9) _____ revolutionise leisure, education, work, shopping and health. It has (10) _____ become the main source of instant knowledge on any subject. The Net is excluding the middleman from almost every activity, from car-buying to music, (11) _____ can be downloaded straight from the Net. The Web is now invading our television sets for e-mailing and shopping, and mobile phones offering net access are now (12) _____ . This will almost certainly be a sign of mass market for the Web. (13) _____ , Web cameras and microchips that track your location are getting smaller and (14) _____ , and will soon be put into phones and laptops. Goodness only knows where all this is leading. But it is difficult to deny that, (15) _____ the disturbing divisions between those who have and those who have not, the 21st century will be uniquely endowed to empower practically everyone. If the will is there.

(Adapted from *The Guardian Weekly*, October 28–November 3, 1999)

1 a) since   b) from   c) of   d) in
2 a) the   b) other   c) another   d) others
3 a) At   b) On   c) In   d) For
4 a) anybody   b) nobody   c) none   d) any
5 a) before   b) after   c) while   d) during
6 a) had been   b) will be   c) was   d) has been
7 a) recognised   b) will recognise   c) recognises   d) has recognised
8 a) is proving   b) has proved   c) will prove   d) proves
9 a) must   b) would   c) has to   d) will
10 a) just   b) already   c) still   d) yet
11 a) that   b) –   c) which   d) it
12 a) in sale   b) on sales   c) at the sales   d) on sale
13 a) While   b) Now   c) Meanwhile   d) At this moment
14 a) cheaper   b) more cheap   c) quite cheap   d) cheap
15 a) however   b) despite   c) although   d) instead

Grammatical competence

Part II

This is the end of a letter Kerry, a 32-year-old American teacher, wrote to her friend in Spain. Read the letter and choose the best answer.

> So, how are things with you? (1) _____ of you a lot lately, and feel (2) _____ about not calling you to (3) _____ you know that we finally decided not to buy that car we were so interested (4) _____ . We realised it was far (5) _____ expensive for a second-hand car.
>
> (6) _____ , how are you getting on with your driving? Are you getting more confident about it? Did you (7) _____ buy that computer you needed so badly? I've managed to work (8) _____ how to use Andrew's word processor, and I tell you it (9) _____ letter-writing a lot easier. If I don't like the (10) _____ I wrote something, WHOOSH! Just one push of the DELETE button, and it's all (11) _____ . Of course, I sometimes lose some good information (12) _____ mistake! Well, I'd better stop for now. Please drop me a (13) _____ soon and tell me how (14) _____ are going for you. There is a good chance that I (15) _____ in Spain this summer. Don't forget, you would be more than welcome to come and stay here in California.
>
> Love,
>
> Kerry

1. a) I'm thinking b) I was thinking c) I've been thinking d) I'd been thinking
2. a) bad b) worse c) terrific d) wrong
3. a) leave b) have c) make d) let
4. a) on b) in c) – d) about
5. a) more b) enough c) very d) too
6. a) Beside b) Actually c) Besides d) By the way
7. a) finally b) lastly c) at the end d) also
8. a) off b) out c) up d) over
9. a) has b) makes c) does d) gives
10. a) manner b) form c) style d) way
11. a) gone b) left c) disappeared d) come
12. a) by b) for c) of d) in
13. a) word b) letter c) line d) message
14. a) everything b) all c) things d) matters
15. a) am going b) be c) am d) 'll be

Writing

Task 1

Write a letter of about 125–150 words to a penfriend in an English-speaking country. Include the following information:

- say why you are writing and where you found their address
- describe yourself, your family, the place where you live
- include your hobbies, ambitions, studies / job
- show you are interested in them

Task 2

Use this sentence to begin a story of about 125–150 words.
It was a lovely party!

Oral test

Describe the photo below. You can talk about:

- what the people look like
- their relationship
- their jobs
- what they are doing
- what they did before going to the cinema
- what they are going to do next

Interview: leisure

Read the proverb and talk about the following:
All work and no play makes Jack a dull boy.

- What do you think it means? Comment on the proverb. Is there a similar one in your mother tongue?
- What do you do in your spare time? Compare it to what you used to do when you were a child.
- Describe one of the activities you've recently enjoyed doing.
- How do you think new technologies can influence our free time? And our relationships?
- What are the advantages and disadvantages of having spare time?

s9 Lies

Soap

A fresh start

1. Read the report, and discuss these questions with a partner.
   a) What is Louise's job and what are her responsibilities?
   b) Is she a good employee? Why/why not?
   c) How do you think she got the job?
   d) What are her chances of keeping it?

Ramsdon Maclean plc

Employee Progress Report – No. 1

Name of employee: Louise Anne Hollis-Maclean   **Length of service**: Three months
Job title: Junior Administrative Assistant   **Report by**: Joseph Minsky, Accounts Director

Responsibilities
Photocopying, filing, dealing with phone calls, booking flights and hotel rooms, circulating internal documents, checking payments and ordering stationery.

Punctuality and absence record
Since she started, Louise has been consistently late for work, including six occasions when she was more than an hour late and one day when she did not arrive until midday. Although Louise has one free day a week to attend Westhall College to study for her 'A' levels she has attended fewer than 30% of the lessons.

General performance
There have been numerous problems relating to her performance. The most memorable was when she booked a small bed and breakfast hotel for 100 people attending our annual sales conference. She also booked a one way flight to Hong Kong for the Sales Director, instead of a return. However, the most serious incident was the loss by fire of all client records from A to D. Even now, she does not respect the office no smoking policy.

Relations with others
Both Jo Quilley (Accountant) and Andy Fairbrother (Senior Admin Assistant) have complained to me of Louise's rudeness and aggression and Andy claims she intimidates him into doing much of her work for her.

Conclusion
Louise came to us from prison, after serving nine months for cheque fraud. We saw this as an opportunity to help to rehabilitate a young person who had gone wrong in life. The fact that she was the niece of our Finance Director, Rodney Hollis-Maclean (now retired) was also a factor. Unfortunately, I will not be able to recommend continuing her employment at the end of the trial period.

2. 🔊 17 Louise has applied for new job. Listen to the interview and compare what she says to the report you read. Then write five sentences reporting her lies.

3. Work with a partner. Make up a story which includes a lot of lies. Tell your story. Vote for the best story.

Language awareness

Reporting commands & requests

1 🔊 18 Listen and read. Underline all the commands and circle all the requests in the text. How did you identify them? How do they differ?

Bank robber:	This is a hold-up. Put your hands up! ... Lie down on the floor and don't move!	Man:	B...b...but ... you told us not to speak.
Old Lady:	Could I please stand?	Bank robber:	Hey. Trying to be clever?
Bank robber:	All right, if you have to.	Man:	N-no.
Cashier:	Excuse me, may I go to the bathroom?	Bank robber:	Then shut up. You two, put the money in this bag! Quick! ... Now give it to me! ... Now, listen everybody, don't you move till I'm out, or I'll come back and shoot every one of you. Understand?
Bank robber:	Shut up, everybody! Or I'll kill you all.		
Man:	Please, please, don't shoot us!		
Bank robber:	Then don't say another word. Is that clear? Tell me, is that clear? Why doesn't anybody answer?		

2 This is the statement one of the people in the hold-up gave to the police.

a) Which two verbs are used to report commands?
b) Which two verbs are used to report requests?
c) What grammatical structure follows these verbs?

```
Witness statement
The robber told us to put our hands up. He seemed quite inexperienced and
terribly nervous, so of course we all obeyed him. Next, he told us to lie down
on the floor and not to move. Then an old woman asked him to let her stand, to
which he reluctantly agreed. And then the cashier asked the robber to let her
go to the bathroom. At this, he got very angry and ordered us to shut up, or
else he would kill us. A young man then got hysterical and begged him not to
shoot. He told us again not to say another word, but he then wanted us to
answer a question, and nobody dared to. He told two clerks to put the money in
a bag. Finally, after threatening us again, he left. I've never been so scared
in all my life.
```

What did they say?

Say and *tell* are the most usual verbs in reported speech but there are other verbs that we can use. Look at the sentences below and report what happened using the verbs in brackets.

a) Mary: Paul, this is Marion Smyth. (introduce)

b) Michael: Would you like to come to the cinema this evening? I've got two tickets. (invite)
   Sue: I'd be delighted. Thank you. (accept)

c) Mark: Would you like some more coffee, Barbara? (offer)
   Barbara: No, thank you, not for me. (refuse)

d) Dennis: It's Jo's birthday. Let's buy her some flowers. (suggest)

e) Steve: I'm afraid this bill is incorrect. (complain)
   Waiter: I'm sorry, sir. (apologise)

f) Robert: If I were you, I wouldn't say a word. (advise)
   Simon: Of course not. (agree)

g) Mr Clark: Peter, you broke the window, didn't you? (accuse)
   Peter: No sir, I didn't do it. (deny)

10 Connected

Time

Listening

1 You are going to listen to a journalist talk about his experience as a telecommuter, ie, someone who works at home and connects to the office over the Net. First make sure you know the meaning of the following:

> to commute
> the rat race
> in the nude
> to be available / reliable
> a carrier pigeon

2 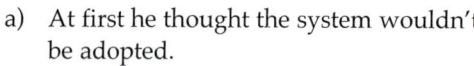 19 Listen to the recording and choose the eight true statements. Mark them with a cross (✗).

a) At first he thought the system wouldn't be adopted.
b) He was very keen on getting this telecommuting job.
c) He felt strange for the first few days.
d) He was happy to be free from routine.
e) He soon realised there were drawbacks in this job too.
f) He felt he couldn't get any breaks from the office.
g) He was constantly e-mailed or phoned.
h) He missed the social side of working in an office.
i) He often found he couldn't get in touch with the office.
j) He found other means of communication.
k) He doesn't think this was a bad experience.

Language awareness

Modals Rewrite the statements below using *can, can't, could, must, mustn't* or *don't have / need to*.

a) No more uncomfortable suits and ties.
b) And goodbye to the Long Island Rail Road.
c) In the office people expect you to disappear from time to time.
d) If you really want to work, it's virtually impossible.
e) It's essential to master the secrets of telecommuting.

New technology

Discussion

1 Match the functions to the phrases.

Functions
1 agreeing   2 interrupting   3 disagreeing   4 asking for clarification

Phrases
a) I completely agree.
b) I'm afraid I don't understand what you mean.
c) I don't agree at all.
d) I agree.
e) I'm sorry, I didn't quite follow what you said about …
f) I think you're right.
g) Sorry to interrupt but …
h) I agree up to a point, but …
i) Could I say something about … ?
j) Excuse me, but I think it's important to add that …
k) I really can't agree with you on that.

2 Work in groups of three or four and discuss:

- how has new technology influenced our lives? (at home, work, school, …)
- what are the advantages and disadvantages of computers? Do they save time, take up all our time or do they threaten our existence? In what ways?

Strong & weak forms

1 🎧 20 When speaking, you normally use the weak forms of *can* /kən/, *could* /kəd/, *must* /məst/, *should* /ʃəd/. You only use the strong forms /kæn/, /kʊd/, /mʌst/, /ʃʊd/ for emphasis. Listen and identify the weak and strong forms of the modal verbs.

a) You must do as you are told.
b) I must pass that exam: it's my last chance.
c) Celebrities can avoid paparazzi, if they want to.
d) Of course he can take a week off work.
e) He should give up smoking, but he won't.
f) You should report his disappearance to the police.
g) They could give me a job as a telecommuter.
h) It's all right, but it could be a lot better.

2 Practise saying the sentences.

Language awareness

Reporting modal verbs

Look at the pairs of sentences below. The second sentence of each pair reports the first one. However, some of the reporting sentences are incorrect. Mark the incorrect sentences with a cross (✗) and correct them.

a) 'You must be ready at six every morning.'
   The soldiers were told to be ready at six every morning.
b) 'Could you swim when you were my age?'
   My daughter asked me if I could have swum when I was her age.
c) 'You don't have to wear a uniform at school.'
   We were told we didn't have to wear a uniform at school.
d) 'You mustn't bring weapons to school.'
   The headmaster told us we didn't have to bring weapons to school.
e) 'Why can't I take my friends up to my room?'
   The young girl angrily asked why she couldn't take her friends up to her room.
f) 'You should take more physical exercise than you do.'
   The doctor advised me that I should have taken more physical exercise than I do.
g) 'We might find an AIDS vaccination very soon.'
   The doctor announced that his team might found an AIDS vaccination very soon.
h) 'You mustn't smoke here.'
   The nurse told us we mustn't smoke there.

S11 Expedition

Journey

Listening

1 Work with a partner or in groups. Have you ever heard of the Sherpas? Discuss what you know about them.

2 🎧 21 Listen to the interview with a climber who has recently returned from an expedition to the Himalayas and answer the following questions:

a) Who are the Sherpas?
b) What's their job?
c) How did they use to make a living at first?
d) Who carries loads on tourist treks at present?

3 Listen to the interview again and organise these facts chronologically:

a) The British hired Sherpas for Everest explorations.
b) Trekking and mountaineering attracted many people.
c) Great Britain colonised India.
d) There was an all-Sherpa expedition to Everest.
e) Sherpas found jobs in a British military post.
f) Edmund Hillary and his Sherpa porter reached the summit of Everest.
g) The Sherpas migrated to India.

Pronunciation

🎧 22 Listen to these sentences and say them using the contracted form.

For example:
We could have been caught in a storm. – *'We could've been caught in a storm.'*

a) He should have been more careful.
b) You shouldn't have mentioned my name.
c) She can't have seen the ice on the road.
d) She must have got fed up waiting so long and gone home.
e) They might have decided not to help us.
f) The police couldn't have identified the murderer so soon.

Out & about

Reading 1 Read the following hotel and entertainment information from around the world and name the places that have:

a) a restaurant that has received an award.
b) a hotel offering keep-fit facilities.
c) Christmas and New Year celebrations.
d) exhibitions.

• AUSTRALIA

The six-day Sydney Harbour Jazz Festival begins on Boxing Day (26 December). Free outdoor concerts are being staged at Garling Harbour and numerous city pubs as part of the event.

• DENMARK

Copenhagen's Tivoli Gardens, famous for their spectacular fairground, beautiful plants and flowers, remain open throughout December for a traditional Christmas fair. Free concerts are being held regularly.

• ENGLAND

At the Barbican Centre, *Native Nations: Journeys in American Photography* (on until 10 January), explores the lives of native North Americans from the 1850s to the present day. At the Tate Gallery, *In Celebration: The Art of the Country House* (on until 28 February), includes 90 paintings, drawings, sculptures and portrait miniatures, from more than 60 historic houses throughout the UK.

Worth a visit on 1 January is the New Year's Day Parade, in which 2,000 cheerleaders, 4,000 street performers and hundreds of classic cars will participate. The parade begins at midday in Parliament Square.

• HONG KONG

Nicholini's, has been named Best Italian Restaurant Abroad, beating thousands of other restaurants from around the world. The award was decided by a panel of food critics appointed by the Italian government.

• JORDAN

The Grand Hyatt Amman is opening this month. The 312-bedroom property is expected to attract mainly business guests as it is linked by a walkway to the new World Trade Centre. Facilities at the hotel include a business centre, meeting rooms and a fitness club.

• SCOTLAND

Edinburgh will host one of the world's biggest New Year festivals this year. The four-day Hogmanay celebrations, which start on 29 December, include processions of pipe bands, street theatre, concerts and a massive fireworks display on New Year's Eve.

• USA

More than 100 interactive exhibits are among the attractions at the Discovery Science Centre, which opens in Santa Ana (California) on 19 December. The museum aims to bring science, maths and technology to life and to make them entertaining.

The Centre Georges Pompidou in Paris has loaned scores of works to the Guggenheim Museum in New York, for an exhibition of 20th-century art (closing 24 January).

(Adapted from *Highlife*, British Airways Magazine, December 1998)

2 Work in groups. Which events do you think are the most interesting / boring? Who would you take to them?

Travelling by plane

Social language 1 🔊 23 Match the sentences on the left to their answers on the right. Listen and check.

a) I'd like to book a flight to Buenos Aires, please.
b) Hurry up! We've got to board the plane half an hour before departure.
c) Have you got anything to declare?
d) Which gate does it leave from?
e) How long to take off?
f) I'd like two seats on the shuttle to Madrid.
g) On the seventeenth. Are there any reductions for children?
h) Would you mind opening that suitcase?

1 I can't tell you, madam. The flight has been delayed.
2 This flight's fully booked. You'll have to wait till the 8.15.
3 Certainly sir. When would you like to go?
4 15% if they're under 12.
5 Don't worry. We've got plenty of time.
6 12, sir. It's at the end of this corridor.
7 Just a few presents and this video camera.
8 Certainly. I'll just find the key.

2 Arrange the pairs of sentences into four dialogues under the following headings:

1 Making a reservation. (2 dialogues)   2 At the departure lounge.   3 On arrival.

Practise the dialogues with a partner.

Expedition UNIT 11   189

s12 Food

Basics

Listening & speaking

1 🔲 24 Cindy and Karen, two flatmates, have decided to go on a diet. Karen has just returned from the supermarket. Listen to the conversation and note down all the food they mention under two headings: countable and uncountable. Then listen again and list the different ways of cooking the food.

2 ~~Cross out~~ the fattening foods and add to the lists five to six other items which could be included in a slimming diet.

3 Have you ever gone on a diet? How much did you actually lose / gain? Can you briefly describe the diet?

Comparing English & Spanish

1 There are many words which Spanish has 'borrowed' from English and vice versa. Sometimes their original form has been kept, while at other times the borrowed word has been modified to become 'more Spanish'. Can you spot the borrowings in these examples?

   a) No sé dónde he dejado el tiquet del parquin.
   b) Cuidado! No te saltes el stop!
   c) Al hacer clic sobre el icono Inicio, se ve la primera página del navegador.
   d) Me encanta chatear en la red.
   e) El mister anota en su bloc cada vez que se marca un gol con un tiro de penalti.
   f) Los pasajeros de clase business tiene acceso a la sala VIP.

   Write more examples.

2 Work in groups of three or four. Find as many of these borrowings as you can to do with food and eating.

   Make a list of food items in English which have a similar name in Spanish.
   For example: *cauliflower*

3 Compare your lists with other groups. Which group has found the largest number of words?

4 Write a restaurant menu including as many borrowings as possible.

Pronunciation

1 🔲 25 Listen to the phrases and notice what happens to the parts <u>underlined</u>:

   a) a carto<u>n of</u> milk
   b) <u>an item of</u> clothing
   c) several bottle<u>s of</u> oli<u>ve oil</u>
   d) a glas<u>s of iced t</u>ea

   Practise saying them.

2 🔲 26 Listen to these phrases and <u>underline</u> the links between the words.

   a) creme caramel and baked apples
   b) tinned anchovies and boiled eggs
   c) a few flavours of ice-cream
   d) iguana eggs in South America

What type of eater are you?

Reading

1 New York dietician Stephen P. Gullo identifies four types of eaters. Read the descriptions. Which one is most like you?

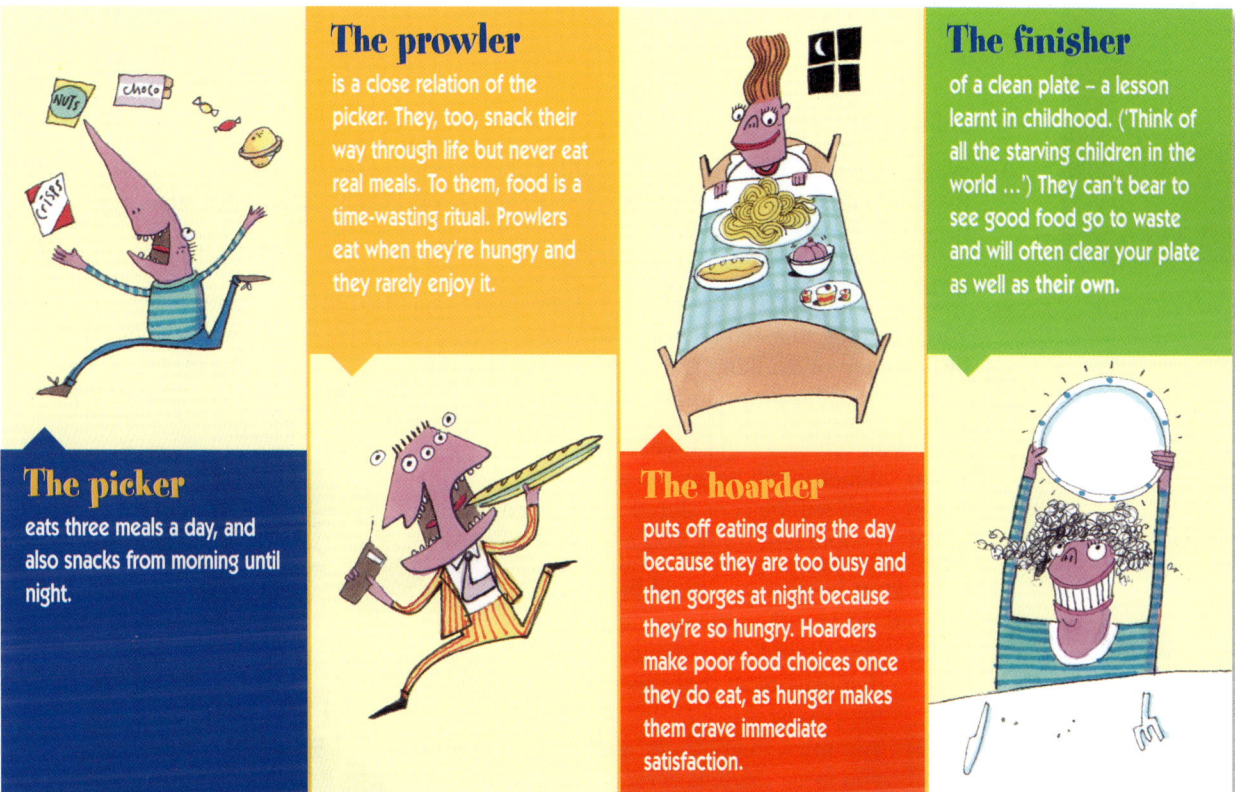

The prowler is a close relation of the picker. They, too, snack their way through life but never eat real meals. To them, food is a time-wasting ritual. Prowlers eat when they're hungry and they rarely enjoy it.

The finisher of a clean plate – a lesson learnt in childhood. ('Think of all the starving children in the world …') They can't bear to see good food go to waste and will often clear your plate as well as **their own**.

The picker eats three meals a day, and also snacks from morning until night.

The hoarder puts off eating during the day because they are too busy and then gorges at night because they're so hungry. Hoarders make poor food choices once they do eat, as hunger makes them crave immediate satisfaction.

(Adapted from *She* magazine, December 1997)

2 Dr Stephen P. Gullo also includes this advice on good eating habits. Read the advice and match them to Gullo's four types:

a) Make time for proper meals. Make mealtimes enjoyable by making your dining area comfortable. Don't eat while watching TV and force yourself to pay attention to what you eat.

b) Don't overload your plate, as you'll feel compelled to eat everything. Eat slowly and allow twenty minutes for your meal. When eating out, order something light. Then you'll have the pleasure of polishing off every last bite.

c) Don't eat on your feet. If you eat standing, you won't pay attention to what you're eating. When faced with finger foods, use your left hand if you're right-handed. You'll have to think twice when the nibbles come round.

d) Have a snack every few hours. That way you won't be starving by dinner time. Get out of the habit of rewarding yourself for missed meals – don't think you can eat extra in the evening because you didn't eat at lunch. Plan meals so you don't satisfy hunger with the first thing you find in the cupboard.

Language awareness

In the article above, Gullo uses both 'pickers' and 'the picker' to refer to an entire class of people. When you use countable nouns to talk about people or things in general, you use either the plural noun without *the*, or the singular with *the*.

Look at the following quotations and decide if they are correct or not. If not, correct them.

a) 'The only thing I like about the rich people is their money.' (Lady Astor)
b) 'The men are those creatures with two legs and eight hands.' (Jayne Mansfield)
c) 'Words are the small change of thought.' (Jules Renard)
d) 'We may live without the friends; we may live without the books; but civilised man cannot live without the cooks.' (Lord Lytton)

S13 Habit

Communication

Listening

1. Work in groups. List what you consider are the main characteristics and customs of the British. Then compare your lists with other groups. Where do national stereotypes come from?

2. 🎧 27 One of the most common stereotypes about the British is their fondness for tea. You are going to listen to what a foreign writer, George Mikes, has to say about the British habit of drinking tea. Listen to the recording and complete the sentences below with the most appropriate response.

   1. If you refuse a cup of tea, …
      a) nobody will be surprised.
      b) you will be considered uncivilised.
      c) people will think you are ill.

   2. If your hostess or a maid brings you tea at five in the morning, …
      a) you should show your displeasure so that this doesn't happen again.
      b) you must thank them warmly.
      c) you must drink it even if you don't want it.

   3. The English are in the habit of drinking tea …
      a) whenever they meet.
      b) only during the day.
      c) at different times during the day and night.

   4. You must always accept a cup of tea …
      a) no matter how you feel.
      b) except if it's hot.
      c) unless you've just had some.

Rising & falling intonation

1. 🎧 28 Listen to these sentences. When does the intonation rise and when does it fall?
   a) Unless you hurry up, you'll be late for school.
   b) If you're offered a cup of tea, you must never refuse it.
   c) As soon as you've done the shopping, we'll be ready to leave.
   d) We won't clean everything up until you've finished.
   e) When a man says 'I'll call you', he probably means the opposite.
   f) You do the vacuuming while I do the washing up.

2. Work with a partner. Make new sentences by rewriting one of the clauses in each of the sentences above.

   For example:
   Unless you hurry up, you'll miss the train.
   Unless you take the bus, you'll be late for school.

Buying a computer

Reading

1 Do you have a computer at home? If you haven't, would you like one? What do people use home computers for? What do you think is important when buying a computer? What advice would you give someone who is going to buy a computer?

2 Here are some tips on how to buy a computer that best suits your needs. Complete the sentences in column A by matching them to their correct endings in column B.

A	B
a) If writing is your main requirement …	1 … if it is not placed two inches away from your face.
b) If you plan to share the computer …	2 … you should remember that buying a computer is like a marathon rather than a 100-metre sprint.
c) Buy a cheaper model which you won't mind replacing in a few years' time …	3 … you'll need to make sure the computer comes with some good word-processing software.
d) If you are going to use it in different places …	4 … you're going to need a modem.
e) Consider the possibility of buying a good office chair …	5 … decide in advance if you'll be able to trust each other.
f) Be aware that a large monitor is a good thing only …	6 … unless you've already got one.
g) If you want to be able to use your computer to access the Internet and e-mail …	7 … if you don't think you'll be using it very much.
h) You can do without a colour printer …	8 … think seriously about paying that bit extra for a laptop.
i) If you are new to computers …	9 … if it's mainly going to be used for printing out invoices or business letters.

(Adapted from *The Mirror*, Saturday December 4, 1999)

3 Write similar advice for someone buying a car or a hi-fi system.

False friends

1 In each of the following translations into English, there is a false friend. Underline the false friend and write down the correct translation of the word.

a) Voy a buscar una empleada para que nos atienda.
   I'm going to look for a shop assistant to attend us.
b) No me gustó el argumento de la película.
   I didn't like the argument of the film.
c) Actualmente los hombres ayudan a las mujeres en las tareas del hogar.
   Actually men help women with the housework.
d) Marge es una de las mujeres más comprensivas que conozco.
   Marge is one of the most comprehensive women I've ever met.
e) Seguro que llegará tarde o no vendrá, es terriblemente informal.
   He'll definitely arrive late or won't come, he's terribly informal.
f) Durante muchos años trabajé como profesora en un instituto.
   For many years I worked as a professor at a secondary school.

2 Complete these sentences with the false friends you underlined listed above.

I'll never forget the first meeting I (1) _____ soon after I was made a student representative at university. I had been told it would be a short, (2) _____ meeting. (3) _____ , I had to listen to a lengthy, (4) _____ report made by a (5) _____ of economics. Unfortunately, everything ended up in a noisy (6) _____ among the different parties. It was a most unpleasant experience.

S14 Fashion

Style

Reading

1. Look at the photograph. Do you think the weather is warm or cold? Are Elizabeth Hurley's clothes appropriate?

2. Read the following article and explain the title.

BUT IT'S COOL!

You may have sometime asked yourself how the stars manage to keep warm in their skimpy dresses. Even when the temperatures are below zero some stars can be spotted moving around in nothing but small scraps of very expensive cloth. Their look for this winter is all backless and strapless, necks and shoulders on display, chests revealed in plunging necklines, dresses slashed to the navel, skirts slit to the thigh. Not a coat in sight.

These stars not only grin and bear it, they even manage to smile warmly at spectators. But how do they do it? One of the organisers of parties for the famous explains: 'We have to make sure that access to the party is really easy so that they can go straight from the car into the venue with minimal time in the cold. If they are likely to spend any length of time outside, elaborate measures are taken. Outdoor heaters and flame torches are installed. If the venue is somewhere potentially draughty, such as a marquee, these may be switched on days in advance'.

There are also precautions the stars can take to avoid facing the flashbulbs in red-nose condition. Most celebrities are expert at looking radiant on the outside while inwardly shivering. The Rudolph syndrome is avoided by applying a small amount of powder to the end of the nose. Some of them will even take a decongestant or antihistamine before an event to prevent their noses from dripping.

However, there are alternatives. Luxurious, long, opera-style capes, which fasten at the neck and can be swiftly flicked back to reveal all, are making a comeback, as are long gloves, which elegantly solve the problem of cold arms. Fur wraps, shawls, ponchos and chiffon capelets are also popular. Not to mention the all-embracing pashmina. But if you really want to face the cameras, prepare to suffer to be sexy. You may be cold, but at least you'll look cool.

(Adapted from *The Sunday Times*, 'Style', January 2, 2000)

Lexis

1. Read the first paragraph again and find the words that mean:

   a) low down cut with a steep V-shape: _____

   b) long deep cut: _____

   c) small pieces: _____

   d) long narrow cut: _____

   e) small in size or quantity: _____

2. Which words or phrases are used in paragraph 3 to refer to the condition of feeling very cold?

Word formation

1 Change the words in the box into adjectives by adding suffixes and make any necessary changes. Look back at the article to check.

draught sex luxury back strap

2 Change the words in the box into adverbs by adding suffixes and make any necessary changes. Look back at the article to check.

warm real potential inward swift elegant

3 Find examples of nouns functioning as adjectives in the article.

Language awareness

Purpose clauses

1 Look at these sentences from the extract:

We have to make sure that access to the party is really easy so that they can get straight from the car into the venue with minimal time in the cold.

Some of them will even take a decongestant or antihistamine before an event to prevent their noses from dripping.

In the first example, you use *so that* to introduce the purpose clause, and in the second example you use the infinitive form. Match the sentences on the left to those on the right using *so that* or the infinitive form. They all refer to paragraphs 3, 4 and 5 in the article.

a) Outdoor heaters and flame torches are installed …
b) The actresses apply a small amount of powder to the end of the nose …
c) Some of them take a decongestant or antihistamine …
d) Actresses wear long gloves …
e) Fur wraps, shawls, ponchos, pashminas are popular ways …

1 keep their arms warm.
2 the actresses won't be cold.
3 fight the cold.
4 their noses won't drip.
5 avoid the Rudolph syndrome.

2 Think of three things you did yesterday and tell your partner why you did them.

Slave to fashion

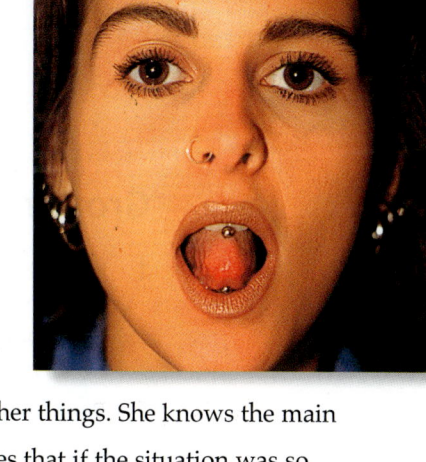

Listening

1 What is body piercing? What part of the body do people generally get pierced? Would you like to have it done?

2 🔲 29 Listen to two young girls talking about body-piercing and complete the summary below.

Sharon's going to have her (1) _____ pierced, but doesn't know whether to have her (2) _____ or (3) _____ pierced. Roberta advises her to (4) _____ before having it done, as it could cause (5) _____ or (6) _____ among other things. She knows the main problem is that there are (7) _____ . Sharon believes that if the situation was so serious, (8) _____ . She finally makes up her mind to (9) _____ .

Discussion

The fashion industry makes huge profits every year. Consumer society has created the need to look young and attractive, and to wear fashionable clothes. Work in groups and discuss the following:

- Should you wear what is in fashion or simply the clothes you are most comfortable in?
- How do the cinema, TV, advertising and the press influence our dressing, shopping and even living habits?
- What makes fashion change?

S15 Memory

Age

Listening

30 Listen to these people talking about their job situation, ambitions and regrets. Put a cross (✗) in the corresponding column whether their statements:

a) refer to the past or the present
b) show a positive or a negative view of things

	Time		View	
	past	present	positive	negative
Speaker 1:				
Speaker 2:				
Speaker 3:				
Speaker 4:				
Speaker 5:				
Speaker 6:				
Speaker 7:				
Speaker 8:				
Speaker 9:				
Speaker 10:				

Growing old gracefully

Reading

1 Look at the photo.
- How old do you think the man is?
- What is he doing?
- What activities do you think you'll be doing when you retire?

2 Read the article on page 197 and complete it with the words and expressions related to time in the box.

> During the next century   as long as
> before   in the end   Now   beyond   longer
> of the 21st century   ageing   from now

Can I live to be 125?

Perhaps not, however, your children may, thanks to scientists looking for longevity genes. But who will want to live that long?

For every generation (1) _____ ours, the
5 first concerns were: Can I grow old? Will my baby reach old age? Please let us grow older!
(2) _____ the average life expectancy in the US has advanced from 47 in 1900 to more than 76 in 1999. (3) _____ , new biological
10 discoveries should ensure that more of us will live to see old age and will encourage us to dream that we might not have to grow old at all.

We are already doing better at preventive medicine and at repairing old bodies –
15 arteriosclerosis, blood pressure, blood sugar, cataracts and so on. In the next century, molecular biologists are likely to make a lot of small alterations and adjustments to our genetic machinery, the result of which may be either
20 mankind's worst failure or the most significant discovery (4) _____ . Researchers may even learn to grow whole new hearts and livers from cells, a prospect I find slightly depressing. Will we walk off the stage of life at last disguised, a
25 living prosthesis – false teeth, false eyes, false everything? Of course, on this question of old age, science is still a baby. There are plenty of biologists who believe that (5) _____ and death are as inevitable as taxes. No one really knows if human
30 longevity will come up against a fixed barrier somewhere or if, like the sound barrier, it is here to be broken. Some gerontologists say the limit of the average life-span is 85 years; others, 95, 100, 150 and (6) _____ .

35 Chances are that my generation will consume all kinds of antiageing drugs – antioxidants, vitamin D, garlic, red wine, melatonin, blueberries – and (7) _____ we'll still live only a little (8) _____ than our parents. I
40 wouldn't want to live (9) _____ Methuselah, myself. But I would like to reach old age alive and kicking.

My hope is that the science of life will mature fast enough so that 30 years (10) _____ ,
45 when my children begin to ask those eternal questions about growing old, I can look at them and say, 'I recommend it'.

(Adapted from *Time*, November 8, 1999)

3 Answer the following questions about the article.
   a) What example does the author give of a scientific advance? (paragraph 2)
   b) The author's view of scientific advances in the future is not very optimistic. Find examples that show it. (paragraph 3)
   c) Who is Methuselah? Is there an equivalent expression in your language? (paragraph 4)
   d) What does the author wish for himself? (paragraph 5)
   e) At the end, the author says 'I recommend it'. What does 'it' refer to?

4 Find words or expressions in the article that mean:
   a) worries (paragraph 2)
   b) number of years a person is expected to live (paragraph 2 and 3)
   c) thought (paragraph 3)
   d) to die (paragraph 3)
   e) full of life (paragraph 4)

5 Work with a partner. Discuss the advantages and disadvantages to individuals and to society of living to be 150.

S16 Exam practice 2

Listening comprehension
Part I

31 You are going to listen to Adrian Mole describing his visit with his parents to a holiday camp. Read the statements and mark the FIVE which are TRUE with a cross (✗).

1 He didn't feel comfortable there. _____
2 The attendants were quite unpleasant. _____
3 He took part in several games and competitions. _____
4 He wasn't allowed to go into the bar where his parents were. _____
5 He didn't have much to eat at lunchtime. _____
6 He bought his own lunch. _____
7 He waited for his parents inside the car. _____
8 An attendant came to pick him up at 4 pm. _____
9 He finally met his parents at the lost children's centre. _____
10 His parents thought the visit had been very funny. _____

Listening comprehension
Part II

32 You are going to listen to three news items. Read the sentences and choose the correct answer. Mark it with a cross (✗).

News item 1:
Fifth Avenue …
a) was constructed in 1824.
b) went as far north as 30th Street.
c) is now 100 years old.

News item 2:
A Eurostar's female employees …
    a) cannot wear trousers to work.
    b) must wear skirts to work.
    c) are now free to wear skirts or trousers to work.

B Eurostar's decision was made after consulting …
    a) passengers.
    b) the female employees.
    c) the union.

News item 3:
A The plane robber …
    a) was not a convict.
    b) said he had escaped from prison.
    c) was soon identified by police.

B The police …
    a) were told the man had an accomplice.
    b) caught the man as soon as he landed.
    c) fear that the other man has left the area.

Listening comprehension

Part III

🔊 **33** You are going to listen to a description of this man's amazing invention. Read the following statements and mark the FIVE which are TRUE with a cross (✗).

1 Paul Moller is a professor at the University of California. _____
2 The university announced that he had built a personal flying saucer. _____
3 His invention could not fly high. _____
4 His new invention appeared in the film *Blade Runner*. _____
5 With his volantor, traffic jams could be avoided. _____
6 This invention could change suburban living habits. _____
7 People could live abroad and be able to commute to work. _____
8 Professor Moller will supervise the first test flight from the ground. _____
9 The volantor will not be allowed to fly over the city. _____
10 It won't take long for the volantor to be on the market. _____

Reading comprehension

Part I

These letters have been written in order to get out of party invitations. Match them with the reasons why they were written.

Getting out of party invitations

a I am sorry to say that my wife, who has recently taken a course on Feng Shui, has discovered that it would be very dangerous to have a lot of people in our house. I am therefore writing to let you know that we have been able to warn you in advance and avoid catastrophe. Thank God it has all turned out for the best!

b *The taxi driver we had booked long ago to take us to and from your party has unfortunately died. Out of respect for his memory, we feel we should stay quietly at home on the evening we would have shared with him. I am sure you will understand our feelings.*

c I regret to say that the taxi driver we had booked long ago to take us to and bring us back from your party has unfortunately died. On the whole, this is no particular loss, as he always drove very slowly and played local radio as loud as possible, but it does mean, of course, that we now have no means of getting to and from your party. I shall go to his funeral. I imagine many of the mourners will be fellow taxi drivers, so I will ask if any of them is free for that day, but I very much doubt it.

d **This is just to let you know that my firm has ordered me abroad and I won't be here on the day of your party. I am so furious I don't even want to speak about it.**

(Adapted from *The Independent*, The Monday Review, 29 November, 1999)

Reasons:
1 to get out of an invitation you accepted months ago
2 to let someone know that you are cancelling an arrangement in order to attend job commitments
3 to cancel a party you are giving
4 to turn down an invitation to a party you are having second thoughts about

1   a) ruined   b) was ruining   c) was ruined   d) had been ruined
2   a) lasted   b) spent   c) went for   d) were
3   a) child   b) children   c) child's   d) children's
4   a) like   b) for   c) how   d) as
5   a) which   b) that   c) when   d) what
6   a) Were   b) There are   c) They were   d) They are
7   a) for mention   b) for to mention   c) to mention   d) for mentioning
8   a) the company pay   b) that the company pays   c) the company paying
    d) the company to pay
9   a) won't accept no   b) will accept no   c) won't accept a   d) won't accept some
10 a) say   b) tell   c) explain   d) recommend
11 a) However   b) Over all   c) Besides   d) Beside
12 a) for   b) into   c) by   d) among
13 a) my advices   b) my advice   c) an advice   d) some advices
14 a) wouldn't worry   b) won't worry   c) didn't worry   d) don't worry
15 a) in   b) for   c) at   d) on

Grammatical competence
Part II

Read the article below about buying Christmas presents and choose the correct alternative.

Presents (1) _____ be opened after lunch, one person at a time, starting with the youngest. Each year, I (2) _____ so terribly sorry for my grandfather. Since he was the (3) _____ , he had to wait until the end and his gifts were so boring and dull, (4) _____ showed complete lack of imagination, such as book tokens and of course, (5) _____ socks. And that was it. Oh, apart (6) _____ the pipe cleaners I always bought him. Eventually, being a horribly materialistic child, I (7) _____ to have nightmares about reaching adulthood myself and finding that everyone bought me socks, (8) _____ . When would it happen, I lay awake wondering: in my twenties, thirties, or did it depend (9) _____ whether you had children or not? Fortunately, (10) _____ having children of my own, my gifts have never become quite that ordinary. (11) _____ I didn't realise then, is that you grow up to care more about what you give than what you get. But only to a point. Although socks are often objects of ridicule as Christmas presents, most of us (12) _____ buy them. Sometimes we try to hide our lack of imagination by choosing expensive cashmere varieties. These, however, tend to fall apart within days (13) _____ , for example, they are not washed properly. I know we (14) _____ criticise people's presents but don't you think that it would be better if we (15) _____ some helpful suggestions in advance?

(Adapted from *The Sunday Times*, Style, 5 December, 1999)

1   a) should   b) could   c) would   d) used
2   a) was feeling   b) feel   c) am feeling   d) felt
3   a) eldest   b) older   c) elderly   d) old
4   a) than   b) that   c) –   d) which
5   a) lot   b) lots of   c) a lot   d) the lot
6   a) of   b) –   c) from   d) those
7   a) start   b) begun   c) began   d) had started
8   a) either   b) also   c) as well   d) too
9   a) in   b) of   c) on   d) –
10 a) although   b) in spite   c) despite   d) even
11 a) Which   b) What   c) That   d) This
12 a) still   b) yet   c) already   d) just
13 a) unless   b) whether   c) as if   d) if
14 a) cannot   b) shouldn't   c) wouldn't   d) don't have to
15 a) made   b) make   c) did   d) do

Writing

Task 1

Use this sentence to begin a story of about 125 words:
When, after a long time, he opened his eyes, he didn't know where he was.

Task 2

Write a review, of about 125 words, of a book for your school magazine. Include the following information:
- a short biography of the author and the reasons for his popularity
- any other information that might be of interest
- a summary of the plot
- what you particularly liked /didn't like about the book.

Oral test

1. Which of these people do you think wrote the postcard? What makes you think so?
2. What is the relationship between them?
3. How are they feeling? Why?
4. Where do you think they come from?
5. Why have they chosen this place to spend their holidays? What is it like?
6. What would your ideal holiday be?

Interview: holidays

- When do you have holidays?
- How do you usually spend your holidays?
- What did you do on your last holiday?
- What has been your best / worst holiday so far?
- What's your opinion about the following quotation: 'A holiday resort is a place where they charge you enough for the eleven months you're not there.' (Herbert Prochnow)
- Do you think holidays are necessary? Why?

Tapescripts

S1 Fame

▭ 01

(See page 165.)

S2 Movies

▭ 02

(See page 166.)

S3 Compatibility

▭ 03

(C = Cecily; G = Gwendolen)
C: Please, let me introduce myself to you. My name is Cecily Cardew.
G: Cecily Cardew? What a very sweet name! Something tells me that we're going to be great friends. I like you already more than I can say. My first impressions of people are never wrong.
C: How nice of you to like me so much after we've known each other such a comparatively short time! Please, sit down.
G: I may call you Cecily?
C: With pleasure!
G: Hmm, and you'll always call me Gwendolen, won't you?
C: If you wish.
G: Then that's all settled, isn't it?
C: I hope so.
G: Perhaps this might be a favourable opportunity for my mentioning who I am. My father's Lord Bracknell. You've never heard of papa, have you?
C: I don't think so.
G: Hmm ... Outside the family circle, papa, I'm glad to say, is entirely unknown. I think that's quite as it should be. The home seems to me the proper sphere for the man, and certainly once a man begins to neglect his domestic duties he becomes painfully effeminate, doesn't he? And I don't like that. It makes them so very attractive. Cecily, mamma, whose views on education are remarkably strict, has brought me up to be extremely short-sighted; it's part of her system; so do you mind my looking at you through my glasses?
C: Oh! not at all, Gwendolen. I'm very fond of being looked at.
G: Ah, you're here on a short visit, I suppose.
C: Oh no! I live here.
G: Really? Your mother, no doubt, or some female relative of advanced years, resides here also?
C: Oh no! I ... I have no mother, nor, in fact, any relations.
G: Indeed?
C: My dear guardian, with the assistance of Miss Prism, has the arduous task of looking after me.
G: Your guardian?
C: Yes, I'm Mr Worthing's ward.

▭ 04

(See page 169.)

▭ 05

1
I'm divorced with two sons, aged 24 and 20. I'm interested in art, the theatre, reading, but I'm also keen on techno music. I'm broad-minded, talkative and fun to be with. However, I don't want to get into a long-term relationship.

2
Maybe because at work I have to compete with aggressive thick-skinned professional women, I prefer feminine, sensitive, quiet types. Of course they must have a variety of interests, including art and outdoor pursuits.

3
I don't want to get into any serious relationships at the moment, so don't talk to me about settling down and having a baby. I just want to meet good-looking guys, er, go clubbing, eat in good restaurants and enjoy life.

4
I came to England about five years ago. I live on my own in a small flat with a balcony full of lovely plants and flowers. I'd really like to meet a man about my age, warm and sincere. I don't mind his nationality, but I'd rather he didn't smoke.

5
I'm one metre 80, strong, and like all sports, especially athletics. It's not long since I left school, so I haven't much experience of life. Maybe that's why I'm attracted to older people, mainly women. I find I can learn a lot from them, if they're fun, I mean.

6
I've been in London since 1992, when I was offered a job as manageress of a fairly large clothes shop. I really don't like living in the city. My dream is to buy a house in the country, with a garden and a large fireplace, and to be able to go for long walks, whatever the weather. You see, I'm a romantic at heart.

S4 Risk

▭ 06

(See page 171.)

▭ 07

Once upon a time a little girl left her home and went into the forest. In the forest she got lost and couldn't find her way home. Then she came across a little house in the forest.

She opened the door and she went in. She saw there was no one there.

In this house lived three bears: Father Bear, Mother Bear and their son, Baby Bear. The bears were not at home. They had gone out for a stroll in the forest.

In the house there were two rooms: one was the kitchen, the other was the bedroom. The little girl went into the kitchen, and she saw three bowls on the table: the first was very big, the second was not so big and the third one was a little blue bowl. By the side of each bowl lay a spoon.

The little girl took up the biggest spoon and began to eat out of the biggest bowl, and then she took up the middle-sized spoon and ate out of the middle-sized bowl, and then she took the little spoon and ate out of the little blue bowl. And she thought that the little bowl had the best porridge of all, and she ate it all up.

The little girl wanted to sit down, and she saw three chairs round the table. She climbed up to the big chair and fell off it; then she sat down on the middle-sized one and was uncomfortable; then she sat down on the third little chair, and she began to smile, it was so comfortable. She began to swing herself to and fro in the chair. The little chair gave way and she fell on the floor.

She got up and went upstairs. In the bedroom there were three beds: one big bed, another, middle-sized and a third small one. She lay down on the little one. It was just the right size, and she fell asleep.

The bears came home, feeling very hungry and wanting their dinners. They took hold of their bowls, looked into them and said:

'Who's been eating out of my bowl?'
'Someone has been eating out of my bowl.'
'Someone has been eating out of my bowl and has eaten all my porridge up and someone has broken my chair.'

The bears went upstairs and Baby Bear caught sight of the little girl, and he squealed as though they were cutting him to bits: 'There she is. Oh! Oh! There she is'. The moment the little girl opened her eyes and caught sight of the bears she rushed to the window. It was open, so she jumped out and ran off.

08

(See page 171.)

S5 Development

09

1
As a child, I found a wonderful place for roller-skating: the forecourt of a supermarket after closing time. An occasional spoilsport would demand I 'clear off' or scream it was dangerous without bothering to explain why. One day a woman stopped to say I might crash into the windows of the supermarket and get hurt. Er, she suggested I should roller-skate in a nearby park. So that's what I did. The thing that was good was that she explained the problem and gave me an alternative. I hope that's what I'd do in that situation.

2
If people take risks when they are adults, why shouldn't they be allowed to take them when they're children? I don't see the difference.

3
Some years ago I was on holiday in France with some friends. We were walking along a cliff path when we saw two children leaping into the foaming sea with great exhilaration. I saw the danger, but thought these kids knew what they were doing. Next morning we learnt they had drowned. I wish I'd said something.

S6 Headlines

10

Everything started when I moved to Liverpool. I was living by myself in a small flat and didn't know anybody there. When I went to get the bus home from work, I passed all those lovely shops. Popping in and buying something small really gave me a boost. It was so much better than going home to an empty flat!
At first, I would only buy make-up, but soon I turned to more extravagant purchases. It got to the point where it was impossible to pass a clothes shop without going in and buying something. Towards the end of my working day my heart would pump and the thought of shopping would give me an adrenalin rush. Just walking into a shop made me feel better. The staff would greet me like an old friend and let me try on as many things as I wanted. Of course I never left without buying something – a bag, a skirt, a pair of trainers.
However, when I got back to my flat a tremendous feeling of guilt would wash over me. I had by now run into debt and owed over 3,000 pounds. Then I lost my job. I was so desperate. What could I do? The only thing that could cheer me up was shopping, so I went into a large department store and spent the little money I had left. Although I knew that what I was doing was wrong and very stupid, by now it all seemed to be beyond my control.

S7 Fiesta

11

(D = Danny; L = Liam; A = Asumpta)
D: Did you know there's a Latin music festival in Kilkenny tonight?
L: No. A Latin music festival?
D: It says here it's the first time one's been organised, and it's a two-day festival. It's closing tonight.
A: Oh, who's playing, does the paper say?
D: Mmm … Let me see … Ah … Pucho and his Latin Soul Brothers. They're on at Langton's at ten.
A: Never heard of them. Er, what kind of music do they play?
D: A mix of Jazz, Latin and Soul, apparently. And … oh … it also says that if we go on the Ruta Loca – whatever that means – we'll be able to see some free gigs at some of the pubs there.
L: Sounds great. Shall we go?
D/A: Yes, let's.
A: How about inviting Kevin and Josie and the twins?
D: Good idea. I'll call Roisin and Eileen and you call the other two.
A: Fine.

12

(A = Asumpta; K = Kevin)
A: Hello, Kevin, we're going to a salsa party tonight and we thought you and Josie would like to come. The twins may be coming too.
K: A salsa party? I can't dance the salsa. Nor can Josie.
A: Oh, don't worry about that. There are loads of bands playing, including a Cuban one, and it's all free. And we could try some cocktails, and you know, by the end of the night we'll be doing the conga. We'll have a laugh, I'm sure.
K: Hah, hah. It sounds grand. OK, I think we'll come. We've nothing on tonight. When does it start?
A: Eight. But we're meeting at my place at half past seven.
K: Seven thirty. Right. Er, by the way, how are we going? Do you want me to drive?
A: Why, yes, great!
K: OK. See you later.
A: Bye.

13

(D = Danny; E = Eileen)
E: Hello.
D: Hello, Eileen. There's a Latin music festival at Kilkenny tonight and I was wondering whether you and Roisin would like to come.
E: Well, Roisin's down with flu, you know, and I'm revising for Friday's exam.
D: Oh, come on, Eileen, don't worry about the exam. Friday's ages away.
E: Yeah, but I'm rather behind. Who else is going?
D: Kevin and Josie. They're driving us there. And Conor said he might join us too.
E: Conor Lindon? I can't stand him. If he's coming, I'm definitely not. Besides, I've loads to do.
D: Oh, come on, don't be such a wimp. Books can wait.
E: No, I'd better stay in and do some work. Some other time, perhaps.
D: But there won't be another time till next year.
E: No, I'm definitely not coming. I'm far too busy. Thanks for the invite, anyway.
D: OK. Suit yourself. Goodbye.
E: Bye, Danny.

S8 Exam practice 1

14

Listening comprehension
Part I
(Tapescript on Teacher's diskette only.)

15

Listening comprehension
Part II
(Tapescript on Teacher's diskette only.)

16

Listening comprehension
Part III
(Tapescript on Teacher's diskette only.)

S9 Lies

17

(I = Interviewer; L = Louise; M = Man)
I: Hello, Louise, please take a seat. Would you like anything to drink? Coffee, tea?
L: Oh, just water, thanks … Ah … sorry, I'm late, but the train I was going to get was cancelled. I'm usually so punctual.
I: Um, OK. Right … Um, I'm just looking at the letter you sent me … Um … can you explain your job title? I'm a little confused by what Director of Development is.
L: Ah, yeah. Well, I'm basically in charge of running the firm: er,

Tapescripts

meeting clients, getting business in, setting budgets …
I: Oh …
L: … um, er, and … and training people up.
I: You say that although you're happy with your job, you'd like more responsibility. It seems that you were given quite a lot of responsibility in your last job.
L: Well, yes, that's true, but after working in the same company for six years you need a change, different challenges …
I: Yes, quite …
L: … and I'd reached the top of the ladder very quickly, and there were no more promotional opportunities.
I: Yes, um … . And how many people were you responsible for?
L: Oh, fifteen.
I: Um. What would you say are your three best qualities?
L: Er … I'm a creative thinker, um, a problem solver and a very hard worker.
I: And your worst?
L: Oh, that's difficult. Um, people say I'm a little impatient, but that's because I'm so eager to get on and make things happen. … Ah, I can't think of anything else at the moment.
I: From your CV, I can't quite see what you did from the period you left Oxford University to starting your job at Ramsdon's. What did you do during that time?
L: Oh, I went travelling. Thailand; Vietnam; Indonesia. Great experience.
I: Three years. Yes, I can imagine.
M: Howard, you're wanted in room 101.
I: Oh, is that the time already? Sorry, Louise, I've got a meeting at 11.30.
L: Oh.
I: Um, W … it was very nice meeting you. Sorry you haven't had a chance to ask me any questions about the company, but if you've got any, please give me a ring. … You know the way out?

📼 18

(See page 185.)

S10 Connected

📼 19

When I first heard that some employers would actually permit their workers to telecommute, I couldn't believe it. But then I became obsessed with the idea, so I did my best to show my boss that, being a total starter and a serious loner, I was the perfect candidate for telecommutation. Finally, one day a computer equipped with a modem arrived at my home. I was a telecommuter at last!

How to describe the incredible liberation I felt in those first days of 'working' at home? Forget about the nine to five rat race. No more uncomfortable suits and ties to go to the office. I could work in the nude if I chose. And goodbye to the dirty, always late and criminally expensive Long Island Rail Road. I was going to work at home. And life was grand.

But what did I know? It turns out that telecommuting is not the golden goose of the Digital Age as some claim it is. No, it's a cruel deception that could send you back to the office begging for your old job unless … unless you understand and are ready to master the Four Dirty Little Secrets of Telecommuting:

Dirty Little Secret One: you're always available to management. When you're in the office people expect you to disappear from time to time: with a newspaper to the bathroom, out to lunch, to chat up the receptionist … But when you're the lucky one working at home, they incessantly e-mail and phone you on your mobile. And there are few defences against this.

Dirty Little Secret Two: if you really want to work, it's virtually impossible. Because it's such a nice day, or it's too hot, or you want to see a particular movie or the garden needs watering. Whatever. In the end, you don't get any work done.

Dirty Little Secret Three: it's lonely. All your friends are at work having long lunches or gossiping about the boss. And you're at home. Alone.

Dirty Little Secret Four: your connection will always fail. So, if you need connectivity to your office system, try something more reliable, like a carrier pigeon or a message in a bottle.

Aside from that, I love telecommuting, I really do. And I'm sure you will, too.

📼 20

(See page 187.)

S11 Expedition

📼 21

(I = Interviewer; C = Climber)

I: Many people may wonder who the Sherpas are. Can you tell us?
C: Yes, of course. The Sherpas are an ethnic group of about 35,000 Buddhists living mainly in Nepal. They work as high-altitude porters for mountain expeditions and also as guides for tourist treks.
I: The general assumption is that Sherpas have been mountain climbers for generations. Is that correct?
C: Well, no. In fact, until Europeans created a job market in the early 1900s, Sherpas had never scaled mountains.
I: What did they use to do then?
C: They raised yaks and traded, and they also worked the land.
I: How did they become porters?
C: Mmm … After Great Britain colonised India in the 1800s, many Sherpas migrated to find work at a military post in Darjeeling, India, just across the border from Nepal. And in the 1920s, the British started hiring them as porters for pioneering Everest explorations. Then, in 1953 a New Zealander, Edmund Hillary, and a Sherpa, called Tenzing Norgay, became the first to reach the summit of Everest.
I: And after that, I suppose the tourist-trekking business became more and more important …
C: Right. And of course their life was changed for ever.
I: Yes, I can imagine. Tell me, what's their job in an expedition?
C: Well, they're guides, cooks, and camp assistants. But they rarely carry loads on tourist treks. They hire porters from other Nepalese ethnic groups, people who would like to become 'sherpas', a term now used for a mid-level camp assistant. The Sherpas who climb on dangerous high-altitude expeditions are the elite now.
I: Has there ever been an all-Sherpa expedition?
C: Yes, in 1991 the first all-Sherpa expedition reached Everest. It was a matter of national pride. In fact 73 Sherpa men had already reached the summit.

📼 22

(See page 188.)

📼 23

(See page 189.)

S12 Food

📼 24

(C = Cindy; K = Karen)
C: Karen! What have you got there! Are you mad?
K: Ah, don't worry. The diet says you have to buy all the food on the list and then eat it over the next ten days.
C: OK. Right, er … ham, carrots, yoghurt, mmm … and what's this? Diet chocolate mousse, and five cartons of skimmed milk. Are we really going to drink all that?
K: Well, we may. And anyway, skimmed milk doesn't go sour.
C. Yeah. Or we can always give it to

the neighbour's cat. What else? Oh, er, potatoes, fresh pasta, … oh, yes, pork chops … and bananas?! Well, I thought all these were fattening, not slimming.

K: Well, it says you can have some fattening foods so long as it's once a day and you don't fry them.

C: Mmmm … Boiled pork chops. Sounds delicious.

K: Don't be silly. We'll grill the pork chops and boil the pasta.

C: And what are we going to have the pasta with, if we can't use any oil or butter, or rich sauces?

K: We'll roast some tomatoes, aubergines, and onions, then we'll chop them, add plenty of spices, some cottage cheese, a little salt, and voilà! We'll have a delicious sauce.

C: Hah. If you say so … Anyway, do you know how much weight we'll lose?

K: Um, one kilo per week, or even more. That makes four at the end of the month. Just in time for the summer.

25
(See page 190.)

26
(See page 190.)

^S13 Habit

27

There are some occasions when you must not refuse a cup of tea, otherwise you are judged an exotic and barbarous bird without any hope of ever being able to take your place in civilised society.

If you are invited to an English home, at five o'clock in the morning you get a cup of tea. It is either brought in by a heartily smiling hostess or an almost malevolently silent maid. When you are disturbed in your sweetest morning sleep you must not say: 'Madam, I think you are a cruel, spiteful and malignant person who deserves to be shot.' On the contrary, you have to declare with your best five o'clock smile: 'Thank you so much. I do adore a cup of early morning tea, especially early in the morning.' If they leave you alone with the liquid, you may pour it down the washbasin. Then you have tea for breakfast; then you have tea at eleven o'clock in the morning; then after lunch; then you have tea for tea; then after supper; and again at eleven o'clock at night.

You must not refuse any additional cups of tea under the following circumstances: if it is hot; if it is cold; if you are tired; if anybody thinks that you must be tired; if you are nervous; if you are happy; before you go out; if you are out; if you have just returned home; if you feel like it; if you do not feel like it; if you have had no tea for some time; if you have just had a cup.

28
(See p 192.)

^S14 Fashion

29

(S = Sharon; R = Roberta)

S: Hey, Roberta, I'm getting my eyebrow pierced.

R: Oh, yeah. Hah, hah.

S: You don't believe me, do you? Well, I am. And I might get something else done at the same time. What do you think? Tongue or lower lip?

R: That's disgusting!

S: What's wrong with it? I don't see the problem. Everyone's doing it.

R: So? … If I were you, I'd find out more about it before getting anything done. You know, you could get all sorts of infections if you're not careful. And it could lead to blood poisoning. I've even heard that some people have been disfigured by piercing …

S: Oh, come off it. You've been reading those scare stories in the press again.

R: Maybe. But there are loads of people who set themselves up as body-piercers, who've had no training in it at all. Who knows what they might do to you … dirty needles …

S: Oh, you sound just like my mum. Will you stop it! If the problem were so serious, don't you think the government would do something to regulate it?

R: Well, maybe they will one day, when someone famous gets disfigured, or killed.

S: Right. That's it … You know what? I'm going to get my belly-button pierced as well, and you'll be the first to see it.

R: Well, don't say I didn't warn you.

^S15 Memory

30

1
I'd feel like a failure if I didn't have a long-term partner, money in the bank, a promising career, a luxury car, a yacht, a villa in Monte Carlo …

2
I wish I hadn't been made to believe that I could do and be anything I wanted. When all I end up doing is working in a boring job for not enough money.

3
If I didn't have promotion opportunities in my job, I'd simply give it up.

4
I've seen many careers ruined by people more worried about their next job than about the job they were doing at the time.

5
I wish people would stop talking about age limits to do things. I don't recognise such limits. I feel as fit and able as when I was 25.

6
Just think, this time tomorrow I'll be married to Susie. If I hadn't moved to New York and gone to your party, I wouldn't have met her.

7
I wish I had management responsibility. I've got some great ideas for the company.

8
If we increase our wealth by 50%, this doesn't mean we'll be 50% richer in any real terms, or 50% happier. It only means we'll have 50% more money to worry about.

9
Young people today are making themselves miserable by their obsessive aspirations for status, money and success.

10
If only I'd studied economics or computer science instead of architecture! I'd have found a job as soon as I left university.

^S16 Exam practice 2

31

Listening comprehension
Part I
(Tapescript on Teacher's diskette)

32

Listening comprehension
Part II
(Tapescript on Teacher's diskette)

33

Listening comprehension
Part III
(Tapescript on Teacher's diskette)

Macmillan Education
Between Towns Road, Oxford OX4 3PP
A division of Macmillan Publishers Limited
Companies and representatives throughout the world

ISBN 0 333 75754 8 (International edition)
ISBN 0 333 96757 7 (Level III)

Text © Sue Kay and Vaughan Jones
Design and illustration © Macmillan Publishers Limited 2000
Heinemann is a registered trademark of Reed Educational and Professional Publishing Limited.

First published 2000

All rights reserved; no part of this publication may be reproduced, stored in a retrieval system, transmitted in any form, or by any means, electronic, mechanical, photocopying, recording, or otherwise, without the prior written permission of the publishers.

Designed by Keith Shaw, Threefold Design
Illustrated by Kathryn Adams p67; Peter Campbell pp85, 86; Tim Davies pp62, 67; Tim Etheridge pp29, 43, 111, 117, 137, 140; Ian Kellas p7; Julian Mosedale pp28, 36, 42, 45, 83, 88, 95, 100, 103, 106, 113, 122, 127, 130; Andrew Peters pp46, 47, 48, 93, 98, 105, 116, 128; Peter Richardson pp64, 78.
Cover design by Andrew Oliver
Cover illustration © Howard Hodgkin

Authors' acknowledgements
We would like to thank all our colleagues at the Lake School, Oxford for their help. In particular Peter Maggs whose thoughtful comments on work in progress were much appreciated. A big thank you to our wonderful intermediate classes who unwittingly helped shape much of the material. We are especially grateful to Jon Hird for the excellent review units, help on the teacher's book and otherwise tireless support. Similarly, we would like to thank Philip Kerr (*Inside Out Workbook*) Helena Gomm (*Inside Out Teacher's Book*) and everybody involved in the *Inside Out Resource Pack*: a great team!
And finally, the biggest thanks go to our families without whose support and understanding none of this would have been possible.

The authors and publishers would like to thank the following institutions for their help in piloting the material and making comments:
Alejandra González, Florencia Lambertini and Gustavo Seminario, Northside School of English, Buenos Aires. Ana Belén Montero, Carmen Arévalo, EOI Bilbao. Andrea Giulano and Alicia Valle de Ghiorzi, Instituto ITELS, Buenos Aires. Armando de León-Sotelo, EOI Alcorcón. Austin Core, Greylands School of English, Southampton. Carlos Trueba, EOI San Sebastián de los Reyes. Carmen Santos Maldonado, EOI Santander. Catherine Downey and Jan Kingsley, ESADE, Barcelona. Ceri Jones, International House, Serrano, Madrid. Charo Martínez, Herminia Blat, José Carte, José Miguel Galarza and Mari-Cruz Iribarren, EOI Pamplona. Claudina Lovalvo, ICANA, Buenos Aires. Dan Austin and Ian Stuart, St Joseph's Hall, Oxford. Dave Willis. Elisa Jiménez, EOI Fuenlabrada. Freda Miller, International House Livorno. Gabriella Lacza, International Language Studio, Budapest. Genoveva Barsanti, LEA Institute, Buenos Aires. Gergó Farkas, Spell Language School, Budapest. Henny Burke, British Language Centre, Madrid. Idilia Bernadeu and Isabel Tornero, EOI II, Barcelona. Jason Worsnop, British Institute, Bilbao. Jennifer O'Brien and Mike Sayer, Regent's School, Oxford. Jim Scrivener, International House, Budapest. Juan Francisco Silgado, EOI Jesús Maestro. Judit Biró, Európai Nyelvek Stúdiója, Budapest. Judit Csepela, Globe Language School. Katalin Schmell, Globus Language School, Budapest. Kate Threadgold, The British Council, Bilbao. Kit Cree, Glen College, Pamplona. Laura Romero and Miguel Angel Almarza, EOI San Blas. Luis Suárez and Niam Glenn, EOI Alcorcón. Macarena Rodulfo, EOI Getafe. Maite Sanjuan, Miquel Bretón and Núria Godoy, EOI I, Barcelona. Marek Doskocz, Lingwista, Warsaw. María Angeles, EOI Ciudad Lineal. María Galbis and María Piteira Troncosa, EOI Gandía. María Lorente and Michael Hellmer, London Institute, Montevideo. María Silvia Stagnaro, Profesoras Asociadas Egresadas del Instituto Lenguas Vivas, Buenos Aires. Marian Cruz, EOI Mostoles. Mónica Harvey de Campisteguy and Patricia Alvárez, Dickens Institute, Montevideo. Mónika Marton, KOTK, Budapest. Nancy Cortell, Info English, Buenos Aires. Nicholas Sheard, English@Oxford, Oxford. Pablo Arroya, EOI Zaragoza. Paola Ferrari and Kate Jones-Page, Centro Linguistico di Ateneo, Parma. Pascual Pérez Paredes, EOI Cartagena. Peter Hall, Alboraya English Centre, Valencia. Philip Kerr and Vince Desmond, International House, London. Philip Rickett, International House/Academia Lacunza, San Sebastián. Rebecca Place, International Centre, Bilbao. Rosina Otegui de Perrier, Geraldine Poole and María Ema Mira, Instituto Cultural Anglo-Uruguayo, Montevideo. Russell Stannard, CLIC Seville. Ruth Sánchez García, EOI A Coruña. Sándor Csupor, Budapest International Language Studio. Sara Klughaupt de Lieberman, Susana R. Margoniner, María Rosa Sánchez, José Luis Formoso, Queen Victoria Institute, Montevideo. Silvina Campagnoli, Leeds School of English, Buenos Aires. Sonia Casal, EOI Alcalá de Guadaira-Seville. Steve Bush, British Institute of Florence. Sue Bailey, University of Strathclyde. Tania Bastow. Teachers at Atlanta Language School, Budapest. Teresa Blanco, EOI Fuenlabrada. Virginia López Grizolia, Silvana Ioli, Interaction Language Studio, Buenos Aires. W. Arnold and Julian Wright, Instituto de Idiomas Universidad Deusto, Bilbao. A special thank you to María Galbis and her colleagues at EOI Gandia, Spain and to our great intermediate class of summer 1998.

The publishers wish to thank Nick Blinco, St Thomas More RC Primary School, Kidlington and Jane Couch.

The authors and publishers would like to thank the following for permission to reproduce their material:
The Purple Agency on behalf of Jade Jagger for an adapted version of a published interview; *The Independent* for the article 'Can student mates be friends for life?' by Zenia Gregoriadis (9th April, 1998); International Music Publications and Polygram Record Operations Limited for *You've Got a Friend* by the Brand New Heavies, words and music by Carole King, © 1971 Screen Gems-EMI Music Inc. USA and London, WC2H OEA; Penguin Books Australia for extracts from *The Little Book of Calm* by Paul Wilson; HarperCollins Publishers Limited for extracts from *Collins COBUILD English Dictionary* © 1995; Michael B. Vederman for his story on website deadmike@deadmike.com; Universal Music Publishing Limited and Music Sales Limited for *River Deep, Mountain High* by Ike and Tina Turner, words and music by Phil Spector, Ellie Greenwood & Jeff Barry, © 1966, Trio Music Co. Inc., Steeplechase Music, Malt Shoppe Music and Mother Bertha Music, Inc., USA, and for *Ugly* by Jon Bon Jovi, words and music by Jon Bon Jovi & Eric Bazilian, © 1997 Human Boy Music and Bon Jovi Publishing/PolyGram Music Publishing Inc., USA; Exley Publications Limited for an extract from *To Mum (the Kindest of Ladies)*, edited by Richard and Helen Exley; David Higham Associates Limited on behalf of the Estate of Roald Dahl for an extract from Boy, published by Jonathan Cape Limited, 1984; Independent Newspapers (UK) Limited for extracts based on articles 'A boyfriend's worst nightmare' by John Christopher (*Independent on Sunday*, 12th October 1997); 'The most frightening feeling in the world' by Hester Lacey (*Independent on Sunday*, 7th September, 1997); 'Valencia burns and the people come out to party' by Nick Taylor (*Independent on Sunday*, 8th February, 1998); 'Global Myths No. 6 – Another story from the travellers grapevine' by Maxton Walker (*Independent on Sunday*, 22nd February, 1998); 'Ageism has withered her' by Sarah Blake (*Independent on Sunday*, 8th December, 1996); International Music Publications for *It's My Party* by Lesley Gore, words and music by John Gluck, Wally Gold and Herb Weiner, © 1982 Arch-Music Co. and World Song Publishing Inc., USA, Warner-Chappell Music, London, W6 8BS; Telegraph Group Limited for an extract based on an article 'I've got a little list' by Alice Hart-Davis (*Weekend Telegraph*, Saturday, 13th December, 1997); Penguin Books UK for an extract from *The Beach* by Alex Garland, © 1997 by Alex Garland; *Focus* Magazine for extract from 'Holidays in hell' (January, 1999); *The Economist*, London, for a chart from article 'Granny knew best, maybe' (9th October, 1999); National Magazine Company Limited for an adapted questionnaire 'Today's woman laid bare' (*Esquire* magazine, June, 1995); Random House Group Limited for an extract from *Come Together* by Josie Lloyd and Emlyn Rees, published by Arrow Books; Candis Magazine, published by Newhall Publications Limited for an extract based on interview with Jon Bon Jovi, (October, 1997); Partners BDDH on behalf of the Harley Davidson Motor Cycles Company for the advertisement *If*.

Whilst every effort has been made to locate the owners of copyright, in some cases this has been unsuccessful. The publishers apologise for any infringement or failure to acknowledge the original sources and will be glad to include any necessary correction in subsequent printings.

The authors and publishers would like to thank the following for permission to reproduce their photographs:
Advertising Archives p124; Art Directors & Trip pp40(fr,r), 55(br,tl) 93(3,4), 104, 133(r); Big Pictures p50; J Birdsall p27(c); Bridgeman Art Library pp25, 80; Bubbles pp27(b), 30, 54(2,4), 60; Colorific p58; Corbis pp73, Warren Morgan 93(1), Galen Rowell 93(2); Julian Cotton pp 15(c), 27(d), 62(l), 68((5,6), 73(br,fbl,fbr); courtesy of Harley Davidson p126; James Davis pp93(5); Eye Ubiquitous p100; Jimmy Gaston p14; Touchstone Pictures/ Ronald Grant Cinema Archive p23; Robert Harding p13; Image Bank p53, 54, 62(r), 77(tr), 108, 129(b); Images Colour Library pp68(2,3,4), 73(mr); London Features International pp4(1,3,5), 5(f); Pam McNee p9(l); Mark Peterson/ Saba/ Network Photographers p129(c); P.A. News p35; People in Pictures p5(d); Popperfoto p5(b); Redferns pp11, 41; Rex pp4(2,4,6), 5(c,e), 12, 47, 55(l), 79, 122, 123, 129(t), 134(t,b); Telegraph Colour Library pp24, 40(l), 50, 54(1), 77(bl), 89(r), 118, 133(fl,l,fr); Topham Picturepoint p63; Frank Spooner pp27(a), 59, 93(6), 103; Tony Stone pp15(tr,m), 31, 32, 40(fl), 68(tl), 73(ml,bl,t,br), 82, 83, 89(c), 93(t), 95, 97, 138; Superstock p89(l).
Commissioned photographs by Haddon Davies pp20, 52, 119, 121; Chris Honeywell p9; David Tolley p43; John Walmsley pp15, 17.

Cartoons on p26, p30, p49, p75, p88, p107 reproduced with permission of Punch Ltd; p18, p37, p44, p81, p83, p96, p108, p109, p110, p124, p125 reproduced with permission of *Private Eye*; p10 reproduced with permission of Harry Venning.